BARACK
OBAMA

THE ROAD FROM MONEYGALL

Stephen MacDonogh

BRANDON

A Brandon Paperback Original

First published in 2010 by Brandon
an imprint of Mount Eagle Publications
Dingle, Co. Kerry, Ireland, and
Unit 3, Olympia Trading Estate, Coburg Road, London N22 6TZ, England
and c/o Dufour Editions Inc, PO Box 7, Chester Springs PA 19425

ISBN 9780863224133

2 4 6 8 10 9 7 5 3 1

Map artwork: Anú Design
Cover design: Anú Design
Typesetting by Red Barn Publishing, Skeagh, Skibbereen

www.brandonbooks.com

Contents

List of Maps

To my daughter Lilya with love

BARACK OBAMA'S IRISH ANCESTORS

7th GREAT-GRANDPARENTS

Joseph Kearney = Cicerly
b. c. 1698   d. 1769
d. 1791

Michael Kearney
d. 1762

Rev. Michael Kearney
b. 1734
d. 1814

Rev. John Kearney
b. 1744
d. 1813

Rev. John Kearney
b. 1770
d. 1838

Rev. Thomas Kearney

6th GREAT-GRANDPARENTS

Thomas   Joseph Kearney = Sarah Healy
b. c. 1725   b. c. 1730   b. c. 1744

John   Patrick
b. 1741

5th GREAT-GRANDPARENTS

William Kearney = Margaret Reeves
b. 1762   b. c. 1774
d. 1828   d. c. 1842

Thomas = Sarah Baxley
b. 1765   b. 1774
d. 1846   d. 1845

James
b. 1767
d. 1779

John
b. 1770
d. 1772

Mary
b. 1772

Joseph
b. 1775
d. 1811

Lambert
b. 1777

John (2)
b. 1779
d. 1780

John (3)
b. 1782
d. 1870

4th GREAT-GRANDPARENTS

John
b. c. 1790

Sarah
b. c. 1793
d. 1852

Joseph Kearney = Ph(o)ebe Donovan
b. 1794   b. c. 1807
d. 1861   d. 1876

Thomas
b. 1800
d. 1845

Francis
b. 1803
d. 1848

William
b. 1812
d. 1868

Margaret
b. 1816
d. 1866

Frances
b. c. 1820

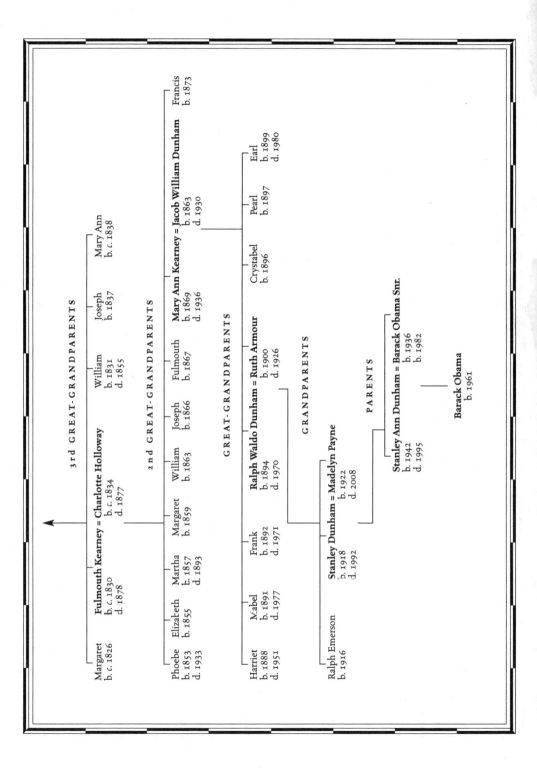

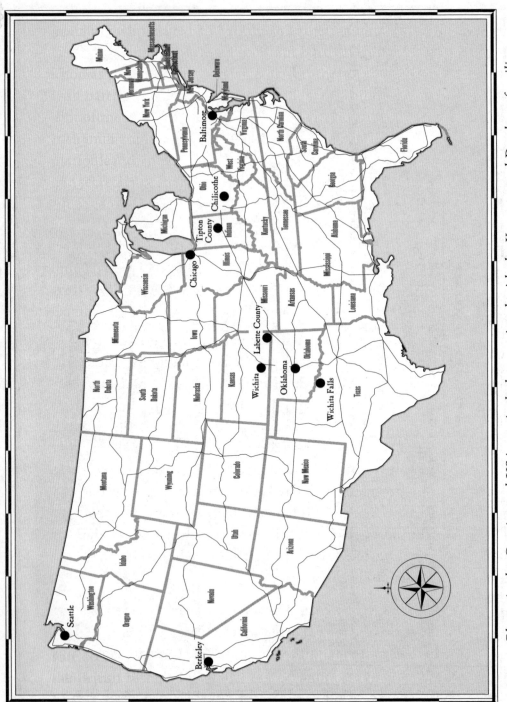

Places in the Continental USA particularly associated with the Kearney and Dunham families

Introduction

In key speeches, Barack Obama has evoked an America made up of many strands. He has emphasised the unity of Americans of diverse backgrounds, religious and ethnic traditions, and political viewpoints.

> For we know that our patchwork heritage is a strength, not a weakness. We are a nation of Christians and Muslims, Jews and Hindus – and non-believers. We are shaped by every language and culture, drawn from every end of this Earth; and because we have tasted the bitter swill of civil war and segregation, and emerged from that dark chapter stronger and more united, we cannot help but believe that the old hatreds shall someday pass; that the lines of tribe shall soon dissolve; that as the world grows smaller, our common humanity shall reveal itself . . .[1]

America is, however, deeply divided – in considerable part on the issue of differing attitudes to Obama himself.

In the process of writing this book, I spoke with Americans of various ethnic origins who felt inspired, enthralled and moved by the election of Barack Obama. Amongst African

Americans, I encountered a special frisson of emotion that seemed to have risen to the surface from the deep historic well of the collective experience of slavery and discrimination. I visited places in Ohio, Indiana and Kansas associated with the story of Obama's Irish ancestors. I came across ordinary white Americans who seemed still stunned by the fact that they now had a president with a black face. Many seemed to be in denial, as in a slightly different sense were those who have come to be called "Birthers" – people who deny that Obama was born in the United States and claim that he was ineligible to be elected president. The denial extends further and wider, beyond the lunatic fringe to those conservative circles in which the assumption is that a person of colour cannot be regarded as an American in the same sense that a white person can.

The election of the first African-American president has not swept away racial prejudice. As Obama observes himself, "we cannot help but believe that the old hatreds *shall* someday pass" [my emphasis]. There is every chance that the very fact of his presidency will be seen in retrospect as a watershed on the road to an eventual true racial equality and unity of Americans. But for the moment America is polarised, not so much by race itself as by political perspectives informed by deep-seated racial prejudice.

To much of the rest of the world, Obama's politics are an uncontroversial blend of centre-right policies packaged with an unusually attractive wrapping of presentational appeal, personal charisma and earnest aspiration. To many in America, however, he stands centre-left; to some, at an extreme liberal left. What most agree, nevertheless, is that Obama offers leadership. Some may deplore the direction in which they see him leading America, others may admire it; few would question that he wears the mantle of leadership. And it is how he meets the inevitable challenges of leadership at a particularly precarious time in the affairs of his nation and the world that will surely have a great bearing on how the historic inheritance of deep divisions may be resolved or ameliorated.

He has spoken of an America made up of many strands, and in this book it is the strand of his Irish ancestry that provides the focus, telling a story of emigration from a country disfigured by gross inequalities and devastated by famine, and the experience of building new lives in a new land, animated by hope for the future.

"Our family's story is one that spans miles and generations; races and realities," Barack Obama has said. "It's the story of farmers and soldiers; city workers and single moms. It takes place in small towns and good schools, in Kansas and Kenya, on the shores of Hawaii and the streets of Chicago. It's a varied and unlikely journey, but one that's held together by the same simple dream. And that is why it's American."

It is certainly an archetypal American journey, and it is also very much an Irish story. Joseph Kearney, Obama's great-great-great-great-grandfather, was born in about 1794 in Moneygall, King's County (later renamed County Offaly), Ireland. He lived through the apocalyptic famine years and left a devastated country in 1849 for America, where he settled in Ohio. Joseph's uncle, Thomas Kearney, had been the first of the family to settle in the New World some sixty years earlier, and Joseph's wife Phoebe and son Fulmouth were among the last of the Kearneys to emigrate.

At the time when the Kearneys began to arrive in America, Ireland was on the cusp of great potential change; Theobald Wolfe Tone had articulated a vision:

> To unite the whole people of Ireland, to abolish the memory of all past dissentions, and to substitute the common name of Irishman, in the place of the denominations of Protestant, Catholic, and Dissenter . . .

However, the universal republicanism espoused by Tone and the United Irishmen was defeated. As a result, some of these revolutionaries, and their ideas, made notable contributions in exile to the development of public life in America. But Ireland itself was set on a course to be defined by its differences and divisions, the hope of unity a tattered banner in the wind.

In the years that have followed the departure of the Kearneys from Moneygall, tens of millions of Americans of Irish ancestry have contributed to the life of the United States, in ways more diverse than many might think. Meanwhile, in Ireland the population continued to decline after the Famine as emigration continued. Later, the establishment of two separate partitioned states in Ireland copper-fastened religious difference as the defining conflict line on the island, and the age-old struggle seemed entirely intractable.

In recent years, great hope, effort and commitment brought about a settlement, an end to the armed conflict that had disfigured, in particular, the north of the island and that had poisoned life in the whole island. Nevertheless, this settlement is no resolution: rather it is the reassertion of the sectarian divide as the guiding principle of Ireland's constitutional arrangements. The dream of the unity of the Irish people and of a universal republicanism is as far away as ever.

The story of the journey to the White House from the Irish village of Moneygall seems to be a familiar story of Irish emigration to escape the devastation of the Great Famine. It seems part of that remarkable tragedy in the history of Ireland that had the effect of contributing greatly to the making of America from the mid-nineteenth century.

However, first sight can be misleading. Barack Obama's ancestors did not arrive in America destitute in the wake of the Famine; theirs was a different tale. The story of Barack

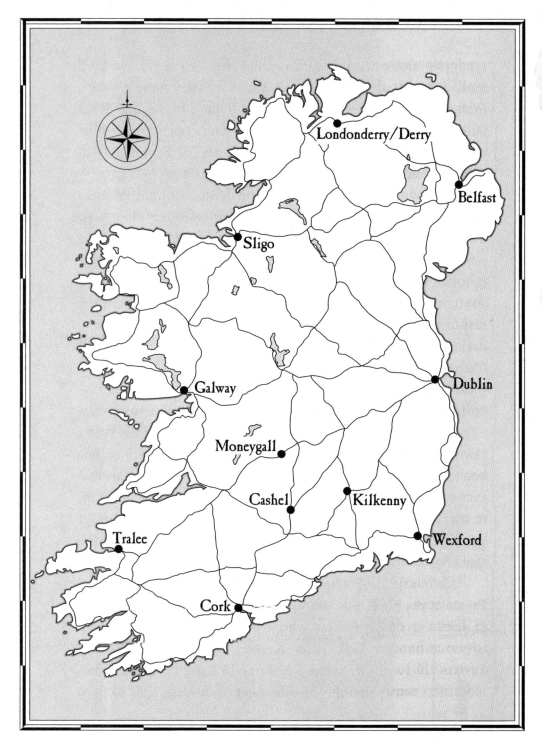

Moneygall, Ireland

Obama's Irish ancestors differs from the commonly accepted narrative of Irish emigration to America. They were a native Irish family, and they were Church of Ireland Protestants (that is, Episcopalians or Anglicans). These facts open up a whole new narrative, a largely forgotten history of Protestants in both America and their native Ireland.

Most present-day Americans and Irish assume that Irish American and Irish Catholic are synonymous. They also assume that Ireland and Catholicism are synonymous. As recently as August 2009, a leading Irish sociologist offered the opinion that the sporting organisation, the Gaelic Athletic Association (GAA), "better defines who we are now than the Catholic Church".[2] His assumption that Catholicism has long defined the Irish people is an assumption that almost all Catholics would consider uncontroversial. Yet more than one million of the five and a half million people who make up the Irish population are Protestants, and so such an assumption excludes from the Irish nation 20 per cent of its people. It is a mundane assumption, almost universally accepted, which has been daily repeated throughout the Irish Catholic educational system for more than a hundred years. As the writer and film-maker Neil Jordan remarked in 2009 in an interview about growing up in Ireland in the 1960s: "Catholicism was like the grass."

The question of whether the Catholic church has defined the Irish people is not simply a matter of numbers. Amongst the definitive Irish writers who articulated the mind and soul of the nation are W.B. Yeats, Samuel Beckett, Sean O'Casey, Bernard Shaw, J. M. Synge – not one of them Catholic. Who, after all, is more definitive as the poet of modern Ireland than W.B. Yeats?

At the end of 2009 RTÉ, Ireland's state broadcasting station, reviewed five decades of momentous events. It declared that John F. Kennedy had been the first Irish-American president of America. A broadcaster with a defining national remit ignored the simple fact that at least eight presidents before him were of Irish ancestry. John F. Kennedy was just the first Catholic president – an achievement in itself and worthy of celebration – but the rest, including the iconic Andrew Jackson (both of whose parents were born in Ireland), were Protestant Irish.

In America, too, the same assumption prevails. Denis McDonough, deputy national security adviser and chief of staff of the US National Security Council, grew up in Minnesota, but his paternal grandparents came from Galway in Ireland, his mother's parents from Cork. Asked what it means to be Irish in America, he responded: "In the first instance it means being Catholic."[3]

The truth obscured by such assumptions of Irishness and Catholicism being synonymous is that Irish Protestants played vitally important roles both in the making of Ireland and the making of America, and the story of Barack Obama's Irish ancestry reveals a newly inclusive understanding of what it means to be Irish in Ireland and to be Irish in America.

— 1 —

Thomas Kearney of Baltimore

Sarah Baxley married twenty-six-year-old Thomas Kearney in St Paul's Episcopal Church on 11 December 1791, the day after her eighteenth birthday, in Baltimore, Maryland. Sarah, from Fairfax, Virginia, was a daughter of John Baxley, a miller from Yorkshire, England, and Mary Sproul from Wilmington, Delaware. Thomas Kearney was from Moneygall, in the King's County, Ireland.

Four days after their marriage, the new United States of America ratified the Bill of Rights, the first ten amendments to the US Constitution, confirming the fundamental rights of its citizens. George Washington was president, and there were only twelve states in the union. The western boundary of the United States was the Mississippi River. Ohio was not yet a state; Florida was a Spanish colony; Texas was part of Mexico. Tennessee was part of North Carolina.

The marriage constitutes the first record in America of Barack Obama's Irish ancestral family. Thomas Kearney, the groom, was born in 1765 in Moneygall, King's County. He was a son of Sarah Healy from Moneygall and Joseph Kearney from nearby Shinrone, and it was in Shinrone church that he was christened. In the graveyard of the same church in January 1791 – the year of Thomas's marriage – his grandfather, also Joseph, was buried at the age of ninety-three. Another Joseph Kearney, his brother William's son, would later follow him to America and become in time the great-great-great-grandfather of Ann Dunham, who was the mother of Barack Obama.

When young Thomas Kearney arrived in Baltimore, it was a vibrant, developing city based around an increasingly busy harbour through which flowed a variety of exports from the state of Maryland. Thomas Kearney was one of many Protestant Irish immigrants to the area. Merchants from the north of Ireland had already played a significant role in the economic development of the area by establishing a network of cross-Atlantic trade that featured the Irish ports of Belfast, Derry, Newry and Dublin. The seed for the flax of Ulster was carried from America on ships, which on their return journey brought both Irish linen and passengers seeking opportunities in America. Exports from Maryland ports, essentially from Baltimore, accounted for two thirds of the wheat and half the flour from the American Colonies imported into Ireland in 1768–72.[4]

A Derryman, Dr John Stevenson, was the leading developer of Baltimore as a business centre, and amongst the materials he imported from Ireland were linen and "fine Irish pickled and dried Salmon". The Ulster Irish merchants following in Stevenson's wake also imported indentured servants in considerable numbers to meet the needs of the rapidly expanding business class. It also became the principal marketplace in America for convicts, who had been sentenced by the British courts to transportation. Both convicts and servants came from a number of different ports, including Waterford, Limerick, London, Dublin and Newry. Convicts generally had significantly longer contracts than indentured servants and so commanded a higher price for those dealing in this human cargo. One historian has described Baltimore at this time as a "Scotch-Irish boom town".[5]

In newspapers in Ireland – especially but not exclusively in the northern counties – merchants also advertised to invite settlers to Maryland. Some of these expressed a specific appeal to Presbyterians and Catholics, emphasising "this Opportunity to go to one of the finest and plentiful Countries in America, where all Kinds of Religions are tolerated".[6]

In the *Londonderry Journal* in 1773, advertisements for a passage on the *Prince of Wales* emphasised Baltimore as providing access to the land of opportunity that lay to the west.

> The town of Baltimore is commodiously situated for a ready Communication with all the back parts of Pennsylvania, Maryland, and Virginia, to which most new Settlers resort. It is a hundred miles nearer than Philadelphia to Fort Pitt on the River Ohio – a new Province of vast Extent, of the most fertile fine Lands in North America, and in the most agreeable moderate Climate, is now settling very fast along the Banks of that famous River, where Tracts of the richest Lands in the World and of greater Extent than most Kingdoms in Europe, are yet unsettled, and will for many Ages to come afford the most happy Asylum for all that choose to exchange a Land of Poverty, for Freedom, Wealth, and Happiness.[7]

On the *Prince of Wales'* arrival, the editor of the *Maryland Journal and Baltimore Advertiser* welcomed those who had come:

> ...to seek in our back extensive and happy Territory, peaceable and comfortable Residences, which those loyal and industrious People could not enjoy in their native Land, from the ill-judged

Oppression exercised over that sinking Country by Great Britain.[8]

An anti-British perspective was shared by almost all the Irish who settled in Baltimore in the 1760s and 1770s, many of them in search of the freedom of religion and civil liberty that they had been denied by the British administration in Ireland. These mostly Presbyterian Irishmen did not confine themselves to trade; they also became enthusiastically involved in the revolutionary politics of Baltimore. Their fellow Presbyterian Irishmen who remained in Ireland at this time would shortly provide the initiative and leadership behind the revolutionary republicanism of the United Irishmen.

Richard K. MacMaster concludes:

> Within less than a decade Baltimore had grown as a port with close ties to Ireland, and with significant trade to the West Indies and southern Europe. Its merchants shipped flaxseed, wheat and flour to Ulster and brought new settlers from there to Maryland and the backcountry. In the same short period a small group of Scotch-Irish Presbyterians became prominent in political affairs.[9]

The Irish influence that was so marked in the 1760s and 1770s did not end there and then. As Timothy Meagher writes in *The Columbia Guide to Irish American History*:

> Through the 1780s and 1790s, Irish immigrants continued to pour through the Delaware River ports of Philadelphia and Newcastle, and through Baltimore in the Chesapeake region.[10]

In the rapidly expanding town of Baltimore, there was no lack of work, and Thomas Kearney set up in trade as a carpenter at a time when tradesmen were in demand for a wide range of construction projects. When he married Sarah Baxley, he also became part of a well-established family that was playing a prominent role in the burgeoning Methodist movement.

Thomas is listed as "carpenter" or "house carpenter" in the *Baltimore Directory* for 1800 through 1804. He lived in or beside Granby Street in Baltimore's inner harbour, just around the corner from the Flag House and what is now the Star Spangled Banner Museum. The Flag House was built in 1793, and it is tempting to speculate that perhaps Thomas may have worked on the construction of the historic building.

Maryland had first been settled by the English in 1634. They soon created a permanent colony, and in 1776, during the American Revolution, it became a state in the United States. It was a slave state where many of the settlers later held Confederate sympathies. During the secession crisis following Lincoln's election in 1860, Maryland was to show strong secessionist and pro-Confederate sympathies. To keep DC from being surrounded by Confederate states, Maryland was essentially placed under martial law, and the leading Confederate supporters were arrested by the military and denied habeas corpus. However, a significant minority – made up essentially of settlers – supported the anti-slavery cause, and following the American Revolution many of the black population were freed, due mostly to manumissions. During the Civil War, Maryland remained in the Union.

There was a history of religious conflict in the area. The first settlers, led by Leonard Calvert, were English Catholics, who came from Cowes, on the Isle of Wight, leaving in November 1633 aboard two small ships, the *Ark* and the *Dove*, and landing in March 1634 at St Clement's Island. There Father Andrew White and the rest of this first group of colonists – seventeen gentlemen and their wives and about two hundred others, mostly indentured servants – celebrated the first Catholic mass in the Colonies.

Ten years after their arrival, Calvert was forced to flee to Virginia when the Virginian William Claiborne led an uprising of Maryland Protestants. He returned at the head of an armed force in 1646, and Maryland soon became one of the few predominantly Catholic regions among the English colonies in North America.

After Virginia established Anglicanism as mandatory, many Puritans migrated from Virginia to Maryland in search of religious freedom, and the government gave them land at Providence (now Annapolis). However, in 1650, the Puritans rebelled and set up a new government that outlawed both Catholicism and Anglicanism. The Puritan revolutionary government persecuted Maryland Catholics, and all of the original Catholic churches of southern Maryland were burned down. In 1655, the 2nd Lord Baltimore sent his Roman Catholic army under Governor William Stone to suppress this revolt, but it was decisively defeated by the Puritan army, and the revolt persisted until 1658, when the Calvert family succeeded in regaining control once more.

The town of Baltimore, named after Cecilius Calvert (Lord Baltimore), was founded in 1729. His title, and hence the name of the city, derived from Baltimore in County Cork, Ireland. It possessed the advantages of a natural harbour on the Chesapeake Bay and a number of potential mill sites on streams dropping over the fall line. Farmers bringing cereal crops to the mills for grinding provided a growing demand for shipping their goods from a new and convenient port.

Sarah Baxley was the seventh of nine children – six boys and three girls. Her parents, John Baxley and Mary Sproul, were intimately involved in the early development of Methodism in America, and St Paul's Episcopal Church was where they regularly attended services, where many of their children were married and their grandchildren christened.

John Baxley was a relatively wealthy and respected citizen, quite prominent in Methodist circles, and he was a Hero of the Revolution, having served as Quartermaster in a battalion of the Maryland militia in Baltimore County. He was also a slave-owner.

It is not known when Thomas Kearney travelled from Ireland to America. He presumably made the journey within a period of about eleven years prior to his marriage – so sometime between 1780 and 1791. Fifteen might seem a young age to emigrate without one's parents, but at the time young men struck out on careers quite early in life. The fact that he married in December 1791 makes it unlikely that he arrived that year. And the fact that his bride was the daughter of an Englishman who had come to Baltimore from Yorkshire suggests that there had been no association between the two families before he arrived in America. It also raises the question of how he had acquired sufficient financial resources to support a wife and family. Had he arrived as a man of some means or had he been in America long enough to acquire means through work or else through military service? Perhaps, too, he may have received some money in his grandfather's will.

We do know that in his new American home of Baltimore he established himself as a carpenter. Many Irish arrived as indentured servants, working to repay their passage and learning at the same time a trade. However, the Kearneys, at the time of Thomas's emigration, were reasonably well off. He was typical of the majority of Irish immigrants of the time. As Kerby A. Miller writes in *Emigrants and Exiles: Ireland and the Irish Exodus to North America*:

> . . . as surviving ships' manifests indicate, the bulk
> of the emigrants of 1783–1814 were substantial

farmers and artisans – weavers, millwrights, tanners – in middling circumstances; moreover, a significant minority were from business and professional backgrounds – merchants, shopkeepers, clerks, schoolmasters, physicians, and so forth . . . overall those who left Ireland in 1783–1814 were Protestants in fairly comfortable circumstances.

It is unlikely that an indentured servant would have been entertained as a suitor for the daughter of a relatively prominent Methodist elder who owned substantial property in Maryland and was a Hero of the Revolution. It may be that the resources of his family in Ireland supported him in his adventure. Irish Protestant families frequently saw emigration to America as offering a positive opportunity both for the individual member and the family as a whole.

John Baxley, a miller born in 1743 in Bowes, Yorkshire, England, recognised the significance of the fast-flowing streams of the area and purchased land at sites well suited for milling. It is thought that he first had a mill on the Brandywine River, and he and his wife Mary Sproul started their married life in Wilmington, Delaware, where their first child was born. They moved to Jerusalem, Harford County, a thriving Quaker settlement. Here John Baxley worked at Jerusalem Mill, the focal point of the community, on the Little Gunpowder River. At some time also they lived in Fairfax County in Virginia, where Sarah was born. He later had mills at Anne Arundel County, on the Magothy River. He had a connection, too, with the Elliott Mills on the Patapsco River in Howard County.

Baltimore town grew swiftly in the eighteenth century, earning profits from providing a granary for the sugar-producing colonies of the Caribbean. It was significantly closer to the Caribbean than other large port cities such as Boston and New York City.

Places associated with the Baxleys of Baltimore

Baltimore played a key role in the American Revolutionary period, becoming the *de facto* capital of the United States from December 1776 to February 1777, when Congress met there in the Henry Fite House. John Baxley was commissioned on 3 June 1777 as quartermaster of Soldiers Delight Battalion of the Maryland militia in Baltimore County, commanded by a leading fellow-Methodist, Colonel Samuel Owings. When George Washington's army was quartered at Valley Forge during the winter of 1777–78, he ground a wagonload of flour at Jerusalem Mill and drove the wagon the seventy miles to Valley Forge, a considerable distance at the time.

John Baxley also took the Oath of Allegiance before a magistrate in Baltimore County, after the Maryland Assembly in 1776 passed an act to prevent the spread of Toryism.

As the port of Baltimore expanded, Baxley diversified his business interests, and in 1781 his name appears in a list of owners of wagons employed in public service there. He became involved in many property transactions – some twenty-five concerning 600 acres in all – between 1784 (when the Land Records of Baltimore County began) and 1795.

After the war, and six years after Thomas Kearney's marriage, the town of Baltimore, nearby Jonestown and the area of Fells Point were incorporated in 1797 as the City of Baltimore.

The early years of Sarah and Thomas Kearney's marriage were marked by tragedy. Their first child, Sarah, born in September 1792, died at the age of just ten months. It must have been a desperately cruel blow for the newly married couple. However, two years later their first son, Joseph, was born, followed in 1797 by Mary, then Thomas Jr in 1800 and Lambert in 1803. This last name, Lambert, came from Thomas Kearney's mother's side of the family, the Healys of Moneygall. An unusual name in Ireland, it was maintained through the generations and may hint of an English or Huguenot connection.

Many of the Maryland settlers of English origin were Catholics. Most of the Irish were Protestants. The Kearneys in Ireland subscribed to the Church of Ireland – that is, they were of the Anglican denomination. There was nothing unusual about a Church of Ireland Protestant marrying into a Methodist family; the relationship between Methodism and Anglicanism was close, Methodism having originated as a movement to revitalise Anglicanism.

John Wesley, the founder of Methodism, was an Anglican, and in the early years in America, most Methodists remained Anglicans. For example, the founder of Methodist societies in Virginia and North Carolina, Rev. Devereux Jarratt, remained an Anglican clergyman. However, a movement towards a more distinct Methodist denomination had begun and developed since the establishment, at the Baltimore Christmas Conference in 1784, of the Methodist Episcopal Church, with Francis Asbury and Thomas Coke as its first bishops. Methodism only formally broke from Anglicanism in 1795.

In *Ireland and the Centenary of American Methodism* (1866), Rev. William Crook listed a number of Irish Methodists in Baltimore at the time who may well have eased Thomas Kearney's assimilation into the new church in a new country.

One prominent religious figure, founder of the Republican Methodist Church and noted campaigner against slavery, was an Irishman of Anglican origin, James O'Kelly.[11] Through a series of divisions and mergers, the Methodist Episcopal Church became the major component of the present United Methodist Church.

Thomas Kearney may have become a Methodist simply because his wife was Methodist, whose parents were both very active in Methodism. Indeed, her father was a preacher, an elder and a class leader. Thomas Kearney would have been by no means exceptional amongst his Church of Ireland country-men in converting to Methodism within a short time of his arrival in America. Methodism was growing in America, especially in the Baltimore area. Anglicanism was associated with the colonial power.

Most of the records of John Baxley's role as an active Methodist are missing, but the broad extent of the Baxley family's involvement is clear from records that have survived. In 1800, John Baxley Jr was a deacon and Bible class leader; his brother George Baxley was a leader for both white and coloured classes. Many classes were held at George's home on Liberty Street, and amongst those listed as attending regularly in about 1800 were Thomas Baxley, Mary Baxley Sr (John Baxley Sr's wife, Mary Sproul), Mary M (George's wife) and Elizabeth (Thomas's wife).

Methodism originated in England in 1739 under the leadership of John and Charles Wesley. It first came to America (and Maryland) in the 1760s, when an Irishman named Robert Strawbridge organised classes in Baltimore and Frederick Counties.

Robert Strawbridge was born in Drumsna, County Leitrim, and according to Abel Stevens in his *History of the Methodist Episcopal Church in the United States of America*,[12] he

> ... provoked "such a storm of persecution"
> among his neighbours as induced him, not long after
> his conversion, to escape their opposition by remov-
> ing from his native place to the county of Sligo,
> where "his labors were signally blessed of God
> through a considerable district." He labored also in
> the county of Cavan, where, for many years, aged
> Methodists delighted to talk of his zeal and humble
> but heroic preaching, and "highly prized his piety

and gifts." They "recognized him as a man of more than ordinary usefulness. He was very ardent and evangelical in his spirit." He subsequently preached in the county of Armagh, residing mostly at Tander-agee. He "sounded the alarm" through all that populous rural district. Terryhugan, mentioned by Wesley as the "mother-church of these parts," was "a place to which he often resorted, and among its lively Methodists, warm in their religious affections, he found many a heart that beat in unison with his own." His name remained embalmed in the memories of the latest Methodists of that generation in Terryhugan. One of their devoted young women became his wife, and emigrated with him to America.[13]

He and his wife Elizabeth Piper were both active in the Wesleyan movement. They emigrated to Frederick County, Maryland, sometime shortly after 1760, where they lived as tenants on land near Sam's Creek. Preaching at his log cabin home near New Windsor, he established a very wide preaching circuit through Baltimore, Frederick and Harford counties and to the edge of the Eastern Shore. He organised Methodist societies in the area, the first Methodist societies in North America. During these early years, Strawbridge also built log meeting houses at Bush and Sam's Creek. A popular and influential communicator, he performed the first known Methodist baptism, of Henry Maynard. It was Elizabeth Strawbridge who was responsible for the first American Methodist conversion, of John Evans. Their influence spread rapidly and widely, and it is highly likely that amongst those who fell under their influence were the neighbouring Baxley family.

Robert Strawbridge was probably always a layperson, and as such he was criticised for administering the sacraments, a practice that was prohibited by the 1773 conference of

Methodist preachers in America. An exception was made in his case, but only then at the discretion of Francis Asbury, who had been sent to the colonies by John Wesley to oversee the faith and who took a dim view of Strawbridge. In his journal entry for June 24, 1774, Asbury wrote:

> [O]ne of these letters informed me that Mr. Strawbridge was very officious in administering the ordinances. What strange infatuation attends that man! Why will he run before Providence?[14]

Strawbridge continued administering the sacraments, ignoring Asbury's disapproval. Remarking on the special provision made for him, Abel Stevens observed:

> A concession so singular shows the extraordinary consideration in which Strawbridge was held, the influence he had obtained over the Societies of Maryland and Virginia.[15]

Behind what might have seemed a clash of personalities lay an important ideological conflict. As Dee E. Andrews writes, in *The Methodists and Revolutionary America, 1760–1800*:

> The sacramental controversy [was] ostensibly a struggle over the powers of Methodist ministry but also a contest between Strawbridge's democratic Irish Methodism and Asbury's loyalty to Wesley's authoritarian "old plan" . . .[16]

Abel Stevens in his *History of the Methodist Episcopal Church in the United States of America* writes:

> Robert Strawbridge . . . contended sturdily for the right of the people to the sacraments, and could not be deterred by Asbury or Rankin from administering them. He had founded the Church in the

regions whence now nearly one half of its members were reported; he had administered to them the sacraments before any English itinerants appeared in the country, and being an Irishman, he shared not in the deferential sympathies of his English brethren for the Establishment.[17]

Asbury and his fellow Methodist leader Thomas Coke were "inclined toward a top-down Federalist-style exercise of authority",[18] and this led them into conflict with another formidable Irishman, James O'Kelly. A celebrated itinerant, a radical opponent of slavery, an anti-British activist and a veteran of the Revolutionary War, O'Kelly mounted a virulent campaign against the Methodist leadership, which he considered were exercising a "lordly power" over the ministers. O'Kelly was not alone in pressing for democratic principles. Another Irish preacher, William Hammett, accused Asbury of episcopal tyranny. But it was O'Kelly who was the more charismatic figure, and in opposition to the Asbury/Coke leadership, he and his followers formed the Republican Methodist Church, taking with them some thirty preachers and twenty thousand members. As Russell Richey has written, O'Kelly's theology "laid claim to a republican language that would increasingly become the Protestant idiom and eventually also the Methodist idiom".[19]

For more than 150 years, both New York and Maryland claimed the honour of being the birthplace of American Methodism. The Centennial of American Methodism was celebrated in New York in 1866. Later, however, it was discovered that a Methodist minister in Ohio in 1813 had met a German farmer who claimed to have been converted by Strawbridge in Maryland in 1763. As a consequence, a 1916 church decision found that the origin of American Methodism was in Maryland, not New York. A shrine to this remarkable

Irishman, the now undisputed pioneer of Methodism on the American continent, stands in Carroll County, Maryland, at the edge of New Windsor. In Ireland, outside a Church of Ireland graveyard in Drumsna, County Leitrim, a monument commemorates his life: "Robert Strawbridge, born Drumsna 1732, died Baltimore, Maryland 1781, founder of the Methodist Church USA."

By 1773, Maryland Methodist membership was at 500, and when the Methodist Episcopal church organised in Baltimore during Christmas 1784, missionary Francis Asbury became bishop. By 1800 membership had increased to 13,046. Congregations were split by race and numbered 6,549 white and 6,497 black members.

Thomas Kearney's father-in-law, John Baxley, a Methodist preacher and class leader, is listed in the 1790 Baltimore County census with four white males sixteen and over, four white males under sixteen, three white females and two slaves. The fact that he had slaves is of relevance to a sharp and sometimes passionate debate within Methodism in Maryland at the time.

White anti-slavery action began in Maryland in the revolutionary era, especially amongst Quakers. Although many Quakers had been slave owners, they came to regard slavery as a violent phenomenon that endangered the souls of the slave owners. Those who had slaves began to manumit (formally free) them, usually after requiring them to fulfil a term of further service. The Maryland Society for Promoting the Abolition of Slavery and the Relief of Poor Negroes and Others Unlawfully Held in Bondage, active from the late 1780s until about 1800, was dominated by Quakers, and it assisted slaves in petitioning courts for freedom.

In Maryland's most celebrated case, Mary Butler was liberated in 1787, on the grounds that she was a great-great granddaughter of "Irish Nell" Butler, who had come to

Maryland in 1681 as a servant of Lord Baltimore. Eleanor Butler was then a sixteen-year-old indentured servant, who fell in love with a black slave on the adjoining plantation. Working as a laundress for the third Lord Baltimore, she told her employer that she planned to wed the man identified in court records as "Negro Charles". Lord Baltimore told her that she would lose her freedom and advised her strongly against it. She persisted, and they were married by a Catholic priest, and subsequently they had seven or eight children; the whole family became the property of Charles's master. Lord Baltimore petitioned the Provincial Assembly to change the law to guarantee that no white woman would ever be forced into slavery. According to the slave laws, the legal status of the children was determined by their mother's status, and this was the provision that Charles and Nell's grandchildren relied upon in seeking to sue for their freedom, eventually resulting in the freeing of Mary Butler in 1787.

Methodists were also active against slavery in the late eighteenth century. In one celebrated instance in 1775, Freeborn Garrettson converted to Methodism and freed his slaves, having heard an inner voice that said, "It is not the will of the Lord that you should keep your fellow creatures in bondage." He became a Methodist circuit rider (travelling preacher) and conveyed his anti-slavery experience and views to thousands. Woolman Hickson, William Colbert and Ezekiel Cooper were also amongst Methodists who preached against slavery, and Daniel Coker, a black Methodist, published *A Dialogue between a Virginian and an African Minister* in 1810, refuting claims of slavery's divine sanction, black inferiority and the alleged inevitability of race war if slaves were freed.

The issue of slavery may have caused life in Baltimore to become uneasy for Thomas Kearney and his wife Sarah. Most of the more established members of the Methodist community accepted slavery, and many of them, like John Baxley, owned slaves, but many less established, less propertied and younger Methodists supported the anti-slavery cause. Given the circumstances of the time, there was some bitterness within families over the issue, and between neighbours and fellow members of the religious community. And as a result of this conflict, many who were supporters of the anti-slavery cause opted to move away from Maryland, choosing to forge new lives for themselves in the relatively unexplored territory known as the Virginia Military District.

There are several reasons why Thomas Kearney and his wife might not have wanted to stay in Baltimore with their young family. Slavery was one of them; land was another. Problems of land tenure in Maryland frustrated a new generation, both American-born like Sarah and new immigrants like Thomas, who saw land ownership as an essential aspect of making a future in America for themselves and their families. As one author about the land situation has written:

> The great surge of population into the West after the War of Independence . . . suggests that acquiring land always remained a compelling aspiration for most tenants in Maryland.[20]

And so, despite enjoying a quite comfortable life in Baltimore, Thomas Kearney turned his attention to the new frontier and its apparently virgin lands.

— 2 —

Poverty and Injustice in Ireland, Opportunity Abroad

Land, landholding and landlordism were the features which disfigured the Ireland Thomas Kearney had left behind in the late eighteenth century. An unjust and inequitable system of landholding largely coincided with a sectarian fault line in a system that had been in place for more than a hundred years but was beginning to come under the strain of popular resistance. Cruelly high rents demanded by the landlord class placed unbearable pressure on artisan families, such as the Kearneys, who were seeing their jobs in the woollen and other industries vanish.

Following the Cromwellian conquest of 1649–53, there had been a major transfer of land in most of Ireland, including King's County, from native, mostly Catholic, Irish owners to Protestant, mostly English, Scottish and Welsh, planters. By 1688 Catholics, who formed most of the population, owned less than a quarter of the land in King's County. Some Irish landholders were ordered at the time to be transported to the west, to counties Clare and Galway. More Irish, however, became tenants, working the land for the planters; while most of these tenants were Catholic, some, like the Kearneys, were Protestant. Others in the Irish population took to the woods and valleys, becoming cattle raiders and agrarian agitators known as "tories".

Despite the confiscations, transportations and other depredations, Catholics were still the majority of the population. Meanwhile, their priests were hunted, jailed and transported. The native former ruling family of the area, the O'Carrolls, deprived of their lands and their status, emigrated in numbers to Europe and the New World. One of them was granted 60,000 acres in Maryland in 1688, and his grandson, Charles Carroll of Carrollton, was a signatory – the only Catholic signatory – of the American Declaration of Independence.

Many of the Cromwellian soldiers and English adventurers granted Irish land under the Act of Settlement found themselves stranded in a sea of resentment, and many sold up their grants of land, sometimes to native Irish. Others persevered, and some prospered.

The Cromwellian settlement had established a society in which the ownership of most of the land was in the hands of people whose ethnic and geographical origin, religion and outlook differed from those of most of the native population around them. These new landowners, having displaced native landowners, appropriated the best land, built mansions and protected their houses and lands with high walls.

Amongst the Cromwellians granted land was a Charles Minchin. His family possessed land already in Gloucestershire, England, and in Tipperary, and he was awarded land in Busherstown, which had been taken from Teige O'Carroll under the Cromwellian settlement. The Minchin estates expanded through additional purchases at Annagh, Ballinakill, Moneygall and Greenhills. Amongst those who became their tenants in Moneygall were the Kearney family.

During the seventeenth and eighteenth centuries, largely as a consequence of the Cromwellian settlement, it had become impossible for the Irish people to maintain their accustomed way of life. Successive rebellions by Irish chieftains were suppressed by the forces of the English Crown, and thousands of men, women and children were killed. The chieftains went into exile, and many of their subjects followed them. In the mid-seventeenth century, tens of thousands were transported to the West Indies. Barbados had not only 30,000 black slaves but also 20,000 white, mostly Irish, indentured servants; St Christopher, too, had 20,000 Irish. In the late decades of the century, many of these Irish moved to the new Carolina colonies, to which many new migrants also came directly from Ireland. Maryland and Virginia received some 25–30,000 Irish, transported by the English as convicts, and about the same number arrived as indentured servants.

Between 50,000 and 100,000 Irish people, three-quarters of them Catholic, the remainder Protestant, arrived in America in the seventeenth century. Most of these Catholic Irish were indentured servants, and only a few were in the merchant class or became prominent in public life. Another 100,000 Irish Catholics came in the eighteenth century, but a larger wave of immigration was of Irish Protestants. Between 250,000 and 500,000 Irish Protestants and Quakers came to America in the eighteenth and early nineteenth centuries. Some of the Protestants were of the Church of Ireland, but a large majority were Presbyterians from Ulster, who came to be referred to as the "Scotch-Irish". Most of them arrived from the north of Ireland during the sixty years from the early eighteenth century to the American Revolution.

Scotland and Ulster had a shared culture, and some of their inhabitants had ancestral links with Dalriada, a Gaelic-speaking area on the northern coasts of Ireland and the western seaboard of Scotland, which lay only an hour apart by sea. In the early seventh century, its extent included County Antrim in Ireland, and Argyll and Bute and Lochaber in Scotland. Regarded as an Irish colony in Scotland, its people were often referred to as Scotti, the Latin name for the people of Ireland.

Most of these "Scotch-Irish" who settled in the south before the American Revolution were Presbyterians, who had been subjected in Ireland to the penal laws that excluded them from public office and denied them recognition of their marriages, funerals and schools. Church of Ireland courts had imposed fines on them, forced couples to confess to fornication, pronounced their children illegitimate. Indeed, they had in one respect been treated with even greater repression than the Catholics, for while the penal laws recognised the ordination of Catholic priests, they did not recognise the validity of Presbyterian ministers.

In America they seem to have encountered no great difficulty in coexisting with other Irish settlers, who were mostly Roman Catholic or Church of Ireland, though they retained an understandable hostility towards all things Anglican. They had much in common with their fellow Irish men and women of different religious backgrounds, and it is important to note that, as Grady McWhiney remarks in *Cracker Culture: Celtic Ways in the Old South*: "Even in eighteenth-century Ireland there was more interaction and friendship between Catholics and Protestants than has generally been assumed."[21]

This arose partly from the fact that only about a third of Catholics attended mass, and the majority were in effect nominal Catholics or not Catholics in any meaningful sense. Writing in *Irish Life in the Seventeenth Century*, Edward McLysaght observed:

> The passionate and exemplary [*sic*] attachment of
> the Irish nation to the Catholic faith dates from a

later time, and was in fact the direct result of the penal laws which were designed to uproot it. At first the opposition to Protestantism was mainly political: men changed from one denomination to the other with as little disturbance of conscience as would have been involved a generation or two ago in England, when the English were still a church-going people, in a transfer from High Church to Low.[22]

Meanwhile in America, the numbers of Anglicans from Ireland, England, Scotland and Wales went into a rapid decline, most joining, as did many of the Catholics, the better organised and more numerous denominations: the Baptists, Methodists and Presbyterians.

What the Presbyterians brought in particular to the New World was a strong distaste for central government, learned from their hard-won experience in Ireland and carried forward by them in America right up to the present day. More Irishmen (nine) signed the Declaration of Independence than any other ethnic group, and all but one of them were Protestant; Charles Dunlap of County Tyrone printed the first copies, and the first man to read it before Congress was Charles Thomson of County Derry, who also designed the Great Seal of the United States. The Belfast *Newsletter* was the first newspaper in Europe to publish the Declaration in full. When the Continental Congress was in need of finances, in July 1775, a plea was sent to Ireland seeking support for the Irish in America. Henry Grattan, the leading Irish parliamentarian of his age, supported the appeal in the Irish Parliament in his first year as an MP, and funds collected in various parts of the country were sent to America. One Irish-born fundraiser, Oliver Pollock from Coleraine, succeeded in raising an enormous sum to help finance the American Revolution and wound up in debtors' prison as a result. Of him the journalist George Johnson

Clarke remarked that "Pollack knew the British in Ireland and that was enough for him."

The circle surrounding George Washington was predominantly Protestant Irish. As historian Mike McCormack has written:

> Early Irish settlers in America fled English tyranny in the old world and were determined it would not follow them to the new. It's no surprise therefore, that when separation from England was first proposed, the Irish were its most enthusiastic supporters. When the issue finally came to rebellion, that support became the backbone of Washington's army. Charles Beard in *The Rise of American Civilization,* wrote, "Native Irish who came by the hundreds, if not by the thousands, bearing the scars of age-old conflict with England, flocked to the American Army when the standard of revolt was raised." When British forces left Boston to destroy the rebels at Lexington and Concord, their Major Pitcairn declared, "We will drive the Yankees and Irish to cover." Not only were there 147 Irish among the minutemen that fateful April 19, but when the "Shot Heard Round the World" was fired and the smoke cleared at Old North Bridge, among the dead were twenty-two Irish who had routed Pitcairn's redcoats and given their lives in America's initial bid for independence.[23]

John Brady, Revolutionary scout, was a son of Irish Presbyterians Hannah and Hugh Brady, who came from Enniskillen in 1730. Richard Montgomery, Revolutionary soldier, liberal Presbyterian and Unitarian and graduate of Trinity College Dublin, came from Convoy House, near Raphoe in County Donegal; his father was member of parliament for

Lifford in Donegal. Hercules Mulligan, the well-known cloth merchant who played a vital role in gathering information for George Washington, was a Protestant born in Antrim in 1740. Thomas Addis Emmet was an elder brother of the Protestant Irish patriot Robert Emmet. John Sullivan, who fired the first shot of the American Revolutionary War, was the third son of Irish immigrants of the Church of Ireland. Charles Thomson, patriot leader in Philadelphia during the American Revolution and secretary of the Continental Congress, who originated the American Eagle emblem, was a Protestant born in Maghera, County (London)Derry. Joseph Reed, a Presbyterian, was a Pennsylvania lawyer, military aide and statesman of the Revolutionary era. He served as a delegate to the Continental Congress and while in Congress signed the Articles of Confederation. Others amongst Washington's most trusted officers included Irish-born Generals Wayne, Irving, Shee, Lewis and Butler.

There were some Irish Catholics, too, in Washington's circle, most notably Commodore John Barry, father of the American Navy, who was born in 1745 in County Wexford; his father was a small tenant farmer. Stephen Moylan, by contrast, came from a wealthy Catholic Cork background, but, like Barry, played a major role, as muster-master general of the Continental Army, secretary and aide to General George Washington.

James Anthony Froude, the British historian, wrote that, "Washington's Irish supporters were the foremost, the most irreconcilable, and the most determined to push the quarrel to the last extremity." It was not just in leadership positions that the Irish played such prominent roles. Ambrose Serle, the private secretary to the British general William Howe, wrote to the British secretary of state: "Great numbers of Irish are in the rebel army," and he suggested that they be banned from leaving Ireland and adding to the rebel forces. David Ramsay, one of the earliest historians of the Revolution, observed, "The common soldiers of the state were, for the most part, Irish." The British general Henry Clinton wrote to his secretary of war that immigrants from Ireland were to be looked on as the most serious antagonists. From a different perspective, Alan Lomax, the great American collector of folk songs, wrote, "If soldiers' folk songs were the only evidence, it would seem that the armies that fought in the early American wars were composed entirely of Irishmen."

Major General Marquis de Chastellux, the principal liaison officer between the French commander-in-chief Comte de Rochambeau and George Washington, observed that "On more than one occasion Congress owed their existence, and America possibly her preservation to the fidelity and firmness of the Irish." General Henry Lee in his memoirs wrote that the Pennsylvania line, "might have justly been called the Line of Ireland". As Mike McCormack has written, "Ireland gave America soldiers to win her freedom."[24] In 1782, George Washington expressed his pride in accepting membership in the Friendly Sons of St Patrick, "a society distinguished for the firm adherence of its members to the glorious cause in which we are embarked".[25] Established in 1771 in Philadelphia, its membership was principally but not exclusively Protestant, and it devoted itself to the support of the victims of starvation, eviction and exile from Ireland.

Irish people emigrated in the pre-Famine times for many different reasons. There were those who saw emigration as an exploration of opportunity. And there were those, like many of the rural poor, who saw emigration as an enforced exile. For the rural cottiers and labourers:

> Their traditional ways of life were breaking down,
> but their outlooks on life, on emigration itself,

43

remained basically passive, fatalistic, and nonresponsible. In general, they were not ambitious to emigrate; rather, they submitted to this new but inescapable "fact" of Irish life as their fathers had endured crop failures and poverty; they would have preferred to remain at home, and they often tried to re-create as much of home as possible in their adopted countries.[26]

Some people – mostly Irish Protestants and relatively Anglicised Catholics – emigrated less under the pressure of changing circumstances than with a view to exploring opportunities to improve their material conditions. It is likely that Thomas Kearney and the family members who succeeded him in making the long journey to America conformed to this relatively positive perspective.

Although not necessarily happy to leave childhood homes, they were ambitious for themselves and their children, and they foresaw only limited or declining opportunities in Ireland. In the face of all the difficulties they knew they might encounter, such emigrants made mature, responsible decisions to go abroad. Consequently, although sometimes discouraged or disillusioned after their arrival in North America, rarely did they regard themselves as involuntary expatriates; they had consciously rejected Ireland for a new life abroad, and, if they failed to achieve material success, they usually acknowledged that they had only themselves to blame for their decisions. . . . [O]nce in North America they often strove for complete assimilation to bourgeois society in their adopted country.[27]

For more than two hundred years before Joseph Kearney – Obama's direct ancestor – left Ireland for America, and more than a hundred years before Joseph's uncle Thomas Kearney arrived in Maryland, there had already been established various forms of emigration from Ireland to America. And the Kearney family's gradual emigration – including that of Fulmouth as late as 1850 – conformed more to the pattern of the eighteenth century than to the post-Famine pattern.

In 1730, a hundred years before Fulmouth Kearney's birth and thirty-five years before Thomas Kearney's birth, members of the North family had emigrated from King's County (Offaly) to Maine in New England. Like the Kearneys, they were Protestants, members of the Church of Ireland in Offaly; unlike them, they were of English origin. Their forebears had been adventurers who arrived in Ireland during the Cromwellian settlement and over the succeeding generations established a substantial network of estates in King's County and Westmeath. It was probably this family tradition of adventuring and land development that led them to make the move to America, seeking new opportunities. Having successfully settled and prospered in Ireland, they now sought similar success at the farther reaches of the British empire.

As Edward T. McCarron writes in *Offaly – History and Society*: "Their Atlantic movement should be viewed as part of an ongoing process: a multi-generational 'safety valve' that sent younger sons and ambitious families outward in search of opportunity."[28]

There were significant differences between the various denominations of Protestants. When Thomas Kearney was born, about a quarter of the Irish people were Protestant. In Cork, up to 40 per cent of the population was Protestant; other Irish towns – Limerick, Drogheda, Kilkenny and Galway – were a bit less than a third Protestant. For the most part these were of the Church of Ireland, but the largest concentrations of Protestants were the Presbyterians of the north of

Ireland, whose numbers were sharply reduced by a species of forced emigration.

In the eighteenth century, long before the Famine, non-conformists or non-Anglicans – especially Presbyterians in the north of Ireland – emigrated under the pressure from the British Crown of the suppression of their religious and civil rights. Several hundred thousand people from Ireland – particularly from the province of Ulster – maintained a steady stream of emigration to America throughout the eighteenth century; some settled in the mountains of the southeastern states and became known as "Billy-Boys of the Hills", or Hillbillies, after their enthusiasm for William of Orange, or "King Billy".

In search both of land and religious freedom, the Presbyterian immigrants had settled at first in New England, New York and Pennsylvania, but later they moved to the frontier wildernesses of Virginia, Georgia and the Carolinas. Noted for their hatred of the British, many fought in the American Revolution and earned a reputation for bravery and rugged individualism. Others settled in Kentucky and Tennessee and became America's first "Indian fighters", producing such American heroes as President Andrew Jackson, Simon Kenton, Daniel Boone and Davy Crockett.

Of the Protestant Irish immigrants in the eighteenth century, two-thirds were Presbyterians, less than one-third Church of Ireland. While much has been written about the Presbyterians – or "Scotch-Irish," as they came to be termed later – very little has been written about the Church of Ireland people, despite the fact that they made significant contributions to the development of public life in America.

Often they have been described by the misleading term Anglo-Irish. Some may have been Protestant Irish of English descent, who came principally from Dublin, Cork, Wexford and the old Pale of Ireland, but others were native or Gaelic-

Irish Protestants who had no English blood; some may have been Protestant Irish from Ulster, of Scottish ancestry. Both Anglo-Irish and Scotch-Irish may in a modern sense be regarded as dubious terms, since they tend to suggest that nationality is based not on the country of a person's birth but on elements of their ancestry that render their Irishness qualified, negated or limited. As the writer Anthony Cronin writes about Anglo-Irish in *Heritage Now: Irish Literature in the English Language,* "whoever invented the term in the first place did no service at all to his countrymen, whoever they were".[29]

Although the Norths were landed proprietors, the majority of the Church of Ireland immigrants were farm labourers, small farmers and artisans; some arrived in America as indentured servants. As landed people, the Norths have left records that allow us to trace their history, and although they were not related to the Kearneys (who left no such records), their story reveals an aspect of the reality of life in Offaly and emigration from it.

The Norths settled in Portsmouth, New Hampshire, where the predominant religious denomination was Anglican and where there were other Irish settlers. Here amongst those they met was Arthur Browne, born in Drogheda and educated at Trinity College Dublin, who was rector of Queen's Chapel and who maintained over the distance of the Atlantic ocean close contact with relations and fellow churchmen in Ireland.

They teamed up with David Dunbar, an associate of Browne's, a fellow Irish-born adventurer who planned to colonise the Maine frontier. North was appointed surveyor general of the King's Woods in 1730, the year of his arrival, which gave him power over a very large expanse of timber land in northern New England.

He began to develop a new settlement at Pemaquid, writing to London that "a great many hundred men of those who come lately from Ireland" wanted to join his development.[30] This was precarious territory, distant from other, more developed communities and subject to Indian raids. Dunbar promised free homesteads to "Protestants from the north of Ireland".

The Norths joined a frontier community of some 150 families, whose farms and clearings were scattered amongst large stretches of oak and pine. Their life was hard and demanding, but redolent of hope and possibility. They succeeded in clearing the wooded wilderness around them, and they developed a leading role in the frontier community, emerging as one of the principal families of the region. A significant aspect of their role was their military capability. This was typical of many of those who had emigrated from Ireland as younger sons of landowners. Commissioned as lieutenant at Fort Frederick in 1744, John North soon became its commander. He led the defence of the fort when it was attacked by both Indians and French.

All the time, the Norths maintained contact with their Offaly homeland, and in general the daughters of the family married fellow members of the Protestant Irish community. Some of these marriages were clearly designed to consolidate estates back in Offaly.

At the same time, these colonists from landed Protestant Irish backgrounds generally integrated well into the frontier society of America. With adventurous and at times ruthless ambition, military experience, education and some legal knowledge, as well as access to capital, they were well equipped to prosper. Captain John North steadily extended a strong network of influence across the territory, encouraging his Cooper relations from west Cork and Tipperary to settle in Maine and providing military commissions and jobs at Fort Frederick for fellow Irish Protestants. Amongst those who joined North at Pemaquid were Offaly natives James and Laurence Parson from Parsonstown – now Birr. Thus close relations were maintained even in the eighteenth century between Protestant Irish settlers, and between them and their Irish homeland.

Edward T. McCarron remarks, in *Offaly History and Society*:

> Their own success and upward mobility in the years that followed was perhaps the strongest legacy of the North migration from Offaly; a migration that sought to preserve and enhance family status and convey that to future generations.[31]

Similar ambitions are likely to have motivated Thomas Kearney to migrate from Offaly, even if his family was not of the same landowning class. As a co-religionist he may have been aware of the Norths and of their success in America; the fact that amongst the Kearney relations were some who had known success in business and politics in Dublin may also have inclined him to follow in their footsteps.

So, who were the Kearneys? The original Gaelic form of the Kearney family name is Ó Cearnaigh, which derives from two different personal names: Cearnach, meaning "victorious", and Caithearnach or Catharnaigh, meaning "warlike" or "a foot-soldier". One of the most celebrated Irish warrior heroes was Conall Cearnach, or "Conal of the Victories", and Cearnach became quite a common name in the early Middle Ages. Conall Cearnach was from Ulster, but the Kearney, or Carney, name occurs quite evenly amongst the four provinces of Ireland.

One group of Kearneys, from the province of Munster, takes its name from a Cearnach who was a descendant of a chieftain named Cas, founding father of the Dalcassians, an alliance of clans that included Brian Boru and the O'Briens. These Dalcassian Kearneys, or Ó Cearnaigh, settled in Cashel in early times, and the tomb of one of their number, Nicholas O'Kearney, who died in 1460, may still be found at the Rock of Cashel in Tipperary, the county that closely borders the part of Offaly in which Thomas Kearney was born.

During the eighteenth century, most of the members of the extended Kearney family were skilled artisans, but some achieved higher social positions. Michael Kearney, a grand-uncle of Thomas who died a couple of years before his birth, had been involved in the politics of Dublin city. Michael's son, John Kearney, served as provost of Trinity College Dublin at the same time as Thomas was plying his trade as a carpenter in Baltimore, and later John Kearney became Church of Ireland bishop of Ossory. He was the great-great-great-great-granduncle of Barack Obama, and his tomb was visited in November 2009 by the US ambassador to Ireland, Dan Rooney.

Two earlier John Kearneys may well have been related, both of them Protestant clergyman and one of them also associated with Ossory. The Rev. John Kearney – also known as Seán Ó Cearnaigh – who was born in 1542, is thought to have attended an Irish bardic school before studying at Magdalene College Cambridge, where he took a BA in 1565; there he was a contemporary of a future bishop of Ossory, Nicholas Walsh. He returned to Ireland, where he became treasurer of St Patrick's Cathedral, Dublin. In 1571 he published, with assistance from Nicholas Walsh and Alderman John Ussher, the first book ever printed in Gaelic in Ireland, *Aibidil Gaoidheilge agus Caiticíosma,* which is sometimes referred to in English as *Alphabet of the Irish Language and Catechism.* This small volume consists of a translation of the Anglican catechism, with an explanation of the Irish alphabet and rules of pronunciation.

AIBIDIL

Gaoidheilge, ⁊ Caiticiosma .i.
foircheadal nó teagaſg Chriosdghe,
maille lé háthioglúb ógmhóe don pia-
gal Chrioroúge, ⁊ ingabcha, dá gach con
da mbé fómánta do peacd Dia ⁊ na
bannpiogā ra pige ro, do tángeam ar
lgoeā, ⁊ ar gaillbépla go gaoideilg, lá
Seaan o keannaig.

[manuscript annotation]

Eprīg : creud rá gcollañ tú a thigéapna?
múrgail : ⁊ na teilg pñ go déog.

Psalm. 43. uer. 23.

Do bugléad ro ágcló gaoideilge, ambq
le Atachhac, ⁊ corpas mgghroin Sheón
yrez aldapman; ór chioñ an óriojchio, an
20. lá do Juin. 1571.

Maille lé prīthghiléio na mór piogna.
1571.

[manuscript annotation: 8ᵒ e·31]

The title page of John Kearney's
Aibidil Gaoidheilge agus Caiticíosma *(1571)*

Alderman John Ussher, who sponsored the publication, took an active part in city affairs, and he worked to promote the establishment of a university in Dublin twenty years prior to the foundation of Trinity College. The first book to be printed in Gaelic had been published in Scotland in 1567 and used Roman characters, but Kearney's used a Gaelic typeface. It is thought that the printer was William Kearney, a relative of John's, who later printed the New Testament in Gaelic and was Queen Elizabeth's printer in Ireland. The New Testament was published by William Daniel in a translation by John Kearney and others. John Ware, under the date 1571, writes:

> This year the Irish Characters for Printing were first brought into the Kingdom by Nicholas Walsh, Chancellor of Saint Patrick's in Dublin, and John Kerne [sic], then Treasurer of the same; and it was ordered that the prayers of the Church should be printed in that Character and Language and a Church set apart in the chief Town of every Diocese, where they were to be Read, and a Sermon preached to the common People.[32]

In 1572, John Kearney had been offered the see of Tuam, but declined it due to the state of unrest in Connaught. He does not appear to have been involved in any further publications and nothing more is known of his life; he died in about 1600.

William Kearney became printer at the newly established Trinity College in the final decade of the century.

Another Rev. John Kearney, born in about 1613, became vicar general of the diocese of Ossory and served in the parishes of Kilmanagh, Dunkitt, Dysertmore and Rosbercon. In 1641, during the Irish rebellion, he lost property to the value of £401 when his house was raided. He died in about 1665, and he was followed into the clergy by his sons Richard, who was rector of Kiltokeghan in 1671, and John, who was vicar of Rosbercon in 1686.[33]

Some Kearneys whose descendants now live in New Jersey, Maryland, Pennsylvania and other parts of the United States, and who gave their name to cities called Kearney in Missouri and Nebraska, were among the earliest settlers in America, but are not believed to be related to the Kearneys of Moneygall and Shinrone.

Thomas Kearney's grandfather Joseph, born in about 1698, had four sons of whom we know. Of these, the eldest, Thomas, born in about 1725, took over the family business of wig- or peruke-making. Joseph, born in about 1730, worked in the woollen industry as a comber.

Michael Kearney, who was a brother of Joseph Sr, joined the Guild of Barber Surgeons and Periwigmakers in 1717 and was listed as a "Capillamentarius" – a hairdresser – in the Freemens' Rolls in 1718. As a freeman of Dublin, he had the right to practise his trade and conduct business in the city, and he had a vote in elections for the city council. He quickly became active within the guild of his trade, and in 1720 he was elected house warden. In 1724, he led a public campaign against the master and warden of his guild. Although suspended, he enjoyed the support of many of his fellow guild members, and in 1726 he was elected by an overwhelming vote as master of the Guild of Barber Surgeons.[34]

A pamphlet attacking Michael Kearney, entitled *Hue and Cry,* was published in 1726, shortly after his election.[35] A piece of political satire, it is deliberately defamatory, and one verse reads:

> His head is still running
> On tricking and cunning
> But he mayn't escape let me tell you

> For the Fox has been caught
> And pay'd dear at last
> For the Geese he had put in his Belly.

In the 1750s he was one of a number of local businessmen, known as Dublin guildsmen, who resisted the attempts of the aristocracy to gerrymander elections to Dublin City Council. In this campaign he made common cause with Charles Lucas, an interesting and significant figure of the time, a pamphleteer and politician of Cromwellian stock who

> ...gained the enmity of the Irish government when he published his "Address to the Free Citizens of Dublin" in 1749. In it he questioned the right of the king to legislate for Ireland. His enemies in the Irish House of Commons and Dublin Corporation were pleased that Lucas had pushed his luck too far. They pounced and declared that his pamphlet was treasonable and they denounced Lucas as an enemy to his country. The citizens of Dublin however supported Lucas and there were public demonstrations in his favour.[36]

However, he had to flee to Holland, returning in 1761 on the accession of George III to Ireland, where he was elected to the Irish House of Commons to represent Dublin city. Lucas had succeeded in gaining the support of many of the guilds in Dublin, and Michael Kearney continued to be a prominent member of the Guild of Barber Surgeons until his death in 1762.

Following his death, his wig-making business was taken over by his nephews from the King's County, who prospered in the business up to and including the 1780s. However, the fortunes of the Kearney family declined quite rapidly after the 1780s.

Wigs fell out of fashion: all but the legal profession and the political elite preferred to dress their own hair rather than wear a wig. Meanwhile, the abolition of the Irish parliament under the Act of Union of 1801 meant that Irish MPs now sat in Westminster, so the Irish political establishment moved from Dublin to London, taking with them the market for wigs.

However, the Kearneys were not destitute. Michael Kearney had invested in property in Tipperary, Offaly and in the city of Dublin. He was able to provide good dowries for his daughters and university education for his two sons. Michael, born in 1734, was educated at Ballitore School in County Kildare, a Quaker school established in 1726 by Abraham Shackleton (1697–1771), which catered especially for Quakers but also for Protestant and Catholic children. Pupils came from as far away as Bordeaux, Jamaica and Norway to study in the school. He entered Trinity College Dublin in 1748, was elected to a scholarship in 1750, graduated with a BA in 1752 and became a fellow in 1757. He was professor of modern history at Trinity from 1769 to 1778, regius professor of law from 1776 to 1781 and Archbishop King's lecturer from 1774 to 1777. He resigned from these last two positions in 1778 and effectively retired to the living of Tullyaughnish, a country parish in Raphoe; in 1798 he became archdeacon of Raphoe.

A scholar with a wide range of intellectual capacities, he took up the question of the alphabet in a paper he contributed to the *Transactions of the Royal Irish Academy*. He may perhaps have been stimulated to address the matter by the fact that his possible ancestor, Rev. John Kearney, had two centuries earlier written a book on the alphabet in Irish. He also contributed a paper on Sir Joshua Reynolds' *Discourses* and in 1776 published a book of *Lectures Concerning History*.[37] Nevertheless, he was felt by contemporaries to have failed to fulfil his potential. He died in 1814, and the author of his obituary in the *Gentleman's Magazine* observed that he was

... deeply read in divinity, versed in all the sub-
tleties of metaphysical disquisition, unequalled as a
historian, skilled alike in the learned and modern
languages and critically acquainted with English literature.[38]

But inexplicably he had spent his last thirty-six years in a
small country parish isolated from his intellectual peers.

His younger brother John, born in 1744, was educated at
the Rev. Thomas Benson's school in Dublin and followed
Michael into Trinity College Dublin in 1757. He was elected
a scholar in 1760, graduated with a BA in 1762 and was elected to a fellowship in 1764. He was co-opted as a senior fellow
in 1782 and was also professor of oratory (1781–99) and
Archbishop King's lecturer in divinity (1782 and 1787). In
1785, he was a prime mover in a campaign to have an Irishman – James Caulfield, Lord Charlemont – rather than an
Englishman appointed chancellor of the university. Conscien-
tious and popular, he apparently recognised and encouraged
the gifts of one of the undergraduates of the time, Thomas
Moore, who became Ireland's most famous balladeer and
poet. Moore was one of the first Roman Catholics to attend
Trinity, and he described John Kearney as being full of "dry
drollery"; his wife as being "lively, literary and musical", and
their house as "the resort of the best society in Dublin". John
Kearney published two sermons, one of which, in May 1798
– like a poem he published anonymously in the same year –
expressed his opposition to the United Irish rebellion and what
he called "the rage of democracy and the zeal of fanaticism".

He was appointed provost in 1799, and both he and a
majority of the fellows in Trinity opposed the Act of Union
that united the kingdoms of Great Britain and Ireland to
create the United Kingdom. The Provost's House, which
became his home, had been built in 1760 and survives in

good condition as the functioning residence of the current provost. A solid Palladian building with a central Venetian window and doric pilasters, internally it is one of the most elaborately decorated houses of its period, remarkable for the quality of its plasterwork.

In 1806, John Kearney resigned as provost to take up the appointment of bishop of Ossory, moving in to the bishop's palace in Kilkenny. The building of the palace had started in the mid-fourteenth century under Bishop Richard Ledred, a controversial figure who pursued the trial for witchcraft of Alice Kyteler. Two hundred years later, a three-storey tower was built at the eastern end of the palace. During the wars of the mid-seventeenth century, the cathedral precinct suffered substantial damage, and by 1660 was "all ruined and nothing standing but the bare walls without roofs". In the following years, however, the building was renovated, acquiring a new roof and new rooms, as well as new windows and doors. In the early eighteenth century, four rooms and the staircase, which can be seen today, were added.

About thirty years before it became Bishop Kearney's home, one of his predecessors, Bishop Newcombe (1775–79) wrote to his brother that he found his

> . . . present situation agreeable and even delight-
> ful . . . adjoining to the rear is as pleasant a garden,
> well walled in and well planted with shrubs. . . . as
> any one would wish to be master of. In the garden
> is a summer house of a very good size with a fire-
> place, fit for drinking tea or a glass of wine and
> from this room a covered way leads to the best
> cathedral in Ireland . . . The country about is very
> pleasant and everything conduces to health and
> cheerfulness.[39]

Bishop John Kearney, as was often the practice at the time, used his appointment to the benefit of other members of his family. His first son, also John Kearney, rector of Castle Inch, became chancellor of Ossory in 1809 and served until his death in 1838 at the age of sixty-eight from cholera; fourteen years earlier his only grandson had also died of cholera at just five years and five months old. The bishop's second son Thomas Henry was prebendary of Ossory from 1810 to 1812 but left no heirs.

Bishop John Kearney died in May 1813 at his palace, and his tomb may be seen on an inside wall of the medieval St Canice's Cathedral in Kilkenny, bearing the epitaph: "The duties of the episcopate he piously discharged, and in the studies of things divine and human he trained his mind with diligence and refinement." Beneath it in the floor lies the tomb of his son John, who died in 1838, his son's wife Elizabeth, who died in 1844, and their young son John James, who died in 1824.

The more privileged line of the family, represented by John Kearney, died out. Meanwhile, the trading Kearneys seem to have lost their business links with Dublin and to have become restricted to the less prosperous territory of Offaly and Tipperary. Two of Michael Kearney's nephews were William Kearney, born in 1762, and his brother Thomas, born in 1765, the same Thomas Kearney who emigrated to America and was married in Baltimore in 1791. William remained in Ireland and became a shoemaker, as later did William's son Joseph, born in about 1794.

The move from wig-making to shoemaking represented a step down the social and economic ladder, especially as it was accompanied by a move from Dublin to the Offaly and Tipperary border. However, the shoemaker enjoyed a position of some importance in the Ireland of the time and could earn a good living. William, as the oldest son, took on his father's trade, but there would probably not have been room in the business for Thomas to work alongside his older brother.

At the same time, the linen industry in Ireland had suffered a temporary collapse, causing widespread unemployment in the northern counties especially, but also in Leinster. This provoked mass emigration in the 1770s, and although there was a marked revival of that industry only ten years later, the decline of the silk, woollen and other industries also led to serious loss of employment, as did the decline of small local breweries in the face of the consolidation of larger breweries in the big cities. As Kerby A. Miller writes in *Emigrants and Exiles: Ireland and the Irish Exodus to North America*:

> ...in the late eighteenth century the Irish woollen industry began a precipitous decline. By the 1790s rural employment in spinning had contracted by 50 percent, because of the disappearance of the once-flourishing export trade in woollen yarn . . . [L]oss of that income reduced thousands of rural families in south Leinster and Munster to what Lord Fitzgibbon described as "a state of oppression, abject poverty, sloth, dirt and misery not to be equalled in any other part of the world."[40]

To make matters worse, in rural Offaly and Tipperary, farmers with long leases falling due found their rents raised four- or five-fold. In the circumstances, Thomas may well have felt that there was little opportunity at home and every reason to use whatever resources he possessed or could muster from relatives to embark on a journey to the New World in the hope of better fortune.

— 3 —

Ireland's Great Turning Point

Around the time of Thomas Kearney's marriage in Baltimore to Sarah Baxley, the people of his native land began to undergo a political struggle, the working out of which would determine the shape of modern Ireland. In September 1791, Theobald Wolfe Tone published a pamphlet entitled *Argument on Behalf of the Catholics of Ireland;* this recognised religious division as Ireland's core problem and advanced the case for unity between Catholic, Protestant and Dissenter. Strongly influenced by Thomas Paine's *The Rights of Man,* it was itself an enormously influential publication.

A group of nine Belfast Presbyterians seeking political reform read Tone's pamphlet and invited him and his friend and fellow activist Thomas Russell to a meeting of the group in Belfast in October 1791. This was the first meeting of what became known as the United Irishmen, and it passed three resolutions:

> FIRST RESOLVED – That the weight of English influence on the Government of this country is so great as to require a cordial union among all the people of Ireland, to maintain that balance which is

essential to the preservation of our liberties and the extension of our commerce.

SECOND – That the sole constitutional mode by which this influence can be opposed is by a complete and radical reform of the representation of the people in Parliament.

THIRD – That no reform is practicable, efficacious, or just, which shall not include Irishmen of every religious persuasion.

All at the first meeting were Protestant, and most were involved in the Belfast linen trade. Two – Tone and Russell – were Anglicans and the rest Presbyterian. Theirs was a vision of a universal republicanism and the separation of religion and politics. A Dublin branch of the United Irishmen was founded in November, and the organisation also linked up with the militant Catholic agrarian secret society, the Defenders, which had arisen out of conflict with sectarian Protestant groups. The movement spread rapidly, and in 1793 the authorities moved to ban it.

The British administration in Dublin applied the carrot as well as the stick, allowing Catholics to vote, to become barristers and to join Trinity College Dublin. In 1795 they abolished the Hearth Tax, and they funded St Patrick's seminary at Maynooth. And in 1794, William Drennan, a leader of the United Irishmen, was arrested and tried for sedition. The Orange Order was founded as a military counterpoint to the spread of the United Irishmen, while the administration secured the loyalty of the hierarchy of the Catholic church with the founding by parliament of the Royal Catholic College of Maynooth in 1795.

In 1796, a French fleet carrying 15,000 troops set sail for Ireland to support a planned rising by the United Irishmen but was unable to land because of bad weather. The British rounded up much of the United Irish leadership and imposed martial law in 1797. Indecision and the arrest of most of the leadership deprived the movement of the ability to strike effectively, and a planned rising on 23 May 1798 was undermined by informers, but tens of thousands did join in a rising and were ruthlessly crushed.

Tullamore, County Offaly, in 1793 had one of the earliest United Irish societies outside Dublin and Belfast. Sir Laurence Parsons, a substantial landlord whose home was Birr Castle, Parsonstown, was an outspoken advocate of political reform and a friend of Wolfe Tone. However, the divisions caused by reports of sectarian attacks by Catholics on Protestants were especially strongly marked in Offaly in 1798 when a Protestant leader of the United Irishmen reacted to such reports by abandoning the republican cause and surrendering information to the government.

The Protestant involvement at all levels in the United Irishmen threatened to undermine the cohesion of the forces of the state.

> It was discovered shortly before the outbreak of rebellion in May 1798 that the United Irishmen of the Clonlisk/Ballybrit district had infiltrated the Shinrone, Castleotway, Nenagh and Roscrea corps and had seventeen of their members in the ranks of the Dunkerrin Cavalry. Arms, intelligence and training were thus received by the republicans while their loyalist opposition was weakened to the same degree.[41]

However, the rebels themselves were subject to debilitating divisions:

> Pressure from the army rocked the internal cohesion of the King's County United Irishmen in April/May and this, combined with certain external

factors beyond their control, greatly reduced their offensive capacity during the rebellion.[42]

It was not only in its leadership that Protestants played an important role in the United Irish Rising of 1798. Rev. Patrick Comerford tells a story from the period:

> . . . in the days when only officers could afford uniforms, there was one way in battle to tell soldiers and rebels apart: if a man spoke in English and said his prayers from the *Book of Common Prayer,* he was fighting with the United Irishmen; but if he spoke in Irish and said Catholic prayers he was fighting with the North Cork Militia [i.e. on the side of the English government].[43]

The tide could not be turned by the arrival of 1,000 French troops in August at Killala, and in October, Wolfe Tone was captured when a French fleet with 3,000 troops was defeated by the British Royal Navy. Having been denied a soldier's death by firing squad, Tone cheated the hangman by cutting his own throat.

In the aftermath of the rebellion, the government and its allies exploited sectarianism in its struggle with the remnants of the United Irishmen. Thousands of Catholics were driven from counties Antrim, Down and Armagh, and hundreds of Protestants suspected of United Irish sympathies were murdered, tortured and imprisoned. The vast majority of the 15,000–30,000 people who were killed during the rebellion were victims of British and loyalist troops, but most attention was reserved for a few instances in which United Irish rebels carried out sectarian massacres, most notoriously in County Wexford at Scullabogue and Wexford Bridge.

Despite the suppression of the rising, the United Irishmen survived in certain counties as an underground movement, but it was further weakened by the British government strategy of playing Catholic against Protestant. Its last gasp came in 1803 with the failure of the rising led by United Irishman Robert Emmet. The movement effectively collapsed, though it was not until the following year that the last armed rebel group was disbanded.

Sir Charles Coote's *Statistical Survey of the King's County* in 1801 noted the Millbrook bolting-mills – where flour was sifted – of Dennis Cassin, Esq. Two years later Cassin was arrested at the time of Robert Emmet's abortive uprising in July 1803 and held without trial in Dublin's Kilmainham Gaol, from which in December 1804 he petitioned the lord lieutenant for clemency.

We do not know what were Thomas Kearney's political views, but as he prepared his family for the challenging journey from Baltimore, he will have been aware of what was going on at home, for not only were the events of the risings reported in the American press, but many more Irish were swiftly emigrating in the face of the suppression of the United Irishmen, bringing news of the great failure with them. Amongst those who emigrated at this time were many of the mostly Protestant, non-Defender members of the United Irishmen, some of whom were soon to play significant roles in American politics. These included Thomas Addis Emmet, brother of Robert Emmet, and James Orr – a brother of a martyred member of the United Irishmen, William Orr – whom Thomas Kearney was soon to meet.

The alliance between Protestant and Catholic was sundered as many Protestants were drawn towards a sense of "British" identity through the fear of having their perceived privileges threatened by the gradually increasing political power of the Catholic majority.

As Fergus Whelan writes in *Dissent into Treason*:

Lovely Lane Methodist Church in Baltimore, the Mother Church of American Methodism (Stephen MacDonogh)

The Rock of Cashel (Joseph Mischyshyn)

The tomb of Nicholas O'Kearney in the thirteenth-century St Patrick's Cathedral at the Rock of Cashel (Stephen MacDonogh)

*Trinity College, Dublin: closely associated with
Rev. John Kearney (1542–1600), Rev. Michael Kearney (1734–1814) and
Rev. John Kearney (1742–1813)* (Joseph Mischyshyn)

The Provost's House (Trinity College, Dublin)

Portrait of Bishop John Kearney (1742–1813)
(Kilkenny Bishop's House Portrait Collection, the Representative Church Body)

The staircase at the Bishop's Palace, Kilkenny (Stephen MacDonogh)

St Canice's Cathedral, Kilkenny (Stephen MacDonogh)

Tomb of Bishop John Kearney, who died in 1813, and beneath it of his son John, his son's wife, Elizabeth, and their son John James
(Stephen MacDonogh)

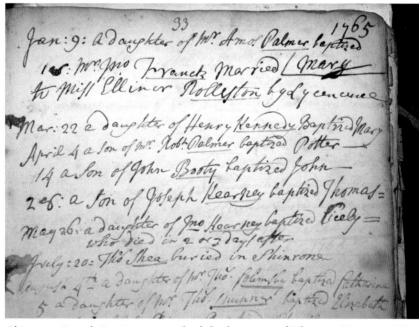

Shinrone Parish Register record of the marriage of Joseph Kearney and Sarah Healy, 1761

Shinrone Parish Register record of the baptism of Thomas Kearney, 1765

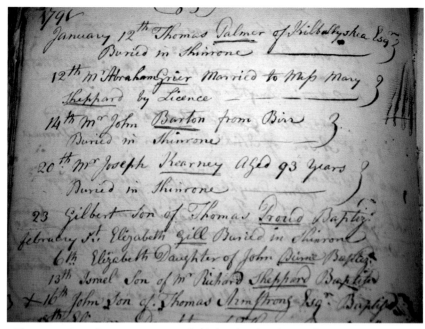

Shinrone Parish Register record of the death of Joseph Kearney in 1791

Shinrone Church of Ireland graveyard, where Joseph Kearney was buried
(Stephen MacDonogh)

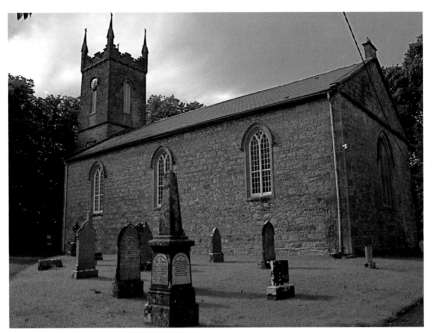

Shinrone Church of Ireland, built in 1820 (Stephen MacDonogh)

Cullenwaine cemetery, where many Kearneys are buried, though none of their gravestones are identifiable (Stephen MacDonogh)

Templeharry Church, built in 1814, where many of the Kearneys were baptised (Stephen MacDonogh)

Templeharry Church (Stephen MacDonogh)

Templeharry Parish Register record of William Kearney's baptism in 1831

Templeharry Parish Register record of Mary Anne Kearney's baptism in 1837

Dunkerrin Church (Stephen MacDonogh)

Borrisnafarney Church, where some of the Healys are buried
(Stephen MacDonogh)

Busherstown House, Moneygall, one of the homes of the Minchins
(Stephen MacDonogh)

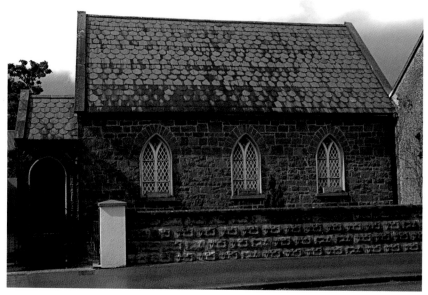

Former Church of Ireland school in Moneygall where the Kearneys attended religious services (Stephen MacDonogh)

House on the site of the Kearneys' house in Moneygall (Stephen MacDonogh)

Some of Emmet's working class citizen soldiers escaped to England and brought their democratic politics into the Luddite and Chartist movements. Within twenty years Daniel O'Connell had led Roman Catholic Ireland to a nationalism that equated the cause of Ireland with the cause of Roman Catholicism, and where there was no space for Dissenters or their universal republicanism.[44]

The Ireland and the Offaly Thomas Kearney had left were changed utterly. Increasingly, Irishness was to be associated with Catholicism, while Protestants were to be regarded as essentially English.

Marianne Elliott, in *When God Took Sides,* wrote that "No one until O'Connell had drawn the link between Irishness and Catholicism quite so publicly or successfully, and he recruited the priests . . ."[45]

The defeat of the United Irishmen and the triumph of Daniel O'Connell's movement led to a growing sense of Irishness being associated exclusively in the public mind with Catholicism and the Catholic community, although many members of the Church of Ireland continued to see themselves as Irish.

The great turning point left Protestant radical republicans bereft of almost any sense of direction and relevance, and this stimulated a new wave of emigration. At the same time that Thomas Kearney was planning to move his family from Baltimore across the Ohio River to the Virginia Military District, many of the most radical and progressive Irish people were leaving Ireland for America.

That the emigrants at this time were disproportionately Protestant owes much to the fact that Catholics were noticeably less inclined to emigrate to America than their Protestant neighbours. For largely cultural reasons, they saw emigration far more negatively than Protestants. A ballad of the time expressed Catholic fears:

An exile, I fly to the banks of Ohio,
Where gloomy dark deserts bewilder my way. . .
Where fell snakes are hissing and dire monsters screaming.
Where death pregnant lightnings are dreadfully gleaming,
And direful contagion destruction proclaiming,
Infest every vale and embitter each day.

Protestants, on the other hand, tended to hold the kind of positive outlook that informed the emigration of the Norths from Offaly, even if they were people of no property.

No figures are available for how many United Irishmen made the journey to America, but it is clear that their influence was enormous, and they brought into the heart of American public life their revolutionary, democratic and republican principles. As Timothy Meagher writes:

> . . . in an age of revolution they had become revolutionaries, and when their dreams for a new Ireland were crushed, they would seek exile in America, the nursery of republicanism and revolution. There, these men and others could boast of their Irish loyalties and scheme for Ireland's redemption. Yet the Ireland that they were loyal to would not be a Catholic, nationalist Ireland, nor would the Irish America they sought to create in the United States be the Catholic nationalist Irish America of the late nineteenth century. These men's vision was of a new beginning for their old country: the birth of a non-sectarian, republican Ireland, backed by Irish Americans of all sects, Catholics and Protestants united by similar, republican sympathies.[46]

They became not just leaders of the Irish in America, but political leaders, pamphleteers, ideologues and activists in the political life of America itself. Within a few years United Irishmen were editors of no less than seventeen newspapers across the nation.

As David Brundage writes in "Recent Directions in the History of Irish American Nationalism:"

> Irish American nationalists have also exerted great influence on political and social developments in the United States itself, with, for example, exiled members of the United Irishmen becoming central figures within Jefferson's Democratic-Republican coalition in the early nineteenth century.[47]

At a time when the new immigrants were able to take advantage of American economic prosperity, their Irish republicanism found positive parallels in American popular politics. They readily supported Jeffersonian principles, attitudes and policies, such as egalitarianism, extension of the franchise, opposition to elites, the rights of states against federal power, a decentralized model of economic growth, anti-Britishness and pro-French and Irish revolutionary sentiments.

Thomas Jefferson's election in 1800 was achieved to a substantial extent with Irish-American support and provided a validation of Irish revolutionary ideals in "this happy country, where Liberty is triumphant and cherished" – as Thomas Addis Emmet expressed it. One of the effects of the United Irishmen's successful intervention in America was to lay the basis for Catholics to begin to look more positively upon the possibility of emigration. As Kerby A. Miller writes in *Emigrants and Exiles*: ". . . even before 1814, Catholics' perceptions of America and of the act of emigration itself were changing and coming to resemble those long held by Irish Dissenters."[48]

In general during this period, Irish Catholic immigrants enjoyed a considerable identity of interest with the Protestant United Irishmen and the "Scotch-Irish". "[I]mmigrants from every part of Ireland shared a sense of fellow feeling."[49]

United Irish exiles such as Thomas Addis Emmet, William MacNeven and William Sampson were resolutely nonsectarian; they championed Catholic emancipation, and they and the Democratic Republicans supported the right of the Irish in America to organise in support of Daniel O'Connell. Emmet, who briefly served as New York State attorney general, became one of the most respected attorneys in the United States. He and fellow lawyer William Sampson, Protestant United Irishmen both, battled for years in the courts of the United States to extend Catholic rights to equal participation in American life. Tom Paine left him, as an expression of his respect, the substantial sum of $200 in his will.

Ireland had surrendered to exile a generation of its finest minds and spirits. The contribution that these publicly minded democrats might have made to the creation of an independent democratic and republican society in Ireland was lost to their native land. How great that loss was is hinted at by the contributions many of them made in their new home of America.

It is hardly surprising that when Thomas Kearney became dissatisfied with life in Baltimore, he did not look back to his native Ireland; instead he looked westwards towards the American frontier.

— 4 —

To the Frontier

Thomas and Sarah Kearney may have felt restricted in what they could achieve in Baltimore, and perhaps like many others at that time they wished to escape from a state in which slavery was the norm – escape into a new territory free of the obscenity of slavery. For whatever reason, their attention turned towards the Virginia Military District, a region some distance to the west which was part of what was known as "the Old Northwest", an area of land that included the present states of Ohio, Illinois, Michigan, Wisconsin and part of Minnesota.

For all the years of white settlement in America, the Appalachian Mountains had formed a substantial barrier to east-west travel, from Pennsylvania to Georgia, and an impediment to settlement west of the eastern coastal region. Indian hostility had also discouraged potential settlers. But all began to change after the Battle of Fallen Timbers in 1794, near what is now Toledo.

One of the most notable military actions that occurred when Thomas Kearney was in his twenties was the campaign of US Army and regional state militiamen against the confederation of Indian nations in the northwestern territories that lay beyond the Appalachians. A series of battles culminated in 1794 at the Battle of Fallen Timbers, where American forces under the command of General "Mad" Anthony Wayne defeated the Indian alliance. General Anthony Wayne was a son of Captain Isaac Wayne (1699–1774), a Protestant born in County Wicklow, Ireland, to Captain Anthony Wayne, a Williamite veteran of the Battle of the Boyne.

It is possible that Thomas Kearney may have seen military service himself during this decisive campaign against the Indians. A great many able-bodied men in Maryland who were in their late teens and twenties between 1780 and 1795 saw some kind of military service. In addition, it was a particular characteristic of Irish Protestants who emigrated to America in the eighteenth century to become involved in military action.

If he did serve in Wayne's army, he may have been one of many soldiers who were rewarded with land grants in the Virginia Military District, part of what would later become the state of Ohio. As Andrew Lee Feight writes in "Land Speculation, Lawlessness, and the Establishment of Seats of Government in Ohio's Scioto Country, 1783–1807":

> Many of the future settlers of the Scioto Country saw service in these campaigns and when the peace had been secured they and thousands of others from Virginia and other eastern states descended upon the Scioto Valley like a host of locusts.[50]

At any time these eager settlers could encounter Shawnee, Cherokee or Delaware Indians, and all around them lay the remarkable earthworks of the much earlier Native Americans.

Between 200 BC and AD 500, there had flourished a prehistoric culture now known as the Hopewell culture (after an early settler farmer who owned the land where one of the mound complexes was located). This culture, which included a network of beliefs and practices shared by various Native American groups, extended over a large part of eastern North America. Its characteristic monuments are mounds of various shapes and enclosures made of earthen walls, often constructed in geometric patterns. The most visible remains are to be found today in the Scioto River Valley, where the most dramatic Hopewell sites feature conical and loaf-shaped earthen mounds up to 30 feet high, along with earthworks in squares, circles and other shapes. Some of the earthen walls stand up to 12 feet high and delineate geometric figures more than 1,000 feet across. Each mound constituted a burial site; after these prehistoric people had cremated their dead, they constructed a mound over the remains and placed in the mounds various artifacts, such as arrowheads, shells, copper figures, mica and pipes.

The Native Americans who now surrounded the new settlers were not descendants of those who had constructed the Hopewell Mounds. They were tribes that had been forced by the actions of white settlers in Pennsylvania and Kentucky out of their own areas and into the Scioto Valley.

The Shawnee in particular had long posed a threat to the white settlers.

> The determination of the Shawnee (and other Ohio Indians) to maintain possession of their lands north and west of the Ohio river posed the most immediate hindrance to the designs of Virginia veterans and other land speculators who sought their fortunes in the Scioto Valley.
>
> Only the extinguishment of Indian land claims to the region would allow for the legal (though not necessarily orderly) survey, sale, and settlement of the region.[51]

Another author, writing about the desire for independence that drove settlers westward in search of land, observed:

> Because almost every white family sought a farm and because the white population doubled every twenty-five years, each new generation doubled the demand for land, putting increased pressure on the beleaguered Indians in the interior. It was a bitter irony that, to obtain the property for independence, settlers violently dispossessed the native tribes, destroying the independence of the Indians whom they found in the supposed wilderness. One people's freedom came at another's expense.[52]

In 1785, Shawnee leaders signed a treaty relinquishing their claims to land in southern Ohio, under the threat that their women and children would be killed. Many Shawnee did not accept the treaty. In response to their alleged breach of the treaty, an America militia force crossed the Ohio River from Kentucky and destroyed Shawnee villages and killed the Shawnee leader Moluntha. In the wake of this action, the first land surveys were carried out in the Virginia Military District.

> The surveying activities of the Virginians, along with other encroachments on to lands claimed by Ohio Indian nations, would then become the primary cause of Indian attacks on American surveyors and settlers in the late 1780s and early 1790s. The Indian raids involved extreme physical violence, hostage taking, and horse thefts, which, in turn, generated a series of military operations against the Indian inhabitants.[53]

Gen. Josiah Harmar led the first federal campaign into the Scioto Valley in 1790. In the following year the first white settlement was established in the Virginia Military District by a group of largely Kentucky settlers under the leadership of Nathaniel Massie at a place named Massie's Station (later Manchester). Conflict continued between a confederation of Indian nations and both regional militias and the US Army, culminating in the defeat of the Indians by General Anthony Wayne at the Battle of Fallen Timbers in 1794.

The next year, Massie brought an armed group to survey lands near what would become Chillicothe and attacked a band of Shawnee who were camping on Paint Creek, an established Indian hunting ground. They killed some of the Indians and looted their property. Later, Massie acquired the lands at the confluence of Paint Creek and the Scioto River.

The Scioto Valley, although characterised by continuing conflict with the Shawnee Indians, was a wonderfully fertile area, which seemed to some a veritable Promised Land. In addition, land surveyors were beginning to survey and divide the land, and most of them were from Baltimore or had connections with the city. What money Thomas might have had with which to buy land if he did not receive a military land grant is uncertain, but his father-in-law, John Baxley, had been the owner of considerable property. Indeed, in later years he had fallen out with his former military commander and fellow Methodist Samuel Owings over the title to land in Mount Royal, Baltimore city, that he had sold for the substantial sum of $2,500. He left no will, but an accounting was made to the Orphans' Court in 1806. His estate appears to have amounted to $36,335, a very considerable sum in its time. What may have happened is that John Baxley may have conveyed property to relatives before his death. Also, as a Hero of the Revolution, he was entitled to claim land, quite likely in the military district, and may have chosen to assign part or all of his claim to his daughter or son-in-law.

By 1798, there was a population of over five thousand adult settlers in the Northwest Territory, or Old Northwest, and representatives were chosen for the legislature, which first met in Cincinnati. Puritans, "Scotch-Irish" Presbyterians, Quakers and Methodists made up a large proportion of the legislature.

Meanwhile, over 40 per cent of the judges and members of the legislative council were Puritans, Methodists or Presbyterians. Edward Tiffin, who was speaker of the house, was also a preacher in the Methodist Church. His brother-in-law, Thomas Worthington, was another influential Methodist, who was a surveyor from Virginia. Before leaving Virginia in 1798, the two men freed their slaves, and several of these now free African-American men accompanied their former owners to the Northwest Territory.

Nathaniel Massie became the leader amongst the first settlers in the Virginia Military District in southern Ohio, a tract of more than four million acres of excellent agricultural land. Jefferson was the guiding spirit of such men, considered the friend of the West. The spirit of individual liberty and opposition to paternal control was a characteristic of the people moving into the area.

The rich bottom land between the Scioto and Little Miami rivers had already begun to attract a number of settlers, most of whom were Virginia Revolutionary soldiers who now claimed their free allotments. This land was not protected, as Cincinnati and Marietta were, by federal forts. So, Virginia's strong and self-reliant war veterans erected their own block-houses and defended themselves against Indian attacks.

By 1799, just before Thomas Kearney and his family came to the Virginia Military District, a remarkable leader had established his influence not only over his own Shawnee people but also the Delawares and other tribes present in the region. Tecumseh, whose name means "shooting star", was born in what would become the state of Ohio in 1768. His father had died at the Battle of Point Pleasant during Lord Dunmore's War in 1774. In the wake of this war, many Shawnee, including his mother, fled from the threatening advance of white settlers, moving westward to Indiana, Illinois and Missouri. Tecumseh, however, remained and was raised by his sister, Tecumpease, and his eldest brother, Chiksika, who trained him to become a warrior.

When he was only fourteen, he experienced his first military action, against an army led by George Rogers Clark, and it was a humiliating experience, as he fled from the battlefield. But he soon became a brave and admired warrior and a Shawnee leader, fighting in 1791 in the victorious Indian campaign against the army of Arthur St Clair. As an emerging leader, he called for resistance against further white settlement, but the next campaign of the Indians in the Northwestern Territory was not so successful. After the Battle of Fallen Timbers in 1794, most of the tribes living in the region signed the Treaty of Greeneville in 1795, surrendering all the land except the northwestern corner of present-day Ohio.

Tecumseh opposed this surrender, and he set about working for a confederacy of Indian tribes west of the Appalachian Mountains to resist white advancement. Tecumseh believed that no single tribe owned the land and that if they united, they would be stronger militarily. He visited most of the Indian tribes west of the Appalachians between Canada and the Gulf of Mexico to gain their support. In this he was assisted by his younger brother, Tenskwatawa, the Prophet, who had a vision in which the Master of Life, the Shawnee's primary god, told him that only if they returned to native customs, giving up all white customs and products such as alcohol and guns, would they drive the whites from the land. Many embraced the

Prophet's message and joined the two brothers at Prophetstown, a village they established in the Indiana Territory.

The governor of the Indiana Territory, William Henry Harrison, led an army towards the village in 1811. Tecumseh was away in the south seeking allies and had ordered his brother not to attack the Americans. However, the Prophet, inspired by another vision, attacked Harrison's army. The Americans defeated the Indians at the Battle of Tippecanoe and destroyed Prophetstown. Harrison's victory played a key role in securing his eventual election in 1840 as president of the United States.

This defeat, and the reluctance of the tribes to put aside their traditional differences to unite, substantially weakened Tecumseh's confederation. Some Indians, including some of his own Shawnee tribe, now preferred white customs. During the War of 1812, Tecumseh allied himself and his followers with the British, hoping that if they won, they would return the Indians' land to them. However, at the Battle of the Thames – near present-day Chatham, Ontario – in 1813, Tecumseh was killed by an American bullet, and his death brought about the end of united Indian resistance against the Americans.

Nathaniel Massie had established the first settlement in this district, at Manchester, north of the Ohio River, in 1790. Another settlement nearly a hundred miles up the Scioto, at Chillicothe, was founded six years later. Massie sold the land around Chillicothe to settlers who braved the dangers of pushing on from the Ohio River into the interior in small tracts at low prices, while some tracts were apportioned by the Virginia government as a reward for military service. Amongst the first one hundred pioneers from Virginia and Kentucky were such men as Edward Tiffin, the first governor; Thomas Worthington, a United States senator; Michael Baldwin, speaker of the lower house; and Duncan McArthur, eleventh governor of Ohio.

Born in Goochland County, Virginia, in 1763, Nathaniel Massie was the son of a large slave-and-plantation-owner. His father was an Anglican vestryman, captain of the militia, and a justice of the peace. Nathaniel set out in his teens to farm land owned by his father in Kentucky. Later he trained as a surveyor and moved to the Virginia Military District in the Northwest Territory; in 1790 he surveyed the site of his first settlement beside the Ohio River, Massie's Station (later known as Manchester). As a surveyor, he generally received a portion of the land he surveyed in payment for his work, and soon he became a large landowner. From Massie's Station, he moved farther into the region, and in 1796, he laid out a town on the Scioto River called Chillicothe. This community grew quickly, attracting other developers such as Joseph Kerr, and became a centre of political life in the Northwest Territory.

Here, near Chillicothe, Kerr established a cattle and hog farm at the meeting point of Paint Creek and the Scioto River. His primary business was in the trade of Scioto Valley farm produce down the Ohio and Mississippi rivers to New Orleans, and from there to Baltimore, Maryland, and other ports in the Atlantic. But he also became one of Ohio's prime land speculators.

Henry Massie, Nathaniel's brother, was the earliest speculator in what became Highland County. This was very close to Ross County, where Thomas Kearney settled. Henry Massie had been among the early settlers at Manchester, and with his brother he engaged in surveying and speculation in the area.

In April 1798, Henry Massie had decided upon the site of what he believed would be the great sister city of Chillicothe. Together with another man from Baltimore – Benjamin Elliott, a business associate of Joseph Kerr – he encouraged settlement and established the town of New Market. He intended the town to rival Philadelphia, Pennsylvania. In promoting his vision of New Market as the county seat,

> Massie succeeded in gaining the interest of Joseph Kerr, one of the early settlers at Manchester who had served as an Adams County Justice of the Peace before going onto a political career that would take him to the Ohio legislature and on to the United States Senate.[54]

. Word of the pioneering developments in Ohio was transmitted enthusiastically to Maryland, and in 1801 Thomas Kearney set out on his first trip to the area. He almost certainly took the Wilderness Road, travelling first southwest from Baltimore, Maryland, to Virginia on a slow journey of more than three hundred miles to Fort Chiswell. From there he was able to start out on the trail that Daniel Boone, with thirty-five axemen, had blazed through the mountains and forests to Kentucky twenty-five years earlier. From Virginia the trail looped southward to Tennessee, then northward to Kentucky, a distance of over two hundred miles, and initially it was little more than a muddy path, along which progress was inevitably very slow. In 1792, the trail was upgraded thanks to subvention by the Kentucky legislature, and in 1796 the road was so improved that it could take wagons. It became the principal route used by settlers to circumvent the Appalachian Mountains and reach Kentucky and from there move north into Ohio.

The Wilderness Road ended at Ohio Falls, at Louisville, and from here Thomas most likely continued along the long and winding course of the river to Portsmouth, where the Ohio River met the Scioto River. For much of his journey north into the Virginia Military District, it would have been easier to travel by river than through the densely wooded land.

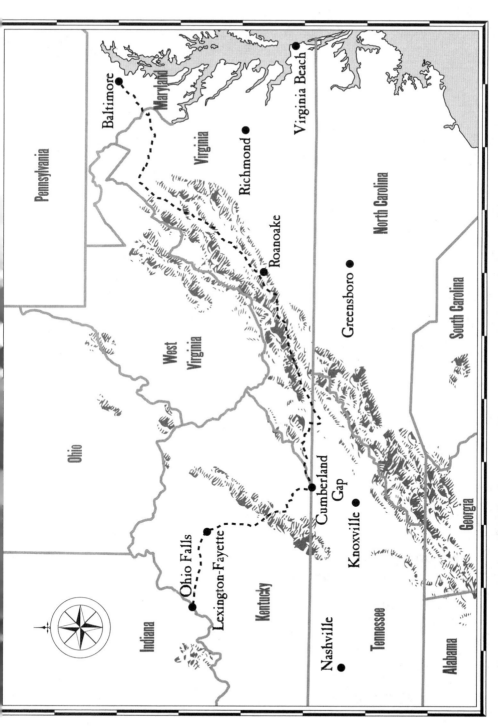

The long journey from Baltimore to the Ohio Falls

Ohio River

Big Sandy River

Levisa Fork

Licking River

Ohio River

Blue Licks

Limestone (Maysville)

Bryans Station

Boonesborough

Lexington

Big Bone Lick

Boones Station

Logan's Fort (St. Asaph)

Kentucky River

Crab Orchard

River

Harrodsburg

Danville

Bardstown

Falls of the Ohio (Louisville)

Ohio River

Salt River

Green River

Cumberland River

The Wilderness Road proper began at the Block House, but to that point converged roads from the northeast, running down the Shenandoah and the Holston valleys, and from the southeast, running up the Yadkin and Watauga valleys.

WILDERNESS ROAD

Cumberland Gap

CUMBERLAND MOUNTAIN

Powell River

Clinch River

Holston River

Clinch River

North Fork

Castle's Woods

Block House

Fort Patrick Henry

Long Island Fort Holston

Moccasin Gap

Martin's Station

To Bissaha

BLUE RIDGE MOUNTAINS

French Lick (Nashville)

WILDERNESS ROAD
AND KENTUCKY
1774–1785

MILES
0   25   50

Drawn under the supervision of SAMUEL COLE WILLIAMS

CUMBERLAND GAP
Drawn under the supervision of
ROBERT L. KINCAID

The Wilderness Road

To the Frontier

The Ohio River was the southern border of Ohio, Indiana and Illinois. It therefore divided free states and slave states. The expression "sold down the river" originated as a lament of slaves who were split apart from their families and sold in Kentucky and shipped via the Ohio River down to New Orleans to be sold again to owners of cotton and sugar field plantations. It came to be called the "River Jordan" by slaves escaping to freedom in the north via the Underground Railroad.

Travelling through the beautiful and fertile Scioto Country today, it can be difficult to picture just how wild this country was when the early settlers advanced into Ohio from the south. Because there were no roads, many travelled on the Scioto, Ohio and Miami rivers, using flatboats, which were sturdy, raft-like tubs. Later an average of three thousand flatboats descended the Ohio River each year between 1810 and 1820, but in the first decade of the century there was little traffic, and explorers of this newly opened territory could have been forgiven for feeling a great sense of trepidation and isolation as they sought to penetrate the wilderness.

> There were no roads; trees were "blazed" for guides to the traveler in the sparsely-settled frontier. There were no bridges, and swollen streams demanded of man and horse that they should swim.[55]

As they pursued their voyage, all they could see on the riverbanks was dense forest of a kind known as "climax forest" – undisturbed, virgin forest of huge trees, in which American beech and sugar maple were the dominant species, with some red oak, red maple, hickory, walnut and cucumber tree. The trunks of trees were often four or five feet thick, and branches were so closely entwined that beneath them was darkness. Almost no underbrush grew, except where openings were made by fallen trees, and then great walls of thorny brambles grew up.

VIRGINIA
MILITARY DISTRICT

Columbus

Chillicothe

Portsmouth

Deerfield

Maysville

Cincinatti

Covington

Ohio Falls

HARDIN

LOGAN

UNION

CHAMPAIGN

MADISON

CLARK

FRANKLIN

FAYETTE

PICKAWAY

GREENE

CLINTON

ROSS

HIGHLAND

PIKE

ADAMS

BROWN

WARREN

CLERMONT

SCIOTO

Scioto River

Scioto River

Ohio River

Ohio River

Ohio River

Little Miami River

From the Ohio Falls to Deerfield

The trees not only crowded the river banks but arched out over both sides of the river, confining boats to a relatively narrow passage down the centre. Sometimes the rivers – Ohio, Scioto, Little Miami – were so full and heavy that only canoes could continue upstream; then, flatboats had to be pulled by hand by ropes from the shore, but with the water's edge so overgrown it was a long and hard task to clear a pathway on the river bank.

From Portsmouth, Thomas Kearney made his way slowly by river and land, through a valley that was fertile with dense forest that had yet to be cleared. Eventually he reached Chillicothe, and from Chillicothe he probably took an old Indian path that led towards Old Chillicothe (now Xenia) along the North Fork of Paint Creek, a route that coincided with what is now a section of US 35. Near the track, the land speculator Henry Massie had recently set up his New Market settlement, at what is now Frankfort. By a strange coincidence, a village in Kearney territory between Moneygall and Shinrone is named Frankfort.

An idea of how it must have been for Thomas Kearney to make the long journey to the Scioto Valley may be gained from a short account in the *Pioneer Record of Ross County, Ohio* of the journey of Levi Hurst who, with his family,

> . . . emigrated to Ross county, from Maryland, in 1801. They came in one-horse carts to Wheeling, where he purchased a flat-boat, in which he floated his effects to Portsmouth, except the horses, which were sent by land. Here he hitched up his carts again, and in nine days reached Chillicothe, in the month of June. He moved into the woods the September following. Wild game was very plenty, and the Indians were hunting in great numbers that fall, so that clearing progressed very slowly.[56]

It is not known whether or how Thomas Kearney acquired land on his first visit to the Scioto Valley in 1801. In *Pioneer Sketches: Life in the Northwest Territory and Ross County, Ohio, 1600s–1896,* George Perkins, in discussing the early families that settled Deerfield Township, observes that "Thomas Carney and S. Howell came in 1801."[57]

It may be significant that another man, Joseph Kerr, who was probably of Irish background and was the same age as Thomas Kearney, made the same journey from Baltimore at the same time as Thomas Kearney, and once in the Scioto Valley became the closest business associate of a third man associated with Maryland, Henry Massie. Had Thomas met either of these men in Maryland? They had been energetically promoting settlement in the area, and it seems unlikely that Thomas would have made such a long and arduous journey without having some information about his final destination.

Joseph Kerr worked as a clerk in an international import-export firm in Baltimore, and during the campaign in the 1790s of General Anthony Wayne against the Ohio Indians, he had clerked for military contractors. It was in the later part of 1801 that Kerr and Thomas Kearney moved to Ohio from Baltimore. Did the two men perhaps travel together? Kerr set up home near Chillicothe on land purchased from Nathaniel Massie, brother of Henry and a prominent land surveyor and developer/speculator who played a leading role in the organisation of the Virginia Military District in the years after the American Revolution.

In 1801 Deerfield had not yet been organised as a separate township – that came in July 1804; so it was still part of Wayne, Union and Concord townships, and it was almost entirely covered with trees.

> The surface is generally level, with just sufficient
> undulation to afford good drainage. Like nearly the

whole area of the Military District, of which Deer-field is a part, it is well watered, and admirably adapted to all classes of diversified agriculture. The principal stream is Deer Creek, an affluent of the Scioto, which drains it from the south-central portion to the eastward.[58]

Although not yet a township, Deerfield was settled in 1801 by the man who would soon come to be recognised as its most prominent citizen.

White Brown . . . was a man of marked intelligence and strong religious principles, one of the few who willingly yield personal interest and make financial sacrifices for the sake of principle. Mr. Brown was reared under the influence of slavery, and was himself the owner of forty slaves in his native state of Delaware. The institution became so repugnant to him that he decided to seek a home on free soil, and this led to his removal to Ohio.[59]

He purchased a five hundred acre tract of land on Deer Creek that had been surveyed by Massie and McArthur, and he built one of the first houses to be erected in the township. White Brown was a Methodist, and it would have been difficult for Thomas Kearney to have visited what would become Deerfield without meeting his redoubtable co-religionist.

In 1803, White Brown erected a log barn near his house, which became

. . . the birthplace of religious services in that whole region. Within its walls, from 1803 to 1818, were held the services of the pioneer Methodist Episcopal church in Deerfield. Rev. Stephen Timmons was probably the first to gather the settlers of the new country into this rude and primitive sanctuary, to hear the preaching of the word of God. The log walls afterward echoed to the eloquence of such men as Bishops Francis Asbury, Whatcoat, and McKendry, as well as George and Lorenzo Dow, and the Finleys father and son.[60]

From Christmas 1802, camp meetings were held annually on the Brown farm, and the neighbourhood very soon became a stronghold of Methodism.

The *Pioneer Record and Reminiscenses of the Early Settlers and Settlement of Ross County, Ohio* (1871) by Isaac J. Finley and Rufus Putnam recorded:

> Benjamin Grimes, Curtis Williams, James Tender, Thomas Junk, David Hagar, John McCarthy, M. P. Junk, Amos Serapes, William Jones, Michael Bush, John Bush, S. Mangold, John Farlow, David Plilly, Edward Young, C. Stratton, Martin Peterson, John Holloway, G. Vincent, John Junk, Henry Colsten, J. Clemens, Aaron Beatonham, Lemuel Holloway, Thomas Carney, S. Chester, and Rufus Betts were all early pioneers, and nearly all in the war of 1812.[61]

Thomas, M. P. and John Junk were Irish Methodists, probably of Huguenot origin (the surname is found in Ireland from 1685, the year of the revocation of the Edict of Nantes). Thomas Carney was, of course, Thomas Kearney; by 1812 he was forty-seven years old, and it seems that he was one of the few who did not serve in that war. The Holloways had a farm adjoining the Kearneys.

Amongst the pioneers who settled Ross County in the early years were many with Irish names, and many more with names that could have been either Irish or Scottish or a bit of both. The early settlers known to have come from Ireland included names such as Barrett, Brown, Cahill, Collins, Cooney, Corcoran, Corken, Craden, Creamer, Cull, Devine, Ferguson, Galbraith, Gunning, Hacket, Hays, Henry, Hyde, Kelly, Larimore, Lavery, Lyons, McCarthy, McKinstry, McNally, McNeal, McShane, May, Moore, Morton, Murphy, O'Neil, Orr, Riley, Rutledge, Ryan, Scott, Shannon, Southworth, Sullivan, Thompson and Warfield. Also there were many with common Irish names, the details of whose ancestry are unknown; amongst these were names such as Cogan, Conner, Dailey, Dulaney, Dunn, Fenton, Fitzgerald, Fitzsimmons, Griffin, Kennedy, Malone and Shields.

Yet the question of what constitutes an Irish name is by no means simple. The ideological founder of Irish nationalism was Thomas Davis, and Davis is a Welsh name. The present-day leader of Sinn Féin is Gerry Adams, and Adams is a Scottish name. Bobby Sands died on hunger strike in Ireland in 1981, and Sands is an Anglo-Saxon name. The ideological founder of Irish Republicanism was Theobald Wolfe Tone, and Tone is a name from Normandy via England. The leader of the Easter Rising in 1916 in Dublin was Patrick Pearse, whose surname is Anglo-Saxon. One of Ireland's great Nobel-prize-winning writers was George Bernard Shaw, and Shaw is an English and Scottish name. Probably the best-known Irish president was Eamon de Valera, and a recent president, Mary Robinson, bears a name of English origin.

So spotting Irish presence and influence is not always easy, but in reviewing the scant records of the pioneer settlers of Ross County and elsewhere in Ohio's Scioto Valley, it is clear that the Irish constituted one strand amongst several, and that the strongest strands were German and English. Most of the Irish were of various Protestant denominations. A quite representative sample of the earliest settlers in Ross County includes, in Huntington township, Richard Elliott, who "emigrated from Ireland at an early day, . . . a weaver by trade". In the same township was James Lenox, "who emigrated from Ireland". James Demoss, likely of French Huguenot origin, was a painter who had emigrated from Ireland to Twin Township. Crawford Caldwell of Buckskin Township had "emigrated to Ohio from Ireland in the first settlement of the country; served as a soldier in the war of 1812". He and his brother John married two Irish sisters, Mary and Sarah McClure. And in Deerfield Township was Thomas Carney from Moneygall.[62]

There were many amongst the first pioneers in Ross County whose names were either Scottish or Irish, or maybe both. James Orr was one of the most interesting settlers from Northern Ireland. He arrived with his family in Ross County in 1797, the same year in which his brother William, a United Irishman, was placed on trial in Belfast and convicted after a notoriously flawed trail.

As Henry Holcomb Bennett writes in *A History of Ross County, Ohio*:

> During the latter half of the eighteenth century, five brothers were born and bred near Belfast, whose names were James, Thomas, Alexander, William and John. William became involved in the rebellion of the Irish against English tyranny, which took place in the closing years of the century, and was the first of the patriots executed in 1797. He was falsely charged with treason, found guilty by a drunken jury and sentenced to die by a hypocritical judge.[63]

Following his conviction, he addressed the court:

> If to have loved my country, to have known its wrongs, to have felt the injuries of the persecuted Catholics, and to have united with them and all other religious persuasions in the most orderly and

least sanguinary means of procuring redress; – if these be felonies, then I am a felon, but not otherwise.[64]

He was executed in Carrickfergus, becoming the first Irish patriot martyr. As he stepped to the scaffold he declared: "I am no traitor. I die a persecuted man, for a persecuted country." Thereafter the battle-cry of the United Irish rebels became "Remember Orr!"

The significance of William Orr's trial and execution, and the public response to them, was summed up by T.A. Jackson in *Ireland Her Own:*

> It was in these circumstances that the struggle between the Irish Nation, as represented by the United Irishmen, and its enemies, as represented by the Irish Administration and its supporters, entered upon its final phase.[65]

The Orrs were Presbyterians, like so many of those in the leadership of the Irish revolution against British rule, but in America James Orr and his family became Methodists. They came to Ross County just four years before Thomas Kearney's first arrival, and they settled:

> ...first near the High Banks prairie and afterward on Dry Run about six miles above. James Orr was a man of good education, as well as an accomplished surveyor, and these qualifications made him very useful in the newly settled and poorly organized communities. For a number of years he kept a private school and the ancestors of some of the most prominent families in Ross county were taught by this Irish immigrant.[66]

His son Thomas became a particularly prominent citizen

of Ross County, and in *A History of Ross County, Ohio,*
Henry Holcomb Bennett writes:

> He was the father of twelve children who lived to
> years of maturity, and eleven of them have spent
> their lives in Ross county. No family in Springfield is
> more prominent and well known than the descen-
> dants of the Orrs. Some of them have held honorable
> and responsible political places, and all have been
> prosperous and influential citizens.[67]

A significant element in the migration into Ohio was religious. Moravians, Presbyterians, Baptists and Methodists all
sought to spread their religion in the new territory.

> Hard after the pioneer settlers trod the pioneer
> Methodist preachers. Almost before clearings were
> made or cabins were erected, and long before the
> whoop of the red man and the scream of the panther
> and wild-cat had ceased, the faithful preacher was
> tracking his way from settlement to settlement, hunt-
> ing after the scattered sheep of his Master's fold.[68]

Amongst these evangelists were Methodists from Virginia,
Maryland and Kentucky "who threaded pathless woods, ford-
ed unbridged streams, eyed into shame brutal mobs, sang into
peace thousands of troubled souls, and laid the foundations"
of their churches.[69]

The territory they entered was wild not only with natural
growth but in the character of many of the earliest settlers.

> Ungoverned tracts and ungospeled settlements
> offered sad welcome to the more moral emigrants
> who toiled over the mountains, or floated down the
> river, seeking homes in Kentucky and Ohio.[70]

Just at the time that Thomas Kearney, himself a Methodist, was making his first visit from Maryland in 1801, Methodist preachers were beginning to make forays across the Ohio River into the wilderness of the Virginia Military District. Whatever he found in Deerfield seems to have decided him upon a permanent move. But first, having perhaps already acquired land in Ross County, he had to return to his family in Maryland.

— 5 —

Frontier Settlers

Thomas Kearney returned to Baltimore. Then, in 1804, following the death of his wife's mother, Mary Baxley, he and Sarah and their children set out on the long and very difficult journey from Baltimore. Theirs was an adventure burdened with risk of accident. The rudimentary road system consisted of little more than Indian tracks, which required that they frequently clear fallen trees, remove boulders and level the ground to take the wheels of their wagon – if they had one. It has been suggested from family sources that they may have joined a group led by a man named Rufus Putnam. This would have offered far greater security than embarking on a solo expedition with a young family. Putnam was particularly well qualified to provide leadership and guidance.

Putnam had fought for the British in the French and Indian War. A man of English origin born in Sutton, Massachusetts, he had enlisted in the Continental Army early in the Revolutionary War. He designed earthworks and other defenses for the American forces surrounding the English in Boston, and he assisted George Washington in preparing New York's defenses. He fought in the Battle of Saratoga and rose to the rank of brigadier general. Following the Revolution, he became a leading surveyor for the Confederation Congress, and like other surveyors such as Nathaniel Massie, he used his knowledge to make land purchases. During his time as surveyor general of the state of Ohio and the Northwest Territories, he initiated the "contract method" of surveys, a system that would be followed for the next 110 years in the drawing of a rectangular survey system over the public lands of the United States. In 1786, he was one of a group of men who founded the Ohio Company of Associates to purchase land in the Northwest Territory. As a member of this company, he promoted in Baltimore and elsewhere land acquisition in the Virginia Military District.

Putnam established the first Ohio Company settlement on the banks of the Ohio River at Marietta and constructed a fortification known as the Campus Martius. Following the signing of the Treaty of Greeneville in 1795, the settlement grew, and Putnam became an important political leader in the region. He was appointed to a judgeship by President Washington in 1790, serving at the same time as a brigadier general in the United States Army; in 1796 he became the surveyor general of the United States but was sacked by President Thomas Jefferson in 1803. He participated in the constitutional convention of 1802 and favoured the Federalist Party, and he succeeded in preventing slavery from becoming legal in Ohio.

And so it may be that Thomas Kearney and his young family travelled in convoy under the experienced leadership of Rufus Putnam as they worked their way from Maryland up through the Cumberland Gap to Tennessee. This was a challenging enterprise, especially for a family including children aged one, four, seven and nine. Their later penetration across the Ohio River of the Scioto Valley was harder still, and as they advanced up the valley they ran a real danger of attack by Indians.

> The pioneer wrung prosperity out of hardships that are almost unimaginable to those who live today [1898] far from peril, want, and hard toil. The immigrant, with wife and little ones, climbed the mountain passes, and descended into the plains beyond, or drifted down the current of the Ohio, not without its peculiar dangers of lurking savage [sic] or flooded banks, to enter the unbroken forest where night became dismal with the howl of the wolf and the weird call of the night-bird; and where day meant only ceaseless vigilance, with hand on gun, or stern labor with the ax.[71]

At the time, over 90 per cent of the land mass of Ohio was covered with trees. If they were riding pack horses, their journey of more than sixty miles up the Scioto Valley from the Ohio River at Portsmouth to Deerfield in Ross County would have proceeded at a rate of between eight and ten miles per day. It is unlikely that they could have brought a covered wagon on the available tracks, but if they had, their journey would have been even slower.

The settlers had to clear most of the land of the new territory by their hard labour, but the leaves of the forest had rotted down to create a wonderfully rich humus, and the soil beneath the trees was nourishing and moist. Beside the land that Thomas Kearney had acquired in Ross County, the North Fork of Paint Creek ran constantly full and deep, providing potential power for milling corn and flour, an advantage he would have understood, given the experience of his father-in-law in Maryland.

However, they faced dangers they had not known in either

Ireland or Maryland. The ever-present risk of malaria hung like a mist over the land, and during the first dozen years the threat still remained of attack by Indians. "Milk sickness" or "milk fever", caused by drinking the milk of cows that had eaten white snakeroot (*Eupatorium rugosum*), could cause loss of appetite, weakness, muscle stiffness, vomiting, severe constipation and even coma. Children were particularly badly affected, but adults, too, could succumb; recovery was slow and sometimes incomplete; many an attack was fatal.

When the Kearneys finally reached their destination, there was an enormous amount of urgent hard work to be done. First of all, they had to clear the ground to plant a crop for food for themselves. They cut down small trees and trimmed them out, piling brush and trimmings around the larger trees, which were too big to cut down. They cut a ring or girdle on the bark of these large trees, so that they would die where they stood. Later in the year they would set the brush and trimmings alight to burn them, but in the meantime, the tops of the trees having died, the sun could now break through the dead branches to warm the ground.

Thomas Kearney single-handedly broke the soil for the first time, his children all too young to help. Tree roots made it impossible to use a horse plough. He may have used a German mattock, a tool popular amongst the frontiersmen of Ohio; it had a small axe on one end, a heavy chopping hoe on the other. In his first year he might have cleared about ten acres. Then, by hand and hoe, he planted around the stumps and standing larger trees; probably in early May he planted the crop, so familiar from home, of potatoes. He also planted corn, squash and pumpkin.

Once he had cleared the land, he had to embark on building the cabin. The favoured tree type for log cabins was the yellow poplar or tulip tree (*Liriodendron tulipifera*), which grew strongly in the rich, moist soil of the Scioto Valley and was likely present on his plot. So, some of the small trees Thomas had cleared almost certainly provided the building materials. These logs, a foot to a foot and a half thick, were squared off with an adze. Naturally straight, fine grained and stable, it was easy wood to work. Also known as canoewood, it was used by the Native Americans in Ohio for making dugout canoes.

The cabin would have been no more than twenty feet long, since that was the length of the longest manoeuvrable log; many cabins were just fifteen feet square. The height of the cabin may have been just enough to stand in, but because they had four young children and another on the way, it is likely that they made it a little higher to provide space for a loft for the children.

The ends of the logs

> . . . were cut to overlap with special angle cuts, so they would lock together and hold fast. The angles were shaped so water would drain out and not rot the wood. The logs of the gables for the loft were cut short to give the slope, and to allow cross poles to hold the gables steady and to make a kind of rafter for the shingles. The peak was locked with a "ridge pole." The roof was covered with big clapboard shingles, rived out of oak or ash. They were four foot long, six inches wide or more, and an inch thick. They were held down with cross poles. They kept out most of the rain, partly because the roof sloped enough so the water ran off quickly. In time they warped badly and let in considerable air, but at first they were reasonably tighter. Clay and flat stone built the chimney and a fireplace in one end of the cabin. The fireplace often covered half of the wall of the

cabin. It could burn a "cord-length" piece of wood – four feet. It provided the heat and the light inside the cabin. Hanging out of the chimney was a "lug pole," a forerunner of the fireplace crane, on which pots could be hung above the fire for cooking.[72]

The Kearneys would have enjoyed the support of their neighbours when building the cabin. It seems likely that they may have known some of their fellow white settler neighbours, or may have soon come to know them. After all, many of these neighbours, whether Irish, English, Welsh or German, were fellow Methodists, some of whom had also moved from Maryland. But it was anyway the norm amongst Ohio settlers that neighbours helped in the construction of each new cabin.

The scattered neighbours came with friendly aid to rear the cabin, and it often happened that, where the morning sun shone through the tree branches, by nightfall the rude cabin with one room sheltered the weary pioneer with all his possessions.[73]

Several men working together cut the logs and rolled them to the cabin site, which Thomas Kearney situated near a fine spring – one of the best features of their plot. With hand spikes and skid poles, they raised the logs into place, a hazardous procedure carrying a high risk of accidents. Once the construction of the walls had been completed, the door and windows could be cut out of the logs, a hole being augered through the logs so that the opening could be sawed out with a crosscut saw. Perhaps the Kearneys had brought carefully packed glass window-panes with them from Maryland. If not, a piece of paper or larded hog guts offered a translucent substitute. Heavy clapboard shutters protected the windows. Most cabin floors were earthen, but a more comfortable option was a floor made of split logs known as a puncheon floor.

Settlers relied upon their own abilities to create homemade furniture, for which the tulip tree wood was well suited, and as a master carpenter, Thomas Kearney no doubt ensured that his family's cabin was fully furnished.

> An upright post in the floor, connected by poles to two walls at a corner made a bed, or covered by clapboards made a table. A split log with sticks for legs made a stool or bench, and if a little larger, would make a table. Pots and kettles were opposite the window, often hung from pegs on the wall. The "dutch oven" with short legs, and a lipped lid (to hold hot ashes on top of the cooking food) was a necessity.
>
> A wooden chest, for storage of clothing and bedding, stood against a wall, and provided seating as necessary. The family might have brought with them a few good chairs, from back east, ladder chairs, maybe even cane bottomed. A carved wood shovel and a pair of metal tongs stood by the fireplace. Every cabin had its spinning-wheels: the large wheel for wool, the small wheel for flax and linen. And in the corner stood the loom – necessary for the family clothing. Linsey-woolsey was the common frontier garb.[74]

Their everyday life was unremittingly hard, even after they had cleared and planted part of their land and had constructed their cabin and its furniture. By any standards, most of the settlers were poor; they grew and raised enough plants and animals on their farms to eat and to wear, but they had very little in the way of income.

As Walter A. Hazen has written in *Everyday Life: The Frontier*:

Everyone worked from sunrise to sunset just to survive. Frontier living was especially hard on women. Childbearing took its toll, as did the day-to-day supervision of children. Besides taking care of a multitude of household chores, women sometimes had to help the men and boys planting and plowing. As a result, many frontier women died young. That old saying from the *New England Primer,* "Man may work from sun to sun, but woman's work is never done," was never more true than during frontier days.[75]

Life on these settler farms was characterised by endless labour, but hunting was also an essential element.

For food he had wild game and Indian corn. The bearskin afforded bedding, and the deerskin, until supplanted by wool and flax, made clothing for man and woman.[76]

Few buffalo, or bison, still roamed Ohio: just a few years earlier, in 1800, an exceptionally hard winter had seen most of them devoured by wolves. But deer were plentiful, venison a fine source of meat, so Thomas Kearney hunted deer, perhaps at night, using a bright light, perhaps at dawn or dusk. Where he killed a deer, he bled and gutted it, then hung it up in a tree out of reach of wolves and bears; returning home, he would either bring or send a pack horse to carry it back.

A religious perspective was an essential characteristic of many settlers in approaching the challenges and opportunities of the frontier. Nathaniel and Henry Massie – from whom Thomas Kearney bought land – were amongst the many influential Methodists who shaped life in the Scioto Valley. However, when Thomas Kearney and his family settled in Ohio, there were at first no churches, and "so far these Methodist movements in Ohio were sporadic",[77] but soon travelling preachers, known as itinerants, visited the area, then developed a Scioto circuit and called regularly on pioneer families.

> The Methodist pioneers of Ohio knew nothing of the conveniences and necessities of our modern life. Their homes were cabins of logs about fifteen or sixteen feet square; but so welcome were the visits of the travelling preachers that they were freely opened for public worship and other religious exercises.[78]

In *Pictures of Early Methodism in Ohio*, Samuel Wesley Williams writes:

> Preaching was also had in the log schoolhouses, which were warmed in winter by great fires built in the capacious chimneys. When churches were first erected there were no schools except in favored localities; and small foot-stoves, containing a brazier of coals, or sometimes carried from home to warm those who attended meeting. At night the room where the people assembled was lighted with tallow dips stuck on tin sconces, and hung about the walls. The person who led the service usually stood by a small table upon which was placed a single candle on a brass or tin candlestick. The candles were kept well snuffed by some officious attendant, who usually picked off the burnt wick between his thumb and fingers.[79]

Religious identity was a vitally important element of frontier life at this time, and the story of Ohio cannot be separated from the advance of Methodism, Baptism, Presbyterianism and other varieties of faith, which shaped the lives of so many of the early settlers.

It was no uncommon thing for men and women to walk every week five or six miles to attend class meeting, and at night the same distance to a prayer-meeting, lighting their way through the woods with blazing fragments of hickory bark instead of lanterns. If the latter were used, they consisted of tin cylinders, pricked full of small holes, with a door on one side, through which a bit of candle two or three inches long might be inserted. As there were no matches, the candles were lighted by holding their wicks close to a live coal, and blowing vigorously with the breath. In summer the men and boys often attended the meetings in their bare feet; and the women and girls, if they could afford shoes and stockings, carried them in their hands until they came within sight of the place of meeting, when they washed off the dust or mud in the nearest brook or spring, and finished their toilets, that they might appear more decent in company; but as soon as the services were over, and they set out on their return, their feet were again stripped bare, and in this condition they traveled ofttimes many miles. And the distance was seldom too great or the roads too bad to prevent these devoted disciples from being in their places when the gospel was preached.[80]

In Ross County, Deerfield was a centre of Methodism, and White Brown was its chief proponent. At his farm there were seasonal gatherings, which the Kearneys no doubt attended. Rev. Stephen Timmons, who emigrated to Deerfield in 1802, was the first Methodist preacher on Deer Creek. He served several terms as justice of the peace, and was an early and vociferous opponent of slavery.

[T]he quarterly meetings, when the sacraments were administered and love-feasts [religious meals, also known as Agape feasts] held, were the great occasions of religious interest among the pioneer Methodists. Persons of both sexes, when the season was favorable and the weather warm enough, would come from twenty to thirty miles distance – many on foot – and find some hospitable neighbour to entertain them during the continuance of the meetings. The kind Christian friends in whose vicinity quarterly meeting was to be held were never lacking in such hospitality. Days beforehand they would begin to make ready for it. A large stock of provisions was laid in; the larders were well supplied with bread, cakes, and pies, while butter, cakes, fresh meats, and poultry were prepared against the time for the meeting to begin; and thus a wealthy member could entertain as many as fifteen or twenty of the welcome guests.[81]

In these early years of settlement, the frontiers people who shared a religious commitment very quickly built their own communities of faith and of neighbours. Many of the Kearneys' neighbours were German, some were Irish; others were English, Scottish, Welsh. Some, like Thomas Kearney, had been born outside America; others, like his wife, Sarah Baxley, had been born in America. The shared routines of the religious community combined with a basic neighbourliness to provide a vital social support in circumstances that were challenging and demanding.

Fridays were always strictly observed as fast-days. Preaching began on Saturday morning at 10 or 11 o'clock, and in the afternoon a short service was held, after which the quarterly conference was convened. At night there was again preaching, generally by the junior preacher of the circuit; or prayer-meetings were held at several convenient points in the neighborhood. On Sunday morning the love-feast was held, conducted by one of the preachers; and about 11 o'clock the principal sermon of the quarterly meeting was preached by the Presiding Elder, followed by a sermon, it might be, by one of the other preachers, and then perhaps by an exhortation. The sacraments of baptism and the Lord's Supper were usually administered at the close of the morning services, though sometimes deferred till the afternoon. At night there was again preaching – generally followed by prayer-meeting, exhortation to repentance, collects for penitent seekers, and stirring hymns – not always rendered according to the laws of musical art, but sung with a fervor that almost lifted the soul to the gates of paradise. Frequently popular hymns not found in the regular hymn-book were used.[82]

Methodism grew rapidly in Ohio in the early decades of the nineteenth century, even to the extent of becoming a defining element of the new society of the Scioto Valley. The vigour of the Methodists who had come from Maryland, Virginia and elsewhere produced many new converts.

Often on such occasions, and especially at the camp-meetings, the converts would be numbered by the score. The meeting, protracted for several days, frequently resulted in numerous accessions to the church; and the new members were watched over with a godly jealousy by the class-leaders and the

elder brethren, so that there was little danger of
their turning back on the way. In many there was a
ripe Christian experience, and they were a great
help not only to the fresh recruits, but to the
preacher.[83]

The practice of their religion spread through their lives.

They were strict observers of the Sabbath and
refrained with diligence from many customs which
have since come into vogue. Shaving, brushing
clothes, polishing boots and shoes, bathing, and lay-
ing out the garments to be worn the next day, were
all attended to on Saturday evening. Very little cooking was done; in many families none further than the
making of coffee for breakfast, and of tea, where
milk was not used instead, for supper.

No meal was eaten without the asking of a bless-
ing or the returning of thanks. If the head of the family was absent, his wife took his place. The members
of the household always stood on their feet surrounding the table until this was done. Instead of a
grace offered at the commencement of a meal, a stan-
za was occasionally sung, and thanks given at the
conclusion.

Family devotions were conducted night and
morning. The entire household, including servants
and hired hands, were expected to be present and
join in the services, which consisted of reading the
scriptures, singing a hymn, and offering a prayer. Private devotion was rarely neglected. On entering the
place of preaching, a silent prayer was uttered, the
head bowed down and the face covered. The custom
of kneeling was universally observed.[84]

There was nothing institutional about this frontier religious practice. For much worship in the early years of settlement, the only church was the open air.

> The great woods offered their umbrageous substitute, and under their spreading branches the herald lifted his voice so as to be heard to the outskirts of the assembly. The eager, curious, and ofttimes unkempt hunter-folk heard the message that recalled memories of the home on the other side of the mountains, or stirred hopes of the other home beyond the last sunset.[85]

No doubt here in the wilderness that they sought to tame by their own manual labour, the home Thomas Kearney recalled was not just their former home across the Appalachians in Granby Street, Baltimore, but his home he had left across the ocean in Moneygall in the King's County, Ireland.

— 6 —

Before the Famine

Thomas Kearney's close family in Moneygall and Shinrone were experiencing considerable social and economic change. They also experienced political conflict arising from the inequality and poverty associated with land tenure. The defeat of the United Irishmen was followed by a British strategy to promote division, in particular through building up and encouraging the sectarian anti-Catholic Orange Order.

Thomas was one of ten children of Joseph Kearney and Sarah Healy, some of whom died in childhood; the youngest of his siblings, James, had been born twenty years after him, the eldest, William, just three years before him. As Thomas cleared the land and built the cabin in Ohio, his older brother William in Moneygall was head of the family since the death of their father Joseph. He was forty-two years old, married to Margaret Reeves, with whom he so far had five children: John, Sarah, Joseph, Thomas and Francis. They would have a further three children – William, Margaret and Frances – during the next fifteen years.

The third-born of the family, Joseph, was ten years old and was destined some forty-four years later to follow his uncle

Thomas to America and to bring the rest of his family out to Ohio. For now he had to struggle through a time of private difficulty and public instability.

Throughout the early decades of the century, much of rural Ireland, including Offaly, was in turmoil as a consequence of agrarian disturbances. These were organised by numbers of secret societies named Ribbonmen, Terry Alts, Rockites and United Men. These were made up of labourers and small tenant farmers, mobilised in opposition to the exorbitant rents they had to pay. Much of the countryside was mired in poverty and destitution, and many of the people were well aware that there was no way out of the trap of grinding poverty while they were required to pay such rents.

In 1801, just as Thomas Kearney had made his first exploratory journey into the Scioto River Valley, in Ireland the *Statistical Survey of the King's County* by Sir Charles Coote was published. It consisted of a factual description of King's County (named in honour of Prince Philip II of Spain, and later to be renamed Offaly), concentrating on its natural resources and agriculture, and it drew an unprepossessing picture. It included an account of Shinrone, the town that lay close to Moneygall.

> There were, till lately, two tan-yards, a malt-house, and distillery in this town, but all are now unemployed. A classical school has lately been opened by Mr Carroll, scholar of Trinity College, Dublin. Here is a handsome church, attended by a numerous congregation, and a market-house, but no weekly markets held, though it has a patent for that purpose. All the wheat of the country is manufactured at Killoge mills, and the two great distilleries at Kilcommin consume the barley, and also the entire of the oats, which leaves little other provision for the

poor but potatoes. Dunkerrin is a clean village, the estate of Thomas Rolleston, Esq. who is a very considerable landed proprietor. No species of manufacture here, and the only public building is a good church; 'tis four miles distant from Roscrea. Moneygall, about two miles further, is the estate of William Minchin, Esq. of Green Hills, and borders the county of Tipperary, but, like Dunkerrin, is of inconsiderable extent.[86]

It went on to describe the living conditions of the people.

The habitations of the lower order throughout the barony are mean and indifferent; in many places, but hovels covered with sods and bog-rush, but turf fuel is plenty and very cheap. Their food, potatoes, and they have but oatmeal or milk. Clothing, coarse friezes and stuffs. Cost of potatoes, generally from 3s 6d the barrel of twenty-four stone, to 5s; and of oatmeal, from 12s to 16s per cwt. Clothing, since the commencement of the war, rising every year. The more wealthy farmers live well, but dirty, and they all refuse to inhabit slated houses, many of which have been erected by the gentry, and are very ornamental to demesnes, but that is all their use, as they prefer their clay huts. The peasantry are extremely illiterate, yet in due obedience to the laws. The cottier pays for a cabin and an acre of ground, thirty shillings, the like sum for the grass of one cow, and he has sixpence per day through the year, and eightpence if no grass. If he has none of these advantages, he is termed a spalpeen; his wages are ninepence in winter, and a shilling in summer. The use of spirits is rapidly declining, and ale or strong beer the substitute. The roads are in tolerable order, but have been greatly neglected since the rebellion [of 1798]; and the bridges are very narrow, and so low, as to cast much back water of the adjoining meadows.[87]

The majority of the population were cottiers, who lived in poverty, scraping an existence from whatever they could grow on a small plot of land. Increasingly, they had come to depend on the nutritious potato, which grew well in the climate and kept cottier families fed from July to March, almost their only other food during that period being a little milk or butter. Between April and June, they would eat stirabout (oats boiled in water). They would hardly ever have eaten meat, except perhaps at Christmas and Easter. So when the potato crop was poor, most families suffered severe hardship. But even the variety of potato posed a problem. The Roscrea Medical Officer's Report to the Commissioners in 1835 stated: "I consider the potato called 'Lumper' a fertile cause of stomach disease as it is of a very waxy soapy nature . . . it is not fit to fatten pigs."

The scourge of cholera brought even greater misery, and nearly three hundred died of the disease in Offaly in 1832.

Though most of the people lived in dire poverty, Coote took a positive view of the principal landowners of the region, who belonged, of course, to his own class.

> The whole of the barony, indeed, is extremely well inhabited by a spirited and wealthy gentry, who are all actively employed in the most material point, the reclaiming of their moors.[88]

He noted that the majority of the population spoke Gaelic as their first language:

> The English language is spoken by all sorts; but the peasants, when conversing together, speak in their native tongue only.[89]

However, in the decades succeeding his 1801 report, the use of Gaelic rapidly declined, and English became the majority language.

Another writer about the area, Jonathan Binns, visited Offaly in the 1830s, encountering very high unemployment, poverty and large numbers of beggars.

> Before leaving Philipstown [now Daingean, County Offaly] let me once more avert to the condition of the people in its neighbourhood. They would work . . . if they could get it. Their food is of the poorest description (the coarse potatoes called lumpers) and obtained in quantities barely sufficient to keep the machine of life in languid motion. . . I have seen young and helpless children, almost naked and without food, exposed to the cruel influences of the weather and I have seen old people, afflicted severely by asthmas and rheumatic attacks, lying in hovels without either window or chimney, with nothing for their beds, but the bare damp floor, or a thin layer of straw.[90]

In Moneygall, Joseph Kearney married Phoebe (often written as Phebe) Donovan, and in 1826 their first child, Margaret, was born. Fulmouth was born in about 1830, then William and Joseph.

The people of Ireland, who lived for the most part in such poor conditions, were traumatised in 1839 by an extraordinarily severe windstorm. The night of 6–7 January, when the storm swept across Ireland, causing severe damage to property and several hundred deaths, became known as the Night of the

Big Wind – in Gaelic, *Oíche na Gaoithe Móire* – and lingered long in folk memory. According to Irish folk tradition, judgement day would come on the Feast of the Epiphany, which was 6 January. The apocalyptic storm caused many to believe that the end of the world was at hand. It must have been a deeply frightening experience for the eight- or nine-year-old Fulmouth Kearney in Moneygall.

The foundation stone of the poverty of the plain people of Offaly and all of rural Ireland was the injustice and gross inequality of land tenure, allied to the system of tithes, whereby taxes were levied for the upkeep of the Protestant established church, the Church of Ireland. And it was in the decades surrounding the birth of Fulmouth Kearney that many rural dwellers rose up in revolt against the system. Most of these rebels, who joined secret agrarian societies, were small tenant farmers or labourers, while hedge schoolmasters seem to have played a key role in providing intellectual leadership.

The Cromwellian planters had appropriated the best land from the dispossessed native Irish landowners, and these planters and other settlers had extended their estates to take in more of the quality land. The natives who were not transported were confined in large numbers to quite small tracts of the poorest land.

On a few acres the cottiers and labourers planted potatoes. The labourers worked twelve-hour days, six days a week for farmers and landlords for seven or eight pence a day. Some piecework was available, in mowing, turf-cutting and ditch-making, and there was occasional labour on public projects.

Joseph Kearney, Fulmouth's father, was one of a number of inhabitants of Dunkerrin parish – within which Moneygall and Shinrone lay – who worked as combers or weavers, mostly for woollen manufacturers in nearby Roscrea. While weavers earned sixteen pence a day, combers earned twenty pence. Comparing that wage with the fact that general labourers earned only seven or eight pence, it is clear that the Kearneys did not suffer the same poverty as many of their neighbours. However, the woollen business declined sharply when protective duties were removed. Irish manufacturing had flourished in the late eighteenth century behind a wall of import duties. But the Act of Union provided for the phasing out of the duties by 1824, to create a free trade area encompassing the new United Kingdom. Irish producers had already fallen behind their English and Scottish rivals in technological development, so irrespective of the removal of duties, they were threatened by competition from across the Irish Sea. But the sudden withdrawal of protection meant that the decline was brutally swift. The wool and cotton industries collapsed, with catastrophic effect. By the late 1830s, most of the mills that had once held out the promise of an Irish industrial revolution had closed or were operating at a much reduced level, while the Irish market was now dominated by English and Scottish imports of cotton and woollen cloth.

Some of the combers and weavers emigrated to England, while others turned to general labouring. In this context, it is hardly surprising that several of the Kearneys decided to join their relative Thomas in America. It was Thomas's brother John who made the first move. Seventeen years younger, he was the third John in the family: a brother named John had been born in 1770 but lived just two years and three months; a second John born in 1779 lived only four months; this John was born in 1782 and would eventually reach the ripe age of eighty-eight. Conditions in Offaly showed no signs of improvement, and soon John was followed by several of the children of William and Margaret Kearney: Joseph's brothers William, Francis and Thomas, and their sister Sarah.

Exploitative rents, evictions for non-payment of rents and conditions of poverty were bad enough in themselves, but perhaps the greatest popular loathing amongst the Catholic population of Ireland was reserved for the practice of collecting tithes for the support of the Church of Ireland. This oppositional resentment chimed also with the burgeoning movement for the repeal of the last of the Penal Laws – which prevented Catholics from becoming members of parliament – and the enactment of Catholic emancipation. In 1823, Daniel O'Connell founded the Catholic Association, beginning a campaign marked by open-air mass meetings and marches.

Two events in Shinrone in 1828 attracted national attention and played roles in the movement towards both the abolition of tithes and the achievement of Catholic emancipation.

On 21 September 1828, a huge crowd, decorated with green sashes, ribbons and hats, and drawn from counties Offaly, Tipperary, Kilkenny and Laois, marched through the town of Roscrea, a few miles from Moneygall and Shinrone. At the rally it was announced that a monster meeting would be held in Shinrone one week later. Shinrone at the time had a large Protestant population and boasted a lodge of the Protestant anti-Catholic organisation, the Orange Order. It was now expected that tens of thousands of, mostly Catholic, "Greenboys" from Offaly and the neighbouring counties would converge on Shinrone, and the prospect filled both the government and many local Protestants with considerable alarm. The Duke of Wellington, first lord of the Treasury and lord lieutenant of Ireland, ordered that the military and the police be mobilised to prevent the march of the Greenboys. Two military regiments took up positions in Shinrone, backed up by two to three hundred infantry police and 120 mounted police. Meanwhile, members of the local Orange Order had taken up entrenched positions.

It was widely feared that a violent confrontation would occur, and in an attempt to prevent this happening, the parish priest of Birr, County Offaly, Fr Kennedy (later bishop of Killaloe) and Mr Thomas Lalor Cooke, a prominent Protestant solicitor from Birr – later to be appointed the first sessional Crown solicitor in Ireland – toured the area together, appealing to the population not to travel to the planned monster meeting.

They were successful in heading off the thousands of Greenboys who were advancing or planning to advance on Shinrone from all directions. In Shinrone itself, the Catholic population were persuaded to stay at home. However, the marchers had succeeded in making their point, and their march on Shinrone, although aborted, was widely reported nationally and played a significant role in hastening the passing in 1829 of Catholic emancipation in Ireland.

If the thousands of Greenboys in Offaly advanced the cause of Catholic emancipation, it was the imprisonment and subsequent death of one Shinrone man that notably accelerated the abolition of the tithes.

A large anti-tithe meeting was held in 1832 at the Devil's Bit, a mountain range in nearby Tipperary featuring a celebrated gap, and the Catholic parish priest of Dunkerrin encouraged his parishioners to support the demonstration in numbers. A neighbouring Protestant rector alleged that he had advised the Catholic people of Moneygall that in such circumstances any of them who gave sustenance to the police would deserve to have their house burned over their heads. As it was, the demonstration took place and was massively supported, and the rector complained bitterly that more than ten thousand had passed his house yelling anti-tithe and anti-Protestant slogans.

Such was the support for the campaign of resistance to paying tithes that it became almost impossible in the area to

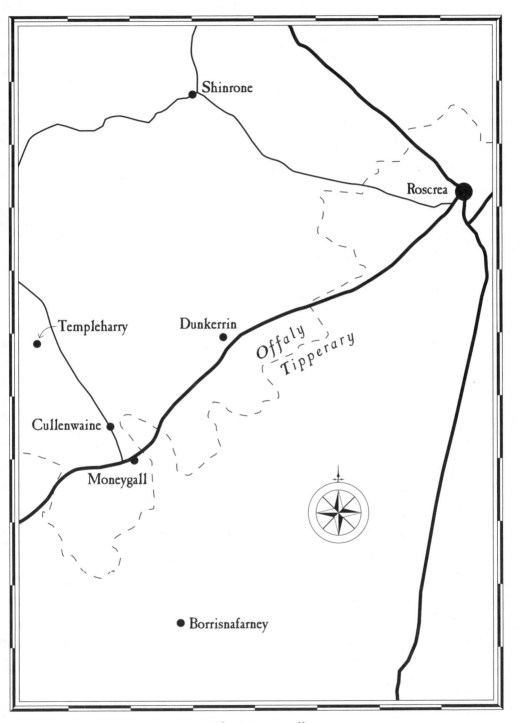

The Moneygall area

deliver warrants against defaulters. The fierce popular opposition to tithes led to attacks on tithe collectors, who were defended by the police and military, who frequently clashed with local people.

The incident which had the greatest impact concerned Thomas Tiquin, a young businessman, a miller, who was described as "one of the finest young men in the King's County, upward of six feet two inches in height, and the idol of his neighbourhood".[91] In November 1835, he refused a demand for tithes amounting to one pound, twelve shillings and eight pence from the Rev. William Brownlow Savage, rector of the Union of Shinrone, Kilcommon and Kilmurry. Tiquin lost an ensuing court case, was arrested and confined in the barracks at Shinrone, then transferred to prison in Dublin, where he was so affected or so ill-treated that he died a short time later.

The funeral procession from Dublin to Offaly turned into a mass demonstration of opposition to the tithes. The coffin was carried in a plain hearse, drawn by four black-plumed horses, and on the sides of the hearse four placards bore the inscription, "Funeral of Mr. Thomas Tiquin of Shinrone, in King's County, who died on Thursday 30th May, 1837, while under imprisonment in the Four Courts, Marshalsea, Dublin. For The Tithes." Thousands of people joined the cortège at various stages along the route, and it was estimated that some 200,000 people took part in the funeral. The tithes were abolished in the following year, and Tiquin became known as "The Last Tithe Martyr".

While a source of resentment and agitation had been removed, the issue of inequitable landholding and rack-rents remained unresolved, and agitation, often violent, continued. Many of the attacks were aimed against landlords and their agents; threatening letters and notices were posted. Separate attempts were made on the lives of George Garvey and another landlord who was visiting him. Shots were fired into the house of George Minchin's herdsman. In 1842, the clerk of the Petty Sessions in Moneygall was shot dead; he was an under-agent for George Garvey and had recently taken over a farm from which the tenant had been evicted. That year notices threatening the landlords and signed "Captain Starlight" were posted on church doors in the area.

As Jonathan Binns wrote:

> King's county has been the scene of many cruel-ties. A man taking a farm, from which another has been ejected, will probably find his horses without ears, or otherwise maimed, and his cattle houghed, that is, the sinews of the hinder legs cut. A grave dug near his house, with a note in it, is considered a friendly mode of warning him of his danger. If these do not produce the desired effect, they set fire to his house, or shoot him; and cruelty has been carried to such excess that whilst the house was burning, the inhabitants have been kept in by monsters armed with pitchforks.[92]

It would be a mistake to see the tithe agitation as a simple matter of Catholic against Protestant; Catholics clearly had special reason to object to the tithes, but Protestants were amongst those who opposed them too. In October 1836, two local farmers were arrested, brought to Dublin and jailed for non-payment of tithes. One of the two, John Hayes from Clonamohan, between Moneygall and Shinrone, was a Protestant. The central issue, despite occasional appearances, was land and poverty, not religion.

Although historians and popular anecdotage have tended to suggest that Protestants and Catholics lived in different worlds, the truth is that in the early nineteenth century, religious affiliation posed virtually no obstacle to interaction and friendship between Catholics and Protestants. Characteristics that marked Catholic-Protestant difference in later eras did not exist at the time when Joseph Kearney was growing up. For example, the propensity for Irish Catholics to have much larger families than Protestants did not exist. As Donald Harmon Akenson writes in *Small Difference,* "the available data suggest that nineteenth- and early twentieth-century Protestants and Catholics did not have divergent family patterns, but, rather, that they held a single common pattern".[93] Cormac O'Grada writes in *Ulster Catholics,* "the large fertility gap [between Catholics and Protestants] so widely noted today was absent".[94] And A.C. Hepburn writes that "We know that the greater propensity of Catholics to have large families is a trend which has emerged only during the twentieth century."[95]

Sexual repression has been so repeatedly described amongst the Catholic Irish that one would think that it was exclusive to that denomination. Yet, as Akenson observes:

> ... the Protestant clergy had methods of enforcing sexual morality that would have made the Catholic priests envious. For instance, take the case of the Presbyterian congregation in the village of Ballycarry in the parish of Templecorran, County Antrim ... There, the kirk session records show, it was the practice of the clergy to have notorious sinners sit in a special pew of shame facing the congregation. This punishment was imposed in the case of a couple who engaged in fornication and those who came to the altar with the girl pregnant.[96]

Ireland abounds in anecdotes that stress the supposed differences in sexual and marital behaviour between Catholics and Protestants, and such tales cohere through repetition to assume the authority of holy writ. Yet, as J.J. Lee concludes, "In the comparative context, the similarities between the sexual and marital mores of Irish Catholics were far more striking than the local differences on which polemicists loved to linger."[97]

The Irish school system had been destroyed in the seventeenth century by the British Restoration government's Act of Uniformity (1666), which required that all teachers must conform to the Church of Ireland. It suppressed not just Catholic education and worship but dissenting Protestantism also. Hedge schools contributed bravely during the seventeenth century to maintaining some form of native Irish education. These were held at first in poor huts in remote places, where the schoolmasters went in fear of the authorities but were supported by the pennies of the community. However, by the early eighteenth century, the noose of sectarian restrictions had significantly loosened, and the number of hedge schools rose dramatically.

In Dunkerrin parish in the first decade of the century, there were at least six schools, to which the scholars brought monthly payments. Four of these – in the townlands of Cloneganna, Coolroe, Templeharry and Moneygall – were Catholic. Two Protestant schools were also active, in the townlands of Dunkerrin and Moneygall; in the second of these, the teacher was Thomas Healy, a relative of Sarah Healy, grandmother of Joseph Kearney.

The relaxation of the Penal Laws in the second half of the eighteenth century meant that Catholic priests were no longer harassed, hounded or transported, and a Report to the Commissioners in 1835 revealed that an average of six hundred people attended the Roman Catholic chapel in Shinrone every Sunday and a further three hundred at nearby Brosna. Church of Ireland attendance was four hundred and fifty in the morning, fifty-five in the evening, and Methodists (Wesleyan and Primitive) accounted for seventy-five.[98]

In the late eighteenth century, the prominent local landed Protestant family, the Minchins, donated a site for a Catholic mass house in Moneygall. John Wesley, founder of Methodism, visited Shinrone in 1749, but it was not until 1790 that a Methodist chapel was built in the village.

Following the 1798 Rebellion, a large rebuilding programme was undertaken by the Church of Ireland. As the established church, it was closely associated with the ruling class and the government, and it was keen to make its authoritative presence felt. St Mary's Church of Ireland in Shinrone, begun in 1819, was part of this building programme. It had twelve family pews for the twelve landowning families in the parish, and the poor of the parish were consigned to the gallery.

The Catholic church was not slow, either, to improve its buildings and to repair damage inflicted during the rebellion. In Shinrone, St Mary's Catholic Church was built in 1810, replacing Kilcommin chapel, which had been burned by the militia in 1798.

The early decades of the century had been a time of rising alarm on the part of the landed Protestant classes at the political tide flowing in favour of Catholic emancipation. The vote had been extended to Catholic forty-shilling freeholders in 1793, and some Catholics had succeeded in building up businesses and sublet land to small tenants; they were now able to educate their children and had increased access to the professions. Some Protestants felt under threat. Some of this alarm may have been shared by some of the small tenant, cottier and labouring Protestants, but largely it was a phenomenon of the political and economic elite, and the clergy. In Dunkerrin a group was formed (a Brunswick Constitutional club, as it was known) to defend Protestant privilege, and its secretary, a local rector, in 1829 – shortly before Fulmouth Kearney's birth – petitioned the House of Lords to grant no more concessions to the Roman Catholics. The Protestant ascendancy, they claimed, was a fundamental element of the "glorious revolution" of 1688.[99]

Apparently contradictory accounts are given regarding relations between Catholics and Protestants in Offaly. W. R. LeFanu, son of the Church of Ireland dean of Emly, wrote, in *Seventy Years:*

> In 1831 came the tithe war, and with it our friendly relations with the priests and people ceased. The former, not unnaturally, threw themselves heart and soul into the agitation. The Protestant clergy were denounced by agitators and priests from platforms and from altars, and branded as the worst enemies of the people, who were told to hunt them like mad dogs from the county; they were insulted wherever they went, many were attacked, some were even murdered.[100]

However, writing in 1836, Jonathan Binns painted rather a different picture, though he seems rather sanguine about Protestant casualties. Referring to the prevalent custom of faction fights, he wrote that they were:

> . . . confined to Catholics – religious differences having nothing whatever to do with them. Taking a district of twenty miles round Philipstown, not more than eight or nine Protestants have been murdered in affrays connected with religion, during the last fourteen years – and no Catholics have been murdered by Protestants. The proportion of the former to the latter is about twenty to one. The Protestants, being few in number, are obliging and quiet.[101]

It can be difficult to disentangle at this distance the motivations of murders and other attacks, but it should be noted that the main targets of the agitation over tithes were the proctors – the middlemen who acted for the Protestant clergy in collecting the tithes – and while some of these may have been Protestant, it was for their role in collecting tithes that they were attacked. Also, it was by no means only Protestants who were the targets of the anger of the people bearing the brunt of evictions. The son of a local middleman who had pursued tenants for non-payment of rents was shot and killed on his way to attend mass in Barna.

Nevertheless, many Protestants may have felt increasingly uneasy during this period of land and tithe agitation and the campaign for Catholic emancipation, which saw a new growth in Catholic confidence. In 1836, the Sisters of Mercy set up as their first foundation outside Dublin a convent and school in Tullamore, County Offaly, establishing themselves four years later also at Birr.

While Protestant owners of substantial properties and the Protestant professional classes may have felt relatively protected by the high walls of their estates and the partiality of the police, military and courts, the situation of Protestant small tenants such as the Kearneys may have been less comfortable. If they were associated by some of their Catholic neighbours with their wealthier and more powerful co-religionists, they may have given some thought to the opportunities that might be offered by emigrating to where elements of their family seemed to be prospering.

In 1844, a redoubtable American woman named Asenath Nicholson visited Ireland and later published an account of her visit, *Ireland's Welcome to the Stranger; or, Excursions through Ireland in 1844 and 1845, for the purpose of Personally Investigating the Condition of the Poor.* Unlike many visitors, she stayed not with the rich and propertied but with the poor, and although an enthusiastic Protestant, she met and stayed with Catholic and Protestant alike. Born in Chelsea on the New England frontier in 1788, she had run a vegetarian boarding house in New York, from where she sailed in 1844 to Liverpool, then King's Town and Dublin, and continuing by the Grand Canal to Tullamore in Offaly.

In all her travels she was moved by the condition of the poor; impressed by their innate qualities, she was horrified by the condition to which they had been reduced by the social conditions of the time and place. She felt that only some kind of revolution could bring about change.

One day she left the house where she was staying in Tullamore to take a coach journey and soon became surrounded by a large crowd.

> It was scarcely eight o'clock when I reached the coach, but the beggars had assembled before me . . . To them a foreigner, or a stranger, whom their shrewdness will readily detect, is a kind of common plunder, and escape is a hopeless undertaking. . . . [L]ike swarming bees, they sallied out from every quarter, till the crowd was immense. . . .
>
> The scene had now become, to say the least, ludicrous, painful, and unseemly. I had travelled by sea and by land among the savages of my own country, the poor abused slaves on the plantations, the degraded, untutored native Canadians; but this eclipsed the whole. I looked down upon the forbidding mass, and saw every lineament of talent, every praiseworthy and noble quality, every soul-speaking glance of the eye, every beauty of symmetry, that God's image ever possessed, united with every disgusting, pitiable incongruity that imagination could depict. . . .

When we had well escaped, "What is this?" I begged the coachman to tell me. "It is the case of all Ireland wherever you travel; a fine country but cursed with bad laws."[102]

Travelling on via Roscrea, she visited Birr.

It rained as I entered the town, and turning into a neat little cottage, found a kind welcome by the cleanly master and mistress, who are Roman Catholics, and was invited to eat, and then they directed me to a Protestant lodging-house. I say Protestant, because the Catholics knowing me to be one, generally selected this sort, supposing I should be better pleased. They told me the people were kind and respectable; this was true, but the rooms were dark and without floors, and two enormous hogs which were snoring in an adjoining closet were called out to take their supper in the kitchen, which made the sum total a sad picture. I was kindly urged to take supper, and sat down with them, took an apple, and passed a solitary evening. Not that I was sorry for my undertaking, but the lack of all social comfort, where comfort should be expected. When I went into my bed-room I felt like bursting into tears; every thing looked so forbidding, and so unlike cleanliness about the bed. Clean sheets were begged, and clean sheets were granted; yet it was a doleful night, and in the morning, after taking some potatoes, and asking for my bill, four pence was the answer. Cheap indeed! I paid her more.[103]

She explored the varieties of religious experience in the area.

Heard the Baptist minister preach to an audience of five, and he likewise broke bread to three. He observed, when he went out, that he felt it his duty to keep the light a burning, the more so, as there were but a few tapers kindled in the island. In the intermission, heard a sermon in the neat Methodist chapel, and that day and evening heard four good sermons. At the house of Mr. W. heard a Roman Catholic, who had been converted from Popery, relate his exercises of mind. A few others had renounced the doctrines, and united with Protestant churches. The priest at whose chapel he attended had left also, and became a Presbyterian clergyman [Father Crotty], that when any become converts from that church, they are the most spiritual Christians of all others, and we must take great stride to keep up with them.[104]

She gave Bible readings when she stayed in a lodging-house in Banagher.

They were Catholics, but they listened to the Word of Life with the most profound attention, and without any opposition. They told their neighbours they fully believed I was inspired of God to come to Ireland, and do them good . . .

They gathered about me in the evening in crowds; and when I had read two hours, such a breathless silence was in the room, that I looked about to ascertain whether all who were behind me had not left it, when I saw the place was filled to crowding, sitting upon the floor; and so quietly had they entered that I knew it not.[105]

Asenath Nicholson visited a second time at the height of the Famine in 1847 as the field agent of the New York Irish

Relief Society, and her second book on Ireland was published in 1850 as *Lights and Shades of Ireland;* the Famine section was reissued in New York in 1851 as *Annals of the Famine in Ireland in 1847, 1848, and 1849.* At the conclusion of her visit she wrote:

> I visited Ireland to see it as it is, so I reported as I found it. I have stayed to witness that which, though so heart-rending and painful, has given me the proof of what common observation told me in the beginning – that there must need to be an explosion of some kind or another.[106]

— 7 —

An Irish Family Sets Down Roots

Thomas Kearney and his family thrived in Ohio, but not without struggle and not without heartache. They had left behind in a grave in Baltimore their first-born child, Sarah, who had died at just ten months old; four other children, aged from nine to one, made the journey with them, and in 1805 their sixth child, William, was the first to be born in their new home in Ohio. However, tragedy struck again at the end of 1807 when their second child, Joseph, died at the age of twelve.

Exactly four months later, another son was born, and they named him Joseph, too. James followed in 1810, a second Sarah in 1812, John in 1815 and Samuel in 1818. In 1815, their oldest surviving child, Mary, was married just prior to her eighteenth birthday to Samuel Hays, whose father Levi was, like the Kearneys and Baxleys, a Methodist from Maryland. He had moved his family to Ohio's Fairfield County just a year after the Kearneys, moving a year later to Perry Township, close to the Kearney family.

The story of the Kearney family's fortunes that Thomas no doubt conveyed to his relatives still in Ireland was

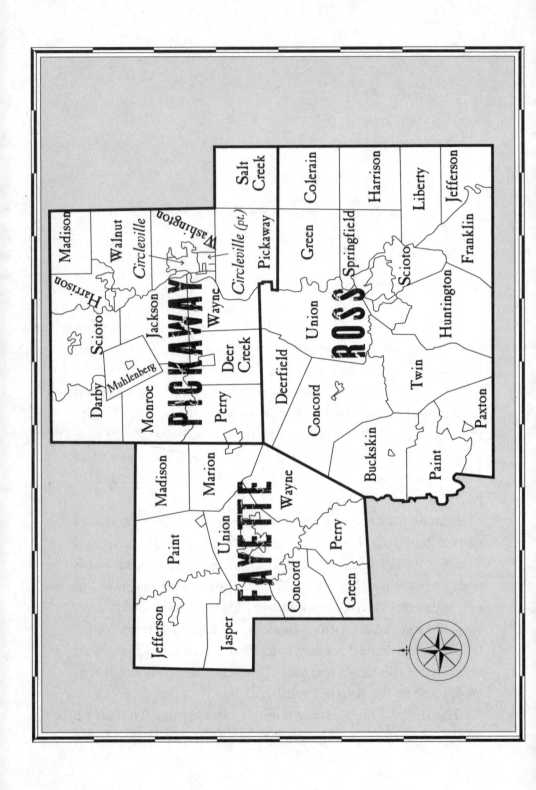

overwhelmingly positive. From a country mired in dysfunctional land ownership patterns, with high unemployment and poverty, he had emigrated to a country in which there was work for every hand. Nothing came easy to these settlers, and the work to forge new farmsteads in the valley was certainly long, severe and energy-sapping, yet there was a sense that application and hard work could bring its own rewards and that it was possible to look forward to a future. The threat posed by the increasingly dispossessed Native American people was rapidly fading as more settlers joined them in clearing more land and establishing more homesteads. In addition, they enjoyed the support of a community of fellow Methodists in Deerfield, the rest of Ross County and the neighbouring Fayette and Pickaway Counties.

Life for the Kearneys and their neighbours remained a struggle – with the elements and with the demands of a complete self-sufficiency. In 1816–17, they endured "the year that had no summer". Every night the temperature dropped to unseasonal lows, and there was at least one hard frost every month. In June, the corn lay dead in the field; in July a new planting was destroyed by another frost; in August, more frost came; and in late September winter arrived, the snows beginning early in October and remaining until April 1817.

The extraordinary weather, which affected the Northeastern United States, New England, the Canadian Maritimes, Newfoundland, China, India and Northern Europe, was caused by an eruption of Mt Timboro in the East Indies. Particles of volcanic ash caused a clouding of large parts of the earth's atmosphere.

In July and August, lakes and rivers were frozen as far south as Pennsylvania. Very dramatic temperature swings occurred, plummeting within hours from 95°F (35°C) to near freezing. Even though Ohio was not as badly affected as

Canada and New England, crops were widely destroyed, and prices of essential foodstuffs rose dramatically. Oats – a vital staple in an economy dependent upon horses – rose from 12¢ a bushel in 1815 to 92¢ a bushel in 1816. For a pioneer family like the Kearneys, now with eight unmarried children aged between one and twenty-one, these must have been terrible times. Many in Ohio survived only because deer had become trapped by the snows and ice and could not escape the hunters. So many were caught and killed that winter that from 1817 on deer no longer featured as a significant source of meat, and the deerskin britches and jacket that had been characteristic of the frontiers people were no longer made.

The Kearneys, like all frontier people, had been dependant upon their own resources since arriving in Ohio. They had not only made their own clothes; they had made the cloth for making the clothes. But in 1817, Clarksburg, the only village of size and importance in Deerfield township, opened its first general store.

Another of their children died young: Lambert, last to be born in Baltimore, died in Ohio at the age of seventeen in 1820.

Many of the details of the life the Kearneys lived in the early decades of the nineteenth century are unknown: how and where they first acquired land; what crops they grew and live-stock they kept; what further land purchases they made in their first twenty years there. But it is known that Thomas Kearney paid taxes on land in Ross County in 1809, 1810, 1816, 1817, 1818, 1820, 1830 and 1840. There is evidence that the family prospered, acquiring more land. In 1828, Thomas Kearney bought land from Henry Massie at the North Fork of Paint Creek on Dogtown Road. In 1831, he bought more land at Paint Creek from John Blue, and in March 1837, he bought land at Concord, Ross County, from William

Shepherd; in August 1837, he bought land bordering that of the Holloways from Wallace Cadwallader. In 1838, he leased land at the North Fork of Paint Creek to Deerfield School. The pattern of his land dealings tells a story of successful settlement and farming, and his success no doubt encouraged his brothers and nephews to follow him out to Ohio from Moneygall and to settle in the adjoining Ross, Pickaway and Fayette counties.

Sometime in the 1830s, Thomas Kearney's brother John (born in 1782) arrived from Moneygall with his wife Deborah. William Jr (born 1812), Francis (born 1803) and Thomas (born 1800) – three sons of Thomas's brother William – left Offaly for the Scioto Valley a few years later. Their brother Joseph, Fulmouth's father, remained at home in Offaly for a few years. Francis was married to Sarah; William Jr to Alice Davis.

Meanwhile, the family of Thomas and Sarah Baxley Kearney had branched out in the decades since their arrival from Maryland. While many of their marriages had been made with neighbours in Pickaway and other bordering counties, Thomas Jr married Nancy Miller in 1825 in Champaign County, Ohio. They moved closer to Thomas and Sarah in the early 1840s, but following their deaths Thomas Jr and family moved to Douglas County, Illinois. Their fourth child, who like the first

An index of some of Thomas Kearney's land deals in Ross County

three children was born in Champaign County, helped organise in 1861 the 13th Illinois Cavalry. He fought in the western theatre of the Civil War (in Arkansas and Missouri); he died of consumption in 1864.

Nancy Miller Kearney appears to have been related by marriage to the famous frontiersman Simon Kenton, and they named their third child Simon, their sixth Kenton.

Simon Kenton was a remarkable example of the Protestant Irish contribution to the making of the American frontier at this time. Probably even more accomplished and significant than the better-known Daniel Boone (another Irish Protestant of the period), his father had emigrated from County Down. He served as a scout against the Shawnee in Dunmore's War in 1774. In 1777, he saved the life of his friend and fellow frontiersman Daniel Boone, and the next year, he was in turn rescued from torture and death. He served on the famous 1778 expedition to capture Fort Sackville and fought with "Mad" Anthony Wayne in the Northwest Indian War in 1793–94, which culminated in the decisive Battle of Fallen Timbers. Kenton moved to Urbana, Ohio, in 1810, and became a brigadier general of the Ohio militia. He served in the War of 1812 as both a scout and as leader of a militia group in the Battle of the Thames in 1813.

Thomas Kearney's son Joseph, now a farmer, married Elizabeth Davis of Pickaway County in 1835, and Samuel, the eleventh and last of Thomas and Sarah Kearney's children, also a farmer, married Elizabeth Peniwell in 1843. Sarah married Eli Holycross in 1851, and in the same year James, another farmer, married Eleanor Hays, a sister of his sister Mary's husband. In the fertile land of the Scioto Valley the Kearneys had already set down strong roots.

In 1827, Sarah's brother George Baxley and his wife Mary visited Sarah and Thomas in Ohio. George had come to own

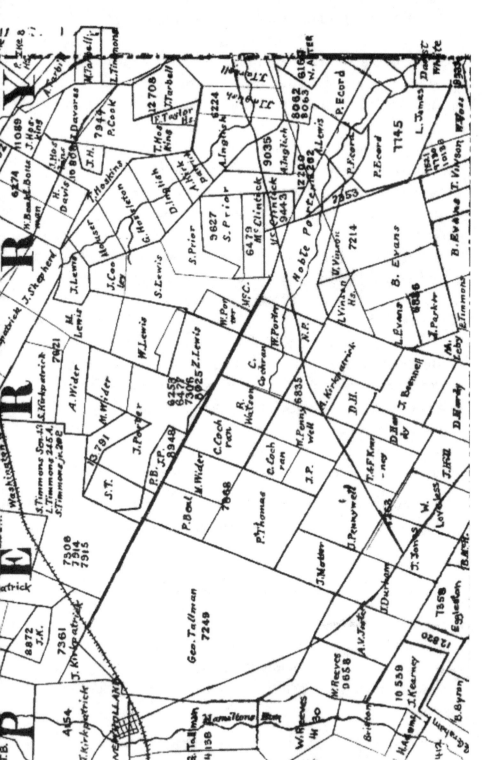

Plat map of part of Perry Township, Pickaway County in 1844 showing Kearney land lower left and lower centre. Deerfield Township, Ross County, borders this map to the south.

several thousand acres of land that had been granted by the Congress as bounty land to those who had served in the Continental Army during the Revolution. George, and his brothers John and Thomas, had enlisted in the Maryland Militia in 1794. George served as a member of Washington's artillery and was at Fort McHenry during the British bombardment on 12 September 1814. A bombshell that landed near him but did not explode was later displayed in the Baxley drug store in Baltimore.

Sarah Sr's brother George Baxley had added to his military grant land holding by acquiring more land in Union County, near Columbus, Ohio, in 1826, and later he deeded a thousand acres of land to his second son, George Washington Baxley (1801–77), who emigrated with his wife Martha Ann Griffith and family to settle on Boke's Creek in Union County in 1840. At the time, his aunt Sarah and her husband Thomas Kearney were in their sixties and seventies and living just about sixty miles away. However, George Washington Baxley seems to have lacked the pioneer qualities of his aunt and uncle. As *The History of Union County, Ohio* records:

> He settled on about five hundred acres, the southern part of Survey 3,238, but not being accustomed to the sturdy labor of a pioneer, did not reduce it to a cultivated state with any great rapidity. He gradually disposed of his land, and at length purchased a mill site at Newton, and removed to that village.[107]

From 1843, he ran a grist mill on Mill Creek for more than twenty years, later combining some farming with serving as postmaster for a time, and he also set up a drug business at Newton.

> Mr. Baxley has immortalized himself by leaving behind him a diary, commencing in 1847, and

continuing for nearly thirty years, containing the passing events of his family and the neighborhood generally. So thorough was his record, that when any neighbor desired to know the date of any event of the past or any particular information upon incidents of the neighborhood, he would refer to Mr. Baxley, who, upon examination of his record, could generally give the desired information. Even the extremes of temperature, and marriages, births and deaths, were all recorded; excessive droughts, or excessive floods were all noted with correctness and precision. He was a peculiar man, exhibiting many eccentricities, yet, withal, a respected citizen and neighbor.[108]

Other members of the Baxley family remained in Maryland and prospered in the fields of milling, grocery and medicine. George and Mary's third son, Henry Willis Baxley (1803–76), was involved in the establishment of America's first dental college, and their fourth son, Jackson Brown Baxley (1814–96), was the leading initiator of pharmaceutical legislation in Maryland, culminating in the enactment of a law requiring the registration of pharmacists. He was to the fore in organising the Maryland College of Pharmacy, and he was the first commissioner appointed and the first president of the Maryland Board of Pharmacy.

The journey that had brought Thomas Kearney from Maryland to Ohio was shadowed in later years by the extraordinary story of the "underground railroad", which brought black slaves along the very same route. Some of those who operated this network of safe houses had come north to Ohio from Maryland because they abhorred slavery. Whether this had been in the thoughts of Thomas and his wife Sarah, we shall probably never know.

The National Park Service lists sixty Underground Railroad historic sites in twenty-one states. Ohio, with eleven, has more than any other state, and Cincinnati is home to the National Underground Railroad Freedom Center. Of the estimated four million slaves in the pre-Civil War South, about 100,000 are believed to have escaped along the Underground Railroad.

Rankin House was the first stop on the route to freedom for an estimated three thousand people. A candle in the window of the house of Rev. John Rankin, high on a hill overlooking the Ohio River, meant the coast was clear, that runaway slaves could find temporary refuge on their flight from the South.

Rankin, a "Scotch-Irish" Presbyterian minister whose grandfather was born in County Derry in 1724, is reputed to have told Harriet Beecher Stowe the story of a runaway slave and her child who crossed the frozen Ohio River, a tale that Stowe recounted later in *Uncle Tom's Cabin*. Rankin House was typical of hundreds of secret meeting places, churches and homes of abolitionists, Quakers, free blacks and others who hid fleeing slaves from bounty hunters.

As they travelled on the Underground Railroad, they shared the route of their path to freedom hidden in lyrics such as these two verses from "Follow the Drinking Gourd", in which the gourd is a code name for the Big Dipper star formation, which points north to the Pole Star.

> When the sun comes back,
> And the first Quail calls,
> Follow the drinking gourd,
> For the old man is waiting
> For to carry you to freedom
> If you follow the drinking gourd.

The riverbank will make a very good road,
The dead trees show you the way.
Left foot, peg foot traveling on,
Following the drinking gourd.

In 1826, Rankin published *Letters on Slavery,* an influential outline of anti-slavery views, and Ohio became even more than ever the destination for those who had freed their slaves. In 1832, William Lloyd Garrison, leader of the anti-slavery movement, published the letters in his newspaper, *The Liberator,* and Garrison later called Rankin his "anti-slavery father", saying that "his book on slavery was the cause of my entering the anti-slavery conflict".[109]

When Henry Ward Beecher was asked, "Who abolished slavery?" he answered, "Reverend John Rankin and his sons did."[110]

More than 500 routes are believed to have gone through Ohio alone, but from the early 1800s until the Civil War, runaways fled to freedom all along the line separating North from South. Some of those routes have been documented but were not general knowledge at the time. One famous passenger on the Underground Railroad was Frederick Douglass, who was to become the most remarkable African-American orator and anti-slavery campaigner.

— 8 —

Frederick Douglass in Ireland

In 1845, when Joseph Kearney was about fifty and his son Fulmouth was fifteen, Frederick Douglass, a remarkable American who was to be a significant intellectual influence on Barack Obama, visited Ireland. Douglass was one of the foremost leaders of the movement that fought to end slavery within the United States. A brilliant speaker, in fact one of America's first great black public speakers, he was himself a former slave, and just before arriving in Ireland he won world fame when his autobiography – *Narrative of the Life of Frederick Douglass, an American Slave* – was published in May 1845.

Douglass was nevertheless exhausted and demoralised when he left the United States. Exhausted by the constant, unremitting racism that surrounded him at every moment, his safety and freedom daily threatened by fugitive slave laws and physical attack by members of the public, he travelled to Europe principally to win support there for the abolitionist cause, but also to gain some rest and respite from the strains and oppressions of his life in America.

He wrote that one of his aims in visiting Europe was "to get a little repose, that I might return home refreshed and

NARRATIVE OF THE LIFE

OF

FREDERICK DOUGLASS,

AN

AMERICAN SLAVE.

WRITTEN BY HIMSELF.

What, ho !—our countrymen in chains !
  The whip on *woman's* shrinking flesh !
Our soil still reddening with the stains,
  ·Caught from her scourging, warm and fresh !
What ! mothers from their children riven !
  What ! God's own image bought and sold !
Americans to market driven,
  And barter'd, as the brute, for gold !—*Whittier.*

DUBLIN:

WEBB AND CHAPMAN, GT. BRUNSWICK-STREET.

1845.

Title page of the Dublin edition of Narrative of the Life of Frederick Douglass, An American Slave.

strengthened, ready to be able to join you vigorously in the prosecution of our holy cause".[111]

Douglass had already experienced positive encounters with the Irish in America. In his autobiography he mentions meeting at a shipyard in Baltimore two Irishmen who were unloading stone and whom he offered to help.

"Are ye a slave for life?" asked one of them.

When Douglass answered that he was, the response was clearly empathetic. So strong was the impression of the Irishmen on him that he resolved "from that time to run away".

Douglass stayed for almost six months in Ireland, where he found not only repose but a reinvigorated sense of direction. Much of this had to do with his reception by progressive Protestant elements in Ireland. The Irish abolitionist movement was regarded as the most militant in Europe, and although Douglas was inspired by the Catholic Daniel O'Connell and the campaign for Catholic emancipation, he found in Ireland an anti-slavery movement that was almost entirely Protestant in membership.

Douglass had also already been inspired and influenced by one of Ireland's foremost revolutionaries, Arthur O'Connor, a leader of the United Irishmen and an MP representing a constituency in King's County in the decade before the birth in that county of Fulmouth Kearney. Although the United Irishmen's rebellion of 1798 failed, it left a legacy of revolutionary precedent for later generations of Irish republicans and nationalists. The United Irishmen's ideological leader, Wolfe Tone, and the movement's activist leader, Arthur O'Connor, were both Protestants, O'Connor coming from the noted Protestant town of Bandon in County Cork but with close family connections with Philipstown in King's County (now Daingean, County Offaly), where his uncle Richard Longfield, later Baron Longueville, lived. Strongly influenced by the American

Revolution, he was a member of parliament in the Irish House of Commons for Philipstown from 1790 to 1795. In 1796, he became a member of the Society of United Irishmen and in the following year published *To the Free Electors of the County of Antrim,* for which he was charged with high treason but won his case.

In early 1798, while travelling to France to solicit aid for a rebellion in Ireland, O'Connor and several others were arrested and charged with high treason in England. O'Connor was acquitted but immediately rearrested and brought to solitary confinement in Dublin's Kilmainham Gaol. He was acquitted again and later that same year published *A Letter to Lord Castlereagh* and *The State of Ireland.* He went to France to seek support for another uprising, and in Paris he was recognised by Napoleon as the accredited representative of the United Irishmen. In 1804, Napoleon appointed him general of division in the French army. He married Eliza, daughter of the Marquis de Condorcet, a French philosopher, mathematician and political scientist, and in his retirement he published many pamphlets on political and social topics.

Frederick Douglass was familiar with both his actions and his writings and at a crucial stage in his life, on the run as an escaped slave, had been inspired by a speech of his. As Patricia J. Ferreira has written:

> . . . he came upon a speech in the *Columbian Orator* on Catholic emancipation in Ireland which had been delivered by Arthur O'Connor in the Irish House of Commons. Douglass was impressed by O'Connor's sentiments and his declaration that he would "risk everything dear to [him] on earth" for Ireland's independence. Douglass wrote that O'Connor provided him with a powerful vocabulary to voice beliefs within his "own soul" which

"boldly" vindicated human rights and "enabled" Douglass "to utter thoughts, and to meet the arguments brought forward to sustain slavery". O'Connor demonstrated to Douglass the powerful way that language can provoke a nation toward change.[112]

Later, he had also been influenced by the oratory of Daniel O'Connell, a lawyer who had built a movement of poor Catholics into a political force that ultimately called for Irish independence. Douglass wrote that "his eloquence came down upon the vast assembly like a summer thunder-shower upon a dusty road . . . and within the grasp of his strong hand, . . . [he] could lead it whithersoever he would . . ."[113]

The influence on Douglass of Irish revolutionary thinkers and activists became amplified by the anti-slavery campaign, led by Quakers and Protestants, which he now encountered, and by the generally positive reception he enjoyed in Ireland.

As Patricia J. Ferreira has written:

> Such interest ultimately helped to instill in Douglass the assurance that enabled him to formulate and articulate a democratic vision for the United States. . . . Although from a young age he possessed the inclination to be a leader, Ireland was the site where this trait blossomed, free of the concern of retribution.[114]

And as she further observes:

> . . . his association with the Irish functioned as a critical component to his own liberation . . . and resulted in a new preface and appendix to the *Narrative* which ultimately demonstrate a shift in the author's sense of self that bespeaks his emerging position as a world champion of human rights.[115]

An important part of that Irish influence was simply the way he was treated. In a letter to William Lloyd Garrison – the leading US abolitionist and publisher of the anti-slavery newspaper, the *Liberator* – he wrote of "a total absence of all manifestations of prejudice against me, on account of my color". The Irish people "measure and esteem men according to their moral and intellectual worth, and not according to the color of their skin". It is clear that the experience had the effect on him of crucially boosting his self-confidence and encouraging him towards a significant leadership role in American life.

> Instead of the bright, blue sky of America, I am covered with the soft, grey fog of the Emerald Isle. I breath, and lo! the chattel becomes a man. I gaze around in vain for one who will question my equal humanity, claim me as a slave, or offer me an insult.[116]

While in Ireland Douglass became associated with Quaker publisher and member of the Hibernian Anti-Slavery Society, Richard D. Webb, who organised his schedule of public speaking engagements and who also published new editions of his *Narrative* to meet the considerable demand created by his speaking tour of Ireland, Scotland and England.

Patricia J. Ferreira observes of the second Dublin edition that it

> contains a new preface and appendix that were not part of the Boston printing and that demonstrate an attitude of self-confidence and self-possession that was not apparent or even available for Douglass to invoke before his stay in Ireland.[117]

It was in general amongst progressive elements of the Protestant Irish that Douglass found the important support that made his Irish visit so significant. In Cork he stayed for a month with a Church of Ireland family, Thomas and Ann Jennings and their eight children. One of the things that made an impression on him there was that although part of a religious minority and hence "different", they acted and spoke as if "everyone else was out of step" – a description of middle-class Irish Protestant attitudes which may well ring a loud bell of recognition even now.[118] Douglass corresponded with Thomas and Ann's daughter Isabel Jennings for the rest of his life. She later observed that Douglass's speaking tour had succeeded in dragging previously reluctant or silent English Protestants into expressing support for the anti-slavery cause.

As Patricia J. Ferreira concludes, "Ireland, physically and spiritually, provided Douglass with one of the first platforms from which he could fully and freely speak."[119]

There was an irony about his experience of freedom amongst the Quakers and Church of Ireland Protestants of Ireland. Quakers in Ireland were few and far between in 1845, largely because of their persecution by the established Church of Ireland and the state.

There had been Quakers in King's County (Offaly) since 1673. They had suffered persecution and had been excluded from the professions, and members had been imprisoned for non-payment of tithes. Also, as Therese Abbott observes in "Quakerism in the Edenderry Area 1673–1831": "The Quakers' pacifistic principles made them easy targets for the Jacobite army and raparees."[120]

By 1691, almost all had been forced out by the attacks of James II's army and their plundering, and most had moved for protection to the Pale, but many returned in the following years, and Offaly's Quaker community entered a second phase, characterised in particular by their development of a new woollen industry and their prominence in the milling business and grocery trade. By 1765, the religious make-up of the Edenderry area was given as: Protestants 689, Papists 2625, Quakers 159 and Presbyterians 22.[121]

But by the time of Fulmouth Kearney's birth in 1830, the Quaker population of Offaly and of Ireland was in steep decline. Part of the reason for this was the troubled circumstances in which many came under attack or feared attack. As soon as any Quakers took up arms to defend themselves, they were expelled from membership of the Quakers. But also Quakers had begun to emigrate. As Therese Abbott writes:

> William Penn had established Quaker colonies in New Jersey and Pennsylvania in the late seventeenth century, so the Quakers felt confident in emigrating to a place where they would find people of a common faith.[122]

One of the elements driving emigration was their persecution under the system of tithes. Many Quakers refused to pay, a few paid under protest, but many found their goods forcibly confiscated in lieu of payment, and this was sufficiently widespread and intense to have an adverse effect on the wool trade in which Quakers were so prominent.

Many Quakers had emigrated to America in pursuit of freedom, and although Frederick Douglass experienced in Ireland a precious sense of freedom in the company of the Quaker Webbs and the Church of Ireland Jennings family, Ireland was hardly a country characterised by political and social freedom, especially for Catholics and Dissenters.

— 9 —

The Great Famine in Offaly

The Famine was the greatest disaster in the history of Ireland. It was also the greatest cause of nineteenth-century Irish emigration to the United States. Ironically, it was from the United States that the potato blight arrived in Ireland.

Originating in the highlands of central Mexico, *Phytophthora infestans*, or potato blight, was first noticed when potato crops around Philadelphia and New York were suddenly and inexplicably destroyed in early 1843; by 1845, it had destroyed potato crops from Illinois east to Nova Scotia, and from Virginia north to Ontario. It crossed the Atlantic with a shipment of seed potatoes to Belgian farmers. It spread through Belgium and into the Netherlands, to northern Spain, the southern tips of Norway and Sweden, and east to Italy. It moved rapidly through Britain and Ireland. For every farmer in Europe who relied on potatoes, the failure of the crop was a disaster, but in Ireland the potato had become the staple diet of the majority of the Irish people, and this meant disaster not just for farmers but for almost the entire population.

Within months, winds spread the rapidly reproducing airborne spores of the disease throughout Ireland, and by September 1845 it was clear that serious food shortage could not be far away. The disease in the crop was widespread, and potatoes that had seemed sound were now discovered to be rotten. People were already taking desperate measures to feed themselves, going back to fields that had already been harvested to seek a few sound potatoes that might have escaped the harvest.

A pattern of crop specialisation and massive population growth had set the scene for the disaster. The remarkable nutritional quality of potatoes and the vast expansion of their planting had fuelled an extraordinary rise in the population, which by 1840 had risen to eight million from just two million in 1700.

Moneygall and Shinrone suffered badly in the Famine, but not as severely as some other parts of Ireland. Barley and oats were grown in the region, and so there was a less than complete reliance on the potato crop. Nevertheless, the advance of the blight threatened disaster here as elsewhere.

In November, a police constable in Shinrone reported to the administration in Dublin Castle: "Disease prevalent. Some crops affected partially. Other serious."

In early 1846, the fears of the previous year began to turn to panic, and many emigrated. Dr John Cowell wrote to the lord lieutenant that "families, a few months ago, having no idea of emigrating to America, are now taking their leave of their land, and others that could make out available means, would do likewise, for fear of dreading the result of want". In February, a Church of Ireland vicar in Offaly wrote:

> The peasantry for months subsisted on the worst description of food, many families are now subsisting on one meal a day. Something must be done or all the horrors of starvation will be experienced by half at least of the population.[123]

Throughout the region, demonstrations were held to protest at the situation. One such demonstration proceeded from Lougheen in Tipperary to Birr in County Offaly, led by a man carrying a loaf of bread on a pole, which was the customary symbol of starvation.

In March 1846, the labourers of Moneygall sent a memorial (an appeal) to the local magistrates, declaring that they were in a destitute condition; they did not want to have to enter the workhouse, and they did not want charity; rather, they appealed for immediate employment. They petitioned the Roscrea Poor Law Guardians, stating that they had neither food nor money to buy food. If they received no help, they would be "obliged, though reluctantly, to encroach on the property of those to whom God has given a superabundance".

A sheep was stolen from Moneygall landlord and resident magistrate George Garvey, and its head left with a note that read: "The poor will not starve while Garvey and other gentlemen have plenty of fat sheep."

George Garvey called a meeting of the local landlords, at which he suggested that Rev. William Minchin, who was receiving rents from his Moneygall lands, make a generous donation. The reverend gentleman declined, saying he had a large family to support and that he gave a lot of employment. Garvey pointed out that he paid his workers only sixpence a day; Minchin stormed out of the meeting. Garvey undertook to donate a ton of grain and indicated that two other landlords would each donate a ton.

Rev. William Minchin, whose home was Green Hills, was the principal landlord in and around Moneygall; most of his land was in tillage, with potatoes being followed by wheat or oats, which gave way again to potatoes. Animal manure and peat mould were used as fertiliser, and some turnips were grown for animal feed. The land supported several tenants on small holdings, one of whom was Thomas Kearney's nephew, Joseph Kearney, a shoemaker who had been born in about 1794 in Moneygall. The son of William Kearney, who had been born in 1762 in Shinrone, and Margaret Reeves, he was married to Phoebe Donovan, a daughter of Fulmouth Donovan and Mary Benn, who were both from Ballygurteen, County Offaly. They had two sons, Fulmouth and William, and two daughters, Mary Anne and Margaret. That the relationship between the Minchins and the Kearneys was closer than the usual landlord and tenant relationship is clear from the fact that in 1843, in Pickaway County Courthouse in Ohio, Thomas Kearney had left in his will "the sum of sixty dollars, and a horse" to his "well beloved niece, Anna Minchin".

The month after the meeting that Rev. Minchin had stormed out of, a relief committee was established in Money-gall, and amongst its members was John Kearney, a relative of Joseph Kearney, and none other than Rev. William Minchin, who had rediscovered an ability to make a donation: he, two other Minchin family members and George Garvey were amongst eight committee members who donated £5 each, while two others donated £10 and one donated £3. This com-mittee, like other relief committees in the Offaly/Tipperary area, was composed of a mixture of landholders and clergy of both Protestant and Catholic churches, with the bulk of the donations coming from the Protestant landed classes.

Although much has been written about the alleged tenden-cy of the Protestant churches to exploit the famine to win con-verts – a process popularly known as "souperism" – it is clear from the composition of the relief committees in Offaly and its surrounds that Protestant and Catholic clergy and laity worked together in these circumstances.

Souperism took hold in the Irish mythology that forms part of our accepted and shared historical memory, and "souper" has long been a term of abuse that to the present day is directed both at Protestants and those Catholics who have in their families any hint of a member having ever been Protestant. And yet it is largely a false memory. Certainly in west Galway and in west Kerry, there were concerted efforts by the Irish Mission Society to gain converts, but the image lodged in Irish consciousness of soup kitchens set up all over Ireland by Protestants who served the soup only to those Catholics who agreed to convert bears no relation to the reality on the ground in places like Offaly and Tipperary. Time and time again the contemporary evidence is of soup kitchens set up as collaborative enterprises involving both the Catholic and Protestant clergy. As Marianne Elliott writes in *When God Took Sides: Religion and Identity – Unfinished History*:

> Narratives conveyed through school textbooks continue to inform people's views of the past, privileging "memory" of historic rights and wrongs, even though, when tested, they often bear no validity in local contexts.[124]

The Catholic priest and Protestant rector worked in tandem to set up soup kitchens in Dunkerrin and Moneygall. They organised Moneygall's soup kitchen in a house opposite where Donovan's shop now stands. Dunkerrin's was housed in a shed opposite the present-day post office. In both places, ten pints of a thick soup were made from 4lbs of ox cheek, half a pound of rice, half a pint of oatmeal, onions, salt and pepper. Another, cheaper soup was made in amounts of fourteen gallons from a half stone of wheat, a third of a stone of oatmeal, a hock bone of bacon with peas, a head of cabbage, three or four leeks, six carrots and salt and pepper.

As part of the ecumenical effort in Moneygall, the Catholic priest, Fr Egan, travelled to Dublin to seek matching funds from the national Relief Office for "upwards of 200 starving families in Moneygall", and he was successful in his efforts.

In Shinrone in late May, another relief committee was set up, which again included both Protestant and Catholic clergy, and amongst their number was Charles Minchin of Clonisk. Mostly they gave direct assistance in return for work, but in some instances they gave to the destitute without any requirement that they work. By August they had collected over £100 in local subscriptions, which were augmented by government donations of nearly £67. Most of this money was used for the purchase of Indian meal, which was then sold on to the starving peasantry.

In a measure to alleviate the destitution caused by the famine, the government provided employment in relief schemes under the Board of Works. The British government was averse to direct famine relief through the provision of food, claiming that it would interfere with free trade, and it required that the starving poor should be made to work for their assistance. In Shinrone in July 1846, some two hundred labourers were employed in relief work, repairing footpaths, building and repairing roads, breaking stones and carrying out general improvements to the village. As the *Tipperary Vindicator* reported in July 1846, "work was never more wanted, as the potatoes in the parish were almost gone". Near by, a major Relief Scheme, employing 150 labourers, addressed the drainage of the Little Brosna river.

In August 1846, a policeman again reported from Shinrone:

> The early [potatoes] were generally injured, far more than last season and the late ones were not larger than good-sized marbles and were nearly rotten to the half. In the months hence, it was feared, there would not be a vestige of the potatoes in existence in the neighbourhood.[125]

The effects of the blight were felt by landless and landed alike. William Stuart Hall of Cardtown, Mountrath, had 162 acres of mountain land under potatoes. Writing, also in August 1846, he reported:

> I shall not readily forget the day I rode up as usual to my mountain property and my feelings may be imagined, when before I saw the crop, I smelt the fearful stench, now so well-known and recognised as the death-sign of each field of potatoes.[126]

While people starved for lack of potatoes, the area around Moneygall – in its barony of Clonlisk and the neighbouring barony of Ballybrit – was a rich grain-growing area. But this grain was grown almost entirely for export out of the region. As it was transported from the Moneygall area through Birr to the canal at Banagher, it attracted the attention of the starving peasantry, and both the police and military were deployed to protect the convoys of grain. By October 1846, attacks on the convoys were preventing or delaying shipments. Meanwhile, all over the country, cattle and corn were transported to ports for export. Colonel Lloyd urged that a halt be called to exportation of grain. Some peasant agitators took direct action; in November, a horse was shot in the yard of a farmer who was transporting flour.

The total failure of the potato crop in 1846 overwhelmed the efforts to provide relief. By the spring of 1847, the nearby Roscrea workhouse was desperately overcrowded, with over 1,000 inmates and others seeking to enter. Auxiliary workhouses were established and soon filled up with emaciated, starving children and adults. Workhouse relief proving insufficient as the numbers of the destitute soared, outdoor relief was provided in the form of daily rations of cooked gruel.

Famine and overcrowded, insanitary conditions inevitably

brought fever, which broke out first in early 1847, and fever hospitals were set up in Roscrea, Dunkerrin and Moneygall.

Some landlords gave direct assistance to the poor. Some set up soup kitchens, others provided dinners, some distributed foodstuffs at cost, and others increased their employment on their estates by way of assistance. Colonel Lloyd of the nearby estate of Gloster gave support to the destitute not only on his own estate but in the barony of Clonlisk. The Church of Ireland in Shinrone distributed the proceeds of a fund for the poor to both Catholics and Protestants. There is no evidence that they made any attempts to convert any of the Catholics to whom they provided aid.

The 1847 potato crop was far less affected by blight, but the previous years' disasters had resulted in a shortage of seed potatoes, and so a severe lack of the staple crop was again experienced in 1848. Soup kitchens and outdoor relief were again provided that year, but hunger and sickness overwhelmed the efforts of the relief committees.

Under the Irish Poor Law Act of 1838, Poor Law Unions had been established in the early 1840s, funded by local rates paid by the mostly Protestant landlords and large farmers. Shinrone, Moneygall and the area around them fell within the Roscrea Union. It was to Roscrea that starving people now flocked for food and accommodation. Built to accommodate a maximum of seven hundred people, numbers rose to more than two thousand, and auxiliary workhouses were rented. These workhouses were governed by Boards of Guardians, who were elected and came mostly from the landlord class. In 1847, officers were appointed to the Board of Health for the Shinrone region, and included landlords and both Protestant and Catholic clergy.

Cottiers and small tenant farmers could no longer pay their rents. Landlords experienced an enormous drop in incomes at the same time as they were having to pay increased rates to finance the workhouses and local relief schemes. Some landlords responded by evicting tenants.

Alienation between the landlord and tenant classes had been general since the Cromwellian settlement, and there had been violent agitation against high rents and tithes. Now the conflict intensified, as landlords and their agents were attacked, and labourers protested against their low wages on the relief schemes. Much of the rural crime and unrest was directed by tenants against landlords and their representatives; some of it was inflicted by tenants on other tenants. The root of the problem was an unjust set of property laws. As was noted in the *Transactions of the Central Relief Committee of the Society of Friends during the Famine in Ireland, in 1846 and 1847*:

> The objects of these agrarian disturbances are various, but they always imply a contest between the landlords and the tenants – whether to obtain the possession of land, to prevent ejectment, to obtain a reduction, to prevent an advance of rents, or from vindictive motives . . . We are convinced that if a good system of laws for the regulation of real property had existed, so large an amount of agrarian crime would never have disgraced our country.[127]

In these circumstances of unrest and conflict, the fact that the major landlords in Moneygall and Shinrone were Protestant may well have made life uneasy for Protestants such as the Kearneys who were not landowners but tenants, cottiers and labourers. Until Catholic enfranchisement in 1793, many Protestant tenants were expected to vote according to their landlords' wishes, in return for enjoying lower rents and better treatment than their Catholic neighbours. However, by the time of the

Famine, that advantage had disappeared. The Catholic neighbours of the Kearneys in Moneygall and Shinrone may have tended to associate them to some extent with their better-off co-religionists, especially as the Kearney and Minchin families were also connected by marriage. However, there is no evidence of any hostility between the Kearneys and their Catholic neighbours, and historians such as Edward McLysaght and J.J. Lee tend to suggest that religious difference was at this time far less significant in dividing people than class interest.

Although Moneygall was owned by a Protestant landlord, there were many landed Catholics in the area, and the conflict between tenants and landlords was a conflict over rents and conditions rather than a sectarian matter. As a close study of landholding in the immediately neighbouring county of Tipperary concluded, "Catholics . . . formed an influential section of landed society."[128]

There is no suggestion that sectarian tensions played any role in the decision of the remaining Kearneys to join their relations in Ohio. At the level of the peasantry and small tenants, there could often be the solidarity of neighbours. It is part of the unwritten history of Ireland that Protestant tenants were evicted by landlords, just as Catholic tenants were. In some instances in various parts of Ireland, Catholic tenants took in and sheltered Protestant neighbours who had been evicted, and *vice versa*.

Over a million people died in the Famine, some of starvation, more of consequent disease. Starvation and disease were followed by evictions, and another million emigrated in the wake of the Famine. America soon received a vast influx of destitute Irish people.

The Famine officially ended in 1848, but severe conditions continued into 1849, which proved to be the worst year for deaths. In 1848, more potatoes were planted, in the hope that blight could be avoided; a "pink-eye" potato was widely planted, in the belief that it would not succumb to the disease. But the blight returned, and the workhouses were once more filled with the destitute. Fever increased and the death toll rose.

At the Dunkerrin auxiliary workhouse, overseen by both Catholic and Protestant clergy, four hundred and fifty children were in residence in 1848; soon it was so overcrowded as to constitute an unacceptable health hazard. An extension was provided but proved inadequate. Rev. William Minchin rented out a building in Moneygall, to which two hundred girls were transferred from Dunkerrin.

Despite the building of additional workhouses, the relief provided was inadequate, and the Board of Guardians here, as elsewhere in Ireland, became involved in late 1848 in a government-promoted scheme to assist young women and girls between the ages of fourteen and eighteen in the work-houses to emigrate to Australia. Sixty were selected in the first round and brought to Dublin, where they boarded the *Devonshire* steamer bound for Plymouth in England. After medical examination there, they were put on board a ship for South Australia, and in late 1849 another fifty were sent to the same destination. Complaints were made about the cruelty of delivering them to a far, foreign land without family or friend to help them, and questions were raised about the morality of providing young women as potential wives and mistresses to the men of Australia, but such were the circumstances they were leaving that most seem to have taken a positive view of the initiative.

The cumulative effect of the years of famine had left the surviving peasantry deeply demoralised and in despair. The prospect of emigration seemed very attractive. Meanwhile, letters that came from America from relatives of families like the Kearneys, while reporting that life was hard, were full of optimism and the excitement of new possibilities.

In 1841, the population of Offaly had stood at 146,857; by 1851, it had dropped by 34,777, or 23.3 per cent. 6,288 people had died in the workhouses; these deaths were recorded, but the deaths of many who died silently of starvation and disease in their homes, by the roadside or in their fields were often not recorded. At least 16,000 had died. In addition, about another 16,000 to 20,000 people had been evicted from their homes during the famine years.

As Tim P. O'Neill writes: "The parish records indicate that no section of the community was immune to the ravages of famine and that the demographic impact was severe."[129] Both Catholics and Protestants suffered side by side.

A letter addressed to Lord Clarendon, the lord lieutenant of Ireland, and signed by nine Catholic and six Protestant labourers from Shinrone, pleaded for the reinstatement of the Brosna Drainage Scheme, a river drainage project on which they had been working and which had kept them from starvation but which had been suspended in June 1848.

> Your memorialists humbly hope that each Catholic and Protestant labourer, so long driven to almost utter despair by reason of all absence of employment in the neighbourhood, may be cheered with good tidings at the approaching relief at Easter of the happy and glorious news of immediate employment, as coffins and funerals are the only sad exhibitions in the vicinity of Shinrone at present.

One of the landlords who now experienced severe difficulties was Rev. William Minchin, and the fact that a member of such a prominent landed family was in financial trouble indicates the seriousness of the crisis for the landlords of the time. It inevitably spelt difficulties for his tenants, amongst whom were the Kearneys.

The Kearney family had suffered a sharp decline in their living standards for several decades. First they had been badly hit by the collapse of their wig-making business following the Act of Union, then by the decline in the income available from hairdressing. Some family members had retained interests in properties, and Thomas Kearney's brother William and nephew Joseph had become shoemakers; Joseph (Fulmouth's father) later moved into the woollen industry as a comber, following the precedent set decades earlier by another Joseph, Thomas Kearney's uncle, who was born in 1730. By the time Fulmouth's father became a comber, the woollen industry was in decline, and later as the world around them was devastated by the Famine, the Kearney family's fortunes had declined substantially by comparison with their situation at the time of Thomas Kearney's emigration. What small interest they still possessed in property might be sufficient to pay their way to America if they could secure a sale in the context of their landlord's approaching bankruptcy.

— 10 —

The Aftermath of the Famine

Thomas Kearney died at the age of eighty-one on 23 September 1846 and was buried in Compton Cemetery in Wayne Township, Fayette County. His wife Sarah had died in January of the previous year at the age of seventy-one. Most of their adult lives had been spent in the Scioto Valley, where with great courage and fortitude they had built a home for their large family, had endured the privations and challenges of pioneer life, and had succeeded as farmers to the extent that they had been able to acquire more land and pass it on to the next generation. They never became prominent or famous; they have left no account of their lives, nor have others recorded their words, their actions or their lives. In this and other ways, they are emblematic of the kind of log cabin pioneers who came to the frontier territories, settled them and developed them.

Thomas Kearney's oldest nephew Thomas, who was born in Moneygall in 1800, and settled in Pickaway County, had died the year before his uncle, in July, at the age of forty-four. He left to his two brothers, Francis and William:

> . . . an equal part of my personal property, and
> also to have an equal share of my property in land

herein described, my farm lying in Ross County Deerfield Township, formerly in the possession of William Shepherd, also my part of that farm former-ly in the possession of William Loveless Junior lying in Pickaway County, Perry Township; also my part of that farm, formerly belonging to Alexander Hamilton, in Fayette County Union Township.

He also left "to my well beloved niece, Anna Minchin, the sum of sixty dollars, and a horse".[130]

His brother Francis Kearney, born in Moneygall on St Stephen's Day in 1803, died in Pickaway County on 3 February 1848, also aged forty-four. In his will he left his house

The Will of Francis Kearney, Pickaway County, Ohio.

On the Wilderness Road

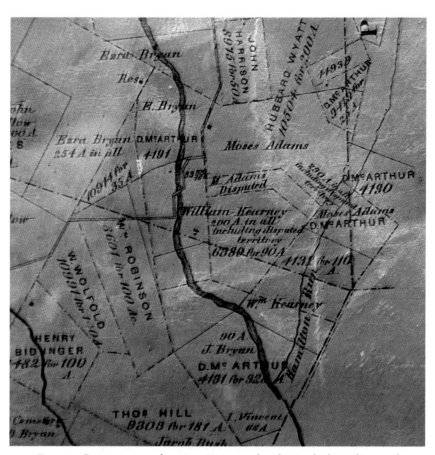

Fayette County map showing Kearney land, "including disputed territory", 1867

Compton Cemetery (Stephen MacDonogh)

Kearney graves at Compton Cemetery (Stephen MacDonogh)

Broken Kearney gravestones at Compton Cemetery
(Stephen MacDonogh)

The grave of Thomas Kearney who died in 1845
(Stephen MacDonogh)

The grave of Francis Kearney, whose will invited Joseph over from Ireland (Stephen MacDonogh)

The grave of Joseph Kearney Sr, born in Moneygall, King's County (Stephen MacDonogh)

Covered bridge at North Fork of Paint Creek (Fayette County)

*Young men at the site of the former Kearney home
on Dogtown Road* (Stephen MacDonogh)

Louisa and Jacob Mackey Dunham

The Dunham House in Kempton, Jefferson Township,
Tipton County, Indiana (Stephen MacDonogh)

Barack Obama and family visiting the Dunham House
(Bob Nichols)

and farm, his "bay mare and the choice cow" to his wife Sarah, who would live another forty-four years before she joined Francis in the graveyard. He also owned a "tract of land lying in Ross County, on the waters of North Fork of Paint Creek", which he willed "to my brother Joseph Kearney (now in Ireland), during his lifetime, if he comes to this country". He also left the sum of twenty-five dollars to Joseph's daughter Margaret – "to be paid to her when she comes to this country". The encouragement is clear: Francis had arrived in Ohio from Moneygall sometime in the 1830s and clearly felt that he had made the right decision in emigrating and wanted his brother to enjoy the benefit of following in his footsteps.

For Joseph, the inheritance offered him the possibility of a welcome escape from the disaster surrounding him in Ireland, and it is not surprising that he took the decision to go out to America. Knowing that land out there was his and knowing that he had other relatives in Ohio must have been a positive encouragement. At his back he must have felt the bleak desolation of famine, agrarian violence and disturbance, the insecurity of their situation with a landlord in financial trouble and the inevitable feeling that there was no life to be had in the future in his native land.

No doubt he contemplated getting the whole family away from the nightmare continuing around them, but his brother's will made clear that there was no house going with the land. Although he had other brothers and relatives in the area, he probably did not know exactly what circumstances would greet him in Ohio, so first he travelled alone to America, rather than commit his whole family to an uncertain move.

In his absence, there were no immediate signs of any improvement in the circumstances facing his family still in Offaly. In early 1849, the weekly death rate in Roscrea workhouse rose from 24 to 45. Poverty reached new levels. Tenant farmers unable to pay rents lacked any property to be seized by collectors. Some landlords moved ruthlessly to evict starving tenants.

There was an outbreak of cholera in Moneygall early in 1849. Rev. William Minchin was first to draw attention to it but was met initially with the disbelief of the Board of Guardians. Soon, however, the medical officer confirmed thirteen cases of cholera, four of whom had already died. An understandable panic spread through the parish. An isolation hospital was established in Roscrea, and while deaths from cholera rose to as many as nineteen a week in May, by June the outbreak was fortunately already in decline.

Joseph and Phoebe Kearney and their children had been living in a house on the main street of Moneygall. Single-storeyed, it measured 20.6 by 12.6 feet and stood seven feet tall, with a thatched roof and stone or lime mortar walls. It was described in a valuation in January 1851 as being in "very bad" condition. The valuer noted that Phoebe Kearney "Has now given up all the land and some other houses that she had."

By this date Joseph had left for America, and it is reasonable to suppose that he and Phoebe had sold their rights to other properties to fund his trip. Travelling alone, he arrived in New York on 25 April 1849 on board the *Caroline Read* and made his way onward to Ohio in the hope of being able to prepare the ground for his family to join him in making a new life in a new country. Within a year, Joseph called the rest of his Irish family over to join him, drawing to a close by 1851 the story of the Kearneys in the land of their birth in Moneygall and Shinrone.

Today the trip to America takes a matter of a few hours and may be taken in some comfort. In the mid-nineteenth century, the journey would have been very much more arduous and lengthy. Joseph had travelled alone at the age of fifty-five, and Fulmouth, aged nineteen or twenty, followed with his sister Margaret and her husband William Cleary on the *SS Marmion*, arriving in New York harbour on 20 March 1850. It was a long, hard journey, first by land and sea from Moneygall to Liverpool; then they had to endure an Atlantic crossing of about forty days. All were leaving behind the place they had been born and reared in, their native home – but they also knew that they were leaving behind a country in a state of abject ruin. Although journeying into the unknown, they were travelling to a destination where Fulmouth knew at least that his father, his uncles and his granduncle awaited them. Some of their relatives had apparently made good lives for themselves and would be able to assist young Fulmouth and the others in settling in.

Like all inbound passenger ships, the *Marmion* was first placed in an anchorage for several days for quarantine purposes. This must have been a time of anxiety and strain for the passengers, who had already endured the strange and often difficult conditions of their transatlantic voyage and presumably yearned to get their feet on to dry land. Once permitted to leave the quarantine area, the ship sailed or steamed closer to the city where State of New York immigration inspectors went aboard and the immigrants made whatever customs declaration was necessary and then continued their onward journey.

From lower Manhattan, near the steamship docks, they would likely have taken the Hudson River Railroad to Albany, the major transportation hub some 140 miles and five-and-a-half hours away on the Hudson. From Albany it was a 328-mile journey, lasting more than thirteen hours, over four interconnecting railroads, to Buffalo. From Buffalo, their next destination would have been Cleveland, reached by a lake steamship, probably overnight. The penultimate leg of their journey brought them by rail from Cleveland to Columbus, a journey of 135 rail miles, lasting seven and a half hours. Washington Court House, the county seat for Fayette County, lay just forty-one road miles to the south.

On arrival, they all moved in with Fulmouth's uncle and aunt, William and Alice Kearney. Their home was in Wayne, a small township in Fayette County, bordering Ross County where Francis Kearney's willed land lay, and where Fulmouth's father Joseph was perhaps engaged in building a house for his family and happy to have the assistance of his son. In January 1851, William and Margaret Cleary had a son, Little Willie, but sadly he died on 13 July at just six months.

Fulmouth's mother Phoebe remained in Ireland for the moment, organising the winding up of their affairs in Moneygall. Their landlord the Rev. William Minchin had, like some sixty other landlords in Offaly, been bankrupted by the Famine. Moneygall and all his lands and properties in Offaly and Tipperary were disposed of in several lots, in Dublin and Roscrea. The *New Ross Standard* reported:

> The next lot consisted of the town and lands of Moneygall, Kilkeeran and Gurrane, held under fee farm grant, containing altogether 305 ac. Ir 6p. stature measure, situate in the barony of Clonlisk and Kings County, with the fairs and markets of said town of Moneygall and the customs thereof, held under a Patent. . . . For this lot the bidders were Messrs Geo. Minchin, Williamson, Clarke, Blackett, Bolton and Greene. Mr Greene was declared the purchaser at £2,800 in trust for Mr Holmes.[131]

Having sold her rights in the house in Moneygall to the new owner Mr Holmes, Phoebe set out for America with her daughter Mary Anne, aged thirteen, and son William, twenty, and a forty-year-old woman named Catherine. They arrived in New York on 28 August on the *Clarissa Courier* and travelled on to Ohio.

It was undoubtedly daunting for these immigrant Kearneys to undertake the long voyage and to face settling into a strange new world. For Margaret and William to experience then the loss of a baby boy, who had been conceived within weeks of their arrival in America with Fulmouth, must have been a deeply felt blow to all those Kearneys who had recently arrived from Moneygall. But at least they had the comfort and support of family members who had already been settled in the area for some years. Indeed, the circumstances facing the Kearneys were a great deal easier than they were for many of the Irish immigrants of the time. They, like many of the Protestant Irish who arrived in the mid-nineteenth century, enjoyed the considerable advantage of following relatives who had arrived earlier. Their integration was eased by their familial ties to those who had arrived in preceding decades. And they faced the challenges of the frontier with the benefit of the support and advice of those who had already endured the challenges of the journey from Maryland to Ohio.

Many more settlers had come to the fertile Scioto Valley since Thomas Kearney first visited it in 1801, and the Kearneys themselves now owned land in three townships of three adjoining counties: Wayne township in Fayette, Perry in Pickaway and Deerfield in Ross County. Fayette County's population had risen from less than two thousand in 1810 to 12,726 in 1850, its growth fuelled by the kind of chain migration that had brought many of the Kearneys themselves. It was named for the Marquis de Lafayette, a Frenchman who was an officer in the American Army in the Revolution. Lafayette also played a role in the French Revolution and was a friend of Arthur O'Connor, the leader of the United Irishmen. Today it is a quiet rural area of wooden houses, farms, barns and silos, and its population stands at about 28,500. Residents report two major ancestries, German (23 per cent) and Irish (15 per cent). Wayne township, now with a population of about 1,370, is one of ten townships in Fayette County. Today the local cultural and social calendar offers the Scarecrow Festival (Washington Court House); Windmill Days (New Holland); Community Days (Jeffersonville); 4th of July Celebration (Washington Court House) and the Fayette County Fair (Washington Court House).

Ross County in 1850 boasted more than 32,000 inhabitants, having been first established in 1798. Named after Federalist Senator James Ross of Pennsylvania, its population today stands at over 73,000. Deerfield, where slightly more than a thousand people now live, is one of sixteen townships in the county, amongst whose communities are Londonderry and Colerain. The name of Pickaway County derives from the Pekowi band of Shawnee Indians. Today some 52,750 people live there, about 1,220 of them in Perry township.

For Fulmouth Kearney, this cluster of three townships in the three contiguous counties offered an opportunity to prosper within the context of a society and a local economy based entirely on agriculture and located in an area of well-irrigated fertile land.

He had arrived into a country in which Protestant Irish immigrants encountered little or none of the sectarian hostility that greeted many Catholics. In the Scioto Valley, most of his neighbours were Methodist or Baptist, and his granduncle Thomas had been part of a vibrant local Methodist community. In the national public sphere, Irish Protestants had already established positions and roles for themselves. They had set up charities to assist their fellow countrymen, such as the Hibernian Society; dedicated to aiding destitute Irish immigrants, largely Catholic, it adopted the motto, *"non sibi sed aliis"* (not for ourselves, but for others).

The Protestant Irish immigrants, most of whom had arrived earlier, in different circumstances, were in general significantly more attuned to existing American values than the Catholic Irish. They proved keen to integrate and to take up positions in civil society. On the other hand, most of the Irish Catholic immigrants were relatively uneducated and often found themselves competing in the early decades after the Famine for the most menial jobs and having to encounter racist stereotyping and hostility.

Attempts to recruit recent Catholic Irish immigrants as field soldiers during the Mexican-American War of 1846–48 and the US Civil War of 1861–65 proved difficult for the US Army, who met with considerable hostility from them. Unemployment forced some Catholic Irish to enlist anyway. In an instance that attracted contrary views, some recent Catholic immigrants from Ireland and Germany deserted from American regiments to form the San Patricio or Saint Patrick's Battalion of the Mexican Army and to fight against the United States. Considered heroes by Mexicans, and traitors by Americans, they may have been motivated principally by an idealistic desire to support the cause of their fellow Catholics in Mexico; or they may have been attracted principally by the valuable incentives of higher wages and generous land grants offered by the Mexican government. Later, Catholic Irish immigrants were also associated with violent draft riots, most notably in New York after President Lincoln ordered conscription in 1863.

The character of post-Famine Catholic Irish settlement in America was strongly influenced by the developments that had taken place in Irish Catholicism in recent decades. Following the Protestant proselytising in Ireland, a devotional revolution in Catholicism expressed itself in waves of Jesuit, Redemptorist and Vincentian missions, especially in the west of Ireland, where proselytism had been concentrated. It was also from the west that the largest proportion of Catholic Irish emigrated to America. Abandoned by government and the state, the only institution these immigrants had been able to rely on were the institutions of the Catholic church. As Irene Whelan writes:

> By the 1860s the Irish had made an institution of the Catholic Church in the United States, and this perfectly suited their needs as an immigrant group facing discrimination in everything from housing to education and employment.[132]

Both the Protestant and Catholic Irish in America before the Famine had tended to be involved in farming, herding and hunting. Also, through a network of familial and communal connections, many of them moved to frontier regions. Those who remained in the cities quickly took advantage of their new country's opportunities and became integrated into the artisan, craft and small business classes.

In Fayette County in 1852, Fulmouth Kearney, who had been working as a farmhand since his arrival two years earlier, married Charlotte Holloway, who had been born in Ohio in about 1833 to a substantial family of early settlers. The justice of the peace at their wedding was a William Kearney, probably the same William Kearney, his uncle, born in Moneygall in 1812, to whose home he had come two years earlier. The young couple moved to live in Deerfield, Ross County, which bordered Wayne Township, next door to Charlotte's brother, Joseph Holloway. Here they had six children: Phoebe, Elizabeth, Martha, Margaret, William and Joseph.

Fulmouth Kearney, his uncles and father and the rest of his family, were typical of the majority of earlier Irish immigrants, in that they settled in rural townships and were involved in the development of frontier territories. Later, predominantly Catholic Irish immigrants to America came to be concentrated in existing cities as the nation became more industrialised and urbanised. In the context of American Protestant prejudice against Catholics, and of the riotous reputation of the newly arrived Catholic Irish, it was not surprising that many of the earlier Protestant Irish immigrants were inclined to make less of their Irishness, and it was in these circumstances that the term "Scotch-Irish" was adopted by many Irish Protestants in America who wished to distinguish themselves from the Catholic Irish.

Many members of the established Protestant church, the Church of Ireland, as also Presbyterians, found that the American Baptist and Methodist churches had a greater relevance to them, their lives and their communities than their own denomination, and many switched allegiance. An additional motivation lay in the fact that most Irish Protestant immigrants were anti-British in their political outlook, and the Church of Ireland was indelibly associated with the British administration in Ireland; not so the Presbyterians, Baptists and Methodists. Many of the pre-Famine Catholic immigrants also chose to join the relatively well-organised and vibrant Baptist and Methodist congregations in their new communities. In leaving behind their Irish churches, both Protestants and Catholics also left behind something of their Irish identity. In forging new settlements, in developing communities in frontier regions, they became defined more by their new roles and social and economic ties in America, less by their country of origin.

So, the Protestant Irish, who accounted for most of the eighteenth-century and early nineteenth-century Irish immigrants, were not inclined to set up Irish institutions, nor did they express themselves through the kind of energetic ethnic church-building that the Catholic Irish quickly became engaged in when they arrived in such numbers in the wake of the Famine.

That is not to say that the Protestant Irish lay low, nor that they forgot their love for their native land. Protestants of Irish descent had already played leading roles in all areas of the forging of the political makeup of America.

Most of the Kearneys who died in Ross, Fayette and Pickaway Counties are buried in Compton Cemetery, a small graveyard at the side of a small country road north of Dogtown Road. Some other Kearneys are buried in nearby New Holland cemetery, amongst them Thomas Kearney's grandson William (son of Joseph), who was born in 1842 and died in 1897. Married to Sarah – one of the neighbouring Holloway family, like Fulmouth's wife Charlotte – this William Kearney served in the Civil War from 1861 to 1864.

Although inclined through circumstances to integrate, Irish Protestant immigrants remained proud of their origins, and this was certainly true of the Kearneys. In the graveyards where most of those early immigrants are buried in Ohio, the names of others buried there may be seen on headstones: English, Welsh and German names. On none of these headstones is there any record of where these people came from. Yet on many of the Kearney gravestones, their origins are proudly etched: "Moneygall, King's County, Ireland."

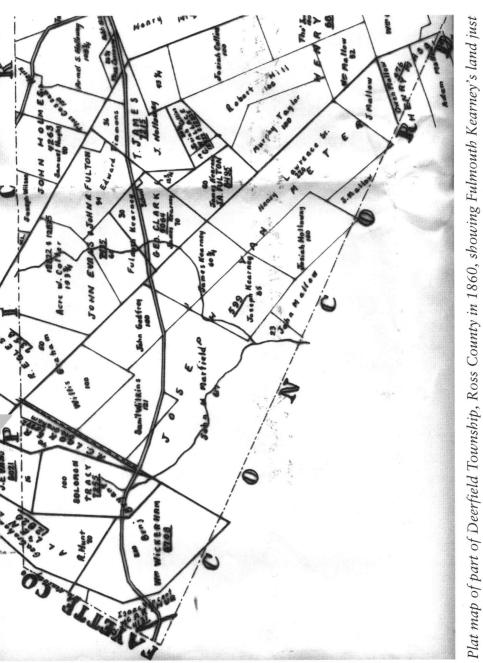

Plat map of part of Deerfield Township, Ross County in 1860, showing Fulmouth Kearney's land just above Dogtown Road and James and Joseph Kearney's land below the road.

— 11 —

Moving On: Indiana, Kansas and Oklahoma

In 1865, Fulmouth Kearney moved to Indiana with his family. It was sixty-four years since his granduncle had been the first of the Kearneys to settle in Ohio.

The extended Kearney family had flourished, and Fulmouth had, since his arrival in 1850, enjoyed the support of his many relatives. However, after fifteen years in Ohio he was still working as a farm labourer, and although he had acquired a little land and built a house on Dogtown Road, he may have found it impossible to buy sufficient land to match his aspirations. It is almost certain that he yearned to be a farmer himself, to take advantage of the opportunities he saw around him in this fertile land of opportunity. But the way in which the land had been settled had not opened up the new era of equal access by white settlers that many had hoped for. Land prices had risen as tens of thousands had flocked to the area, and a few large-scale speculators, such as the Massies, had quickly come to dominate landholding. As Alan Taylor writes in "Land and Liberty on the Frontier",

> the distribution of property in the new state of
> Ohio was about as unequal as that of Kentucky or

western Pennsylvania during the previous two decades: 45 per cent of the men did not own land while the top 1 per cent of the taxpayers owned almost one quarter of the taxable real estate.[133]

This unequal access to the land propelled many settlers to move further westward, and Fulmouth was amongst many who now travelled northwest, to the new frontier where land was much cheaper and where the former Miami Indian Reserve was beginning to be divided up and sold off.

The Indiana Territory had seen some false starts. In 1814, a group of eight hundred people under the leadership of George Rapp had travelled to Indiana on flatboats down the Ohio River. They settled on the banks of the Wabash River with the intention of setting up a Utopian society there in a place they named Harmonie. However, by 1825 they had moved back to Pennsylvania. That year the Welsh Utopian socialist Robert Owen bought the land, renaming it New Harmony, planning to make it into a model community and educational centre. He took over 20,000 acres of land and 180 buildings, including dormitories, two churches, homes, a textile factory, mechanics' shops, a tanning yard, a lecture hall, four mills, a brewery and a distillery. More than a thousand teachers, writers and scholars moved there, as did a motley collection of drifters, farmers, hopers and no-hopers, but the Utopian dream was never realised. Nevertheless, its influence was not entirely lost: most of the settlers at New Harmony stayed, and many of the ideas fostered by the community were adopted – ideas such as public libraries, trade schools, kindergartens and women's clubs.

It was to the southern part of the state that most of the early settlers to Indiana were attracted, but by the mid-1800s they were buying land in the fertile areas of the northern part of Indiana. A new city was chosen for the capital of Indiana:

Indianapolis, situated in the centre of the state, where Fall Creek and the White River met. Amongst the earliest settlers in the northern part of Indiana, fifty miles north of Indianapolis, were a farming family named Dunham, whose lives were to become entwined with the Kearneys and with the ancestry of President Barack Obama.

The move westward to the extending frontier was not easy. As Hon. W.S. Haymond wrote in *History of Indiana*:

> Swamps and marshes were crossed with great exertion and fatigue; rivers were forded with difficulty and danger; forests were penetrated with risk of captivity by hostile Indians; nights were passed in open prairies, with the sod for a couch and the heavens for a shelter; long, weary days and weeks of tiresome travel were endured. Perchance the mother and child were seated in a rough farm-wagon, while the father walked by the side of his faithful team, urging them over the uneven ground. But they were not always blessed with this means of transportation. And, in the best cases, the journey westward was a tedious, tiresome, dangerous one.[134]

The land they had acquired had been held by no previous settler, but was land seized from the Miami Indians and now divided up for sale for the first time.

> [T]he toils and dangers of the pioneer were not ended with the termination of his journey. Perchance the cabin is yet existing only in the surrounding trees. But he never falters. The forest bows beneath his axe; and, as log after log is placed one upon the other, his situation becomes more cheerful. Already the anxious mother has pointed out the corner for the rude chimney, and designated her choice in the location of

the door and window. The cabin grows day by day; and at length it is finished, and the family enters their home.[135]

Fulmouth Kearney travelled two hundred and fifty miles from his Ohio home to Clinton County, in northern Indiana, and while staying there, in 1865, he acquired land in nearby Tipton County. For the sum of $250 he bought from Hezekiah Rector "The south forty of the east fraction of the north west quarter of section no 19 in township no 21 north of range no three east" in Jefferson, Tipton County.

At the time he and his family arrived in Tipton, they were part of a rising population; from 3,532 in 1850, it more than doubled in just ten years to 8,170, and increased to 11,953 by 1870. Tipton County had been formed in 1844, named after John Tipton, a soldier of the Battle of Tippecanoe who later served as United States senator for Indiana. Settlers came from the east and from Europe.

> The Puritan and the Planter, the German, the Briton, the Frenchman, the Irishman, the Swede, the Dane and the Hollander,—each with his peculiar prejudices and local attachments, and all the complicated and interwoven tissue of sentiments, feelings, and thoughts that country, kindred, and home have,—settled down beside and with each other.[136]

Back in Ohio, Francis Kearney's will, which left land to Joseph, Fulmouth's father, was contested in a lawsuit. This action concerning the land at North Fork of Paint Creek in Ross County may have been taken just to get the record straight. There were many disputes about land at the time; indeed, on a map of Fayette County dated 1867, William Kearney is shown as possessing "200 acres in all, including disputed territory". Out of this lawsuit, Fulmouth emerged

This Indenture Witnesseth That, We Hezekiah Rector Elizabeth
Rector his wife Robert K Rector and Mary J Rector his wife
of Tipton County in the State of Indiana Convey and Warrant
to Fulmouth Kearney in Clinton County in the State of Indiana
for the Sum of two Hundred and Fifty Dollars the
Receipt whereof is hereby acknowledged the following Real Estate
in Tipton County in the State of Indiana to wit:
The South forty of the East fraction of the North West quarter
of Section No Sixteen (16) in Township No twenty one
(21) North of Range No three East Containing forty acres
more or less the above Conveyance made subject to an
incumbrance By way of mortgage given to the State of Indiana
for three hundred and twenty one Dollars Borrowed at
Sinking fund Office at Indianapolis Indiana

In Witness Whereof The said Hezekiah Rector Elizabeth
Rector his wife Robert K Rector and Mary J Rector his wife
have hereunto set their hands and seals this 18th day of November
1865.

Hezekiah Rector   [seal]
Elizabeth Rector   [seal]
Robert K Rector   [seal]
Mary J Rector   [seal]

State of Indiana }
Clinton County } ss

Before me Anthony Holmes a Notary Public in and for
said County this 18th day of November 1865 Hezekiah Rector
Elizabeth Rector his wife Robert K Rector and Mary J Rector
his wife acknowledged the Execution of the annexed deed
Witness my hand and Official seal this 18th day
of November 1865   Anthony Holmes
                                      Notary Public

I certify that the deed of which the above and forgoing
is a true Copy was duly Stamped and Recorded
November 20th 1865 at 11 AM

                              M E Clark
                              Recorder
                              &c

*Record of purchase of land in Tipton County, Indiana by
Fulmouth Kearney from Hezekiah Rector, 1865.*

eventually, some years after having made the move to Indiana, as the owner of the land left by his uncle Francis to his father, Joseph, who had died at the end of October in 1861 at the age of sixty-seven.

Like his father before him, and his granduncle Thomas, Fulmouth faced the challenges of the frontier as a pioneer and as the father of a young family.

> For miles in every direction, the eye of the pioneer met only a dense forest, broken here and there by rivers and creeks and small lakes. Dams must be constructed, and mills erected on these streams; and the forest must be cleared away to make room for the cornfield. For the accomplishment of these ends, the pioneer prepares his axe, and day after day he toils on. Tree after tree bows its lofty top. Log after log is rolled into the stream. Through many a long, dreary winter's day, with only a log to serve the double purpose of a chair and table; but, endowed with a spirit of enterprise that knows no faltering, he toiled steadily on.[137]

Another child, Fulmouth (Fullie), was born a year or two after their arrival. They now had children ranging from early teens to an infant in their new home where they no longer had supportive relatives around them. Fulmouth and Charlotte and their family soon became friendly with the neighbouring Dunham family, who had children in a similar age range.

Jacob Mackey Dunham was a farmer who had been born in 1824 in Berkeley County, Virginia (now West Virginia); his wife, Louisa Eliza Stroup, was from Madison County, Ohio, her family of Belgian origin who had arrived in Pennsylvania in about 1733. Jacob's parents, Jacob and Catherine Goodknight Dunham (also from Berkeley County), had been one of the first pioneer families to settle in Tipton in 1847 or 1848. His paternal grandfather Samuel Dunham and two generations before him were born in Woodbridge, Middlesex, New Jersey. Despite their surname, they were descended in the paternal line from a Richard Singletary, who was born in about 1599 in Lincolnshire, England, and had settled in Newbury, Essex, Massachusetts, marrying a Susannah Cooke. Only the first of their seven children, Jonathan Singletary Dunham, was given the new surname, which was probably associated with the village of Dunham-on-Trent, which lies on the border of Lincolnshire and Nottinghamshire. However, family tradition has it that the reason why Jonathan Singletary was renamed Dunham was because he was an adopted child whose natural father's name was Dunham.

In 1869, Fulmouth and Charlotte's youngest daughter Mary Ann was born at their home in Tipton. Two years later, Fulmouth sold twenty acres, consisting of the west half of his original property, to John Goodknight – of the same German (Gutknecht, anglicised as Goodknight) family as Catherine Dunham – who lived close to the Dunhams in the neighbouring township of Kempton, for $600. Having bought the whole property just six years earlier for $250, this represented a tidy profit.

The Dunhams prospered in Kempton and would later become involved in Democratic Party politics. By then their original farmhouse had been replaced by a fine new dwelling built by William Riley Dunham, a nephew of Jacob Mackey Dunham, in the 1880s. This may be seen today, largely restored to its original condition and named "The Dunham House". William Riley Dunham, who served the Democratic Party for several years and represented Hamilton and Tipton County in the Indiana General House of Assembly, was an acquaintance of President Grover Cleveland, who is believed

DEED RECORD.

This Indenture Witnesseth, that *Fulmoth Kearney and Charlotte Kearney his Wife* of *Tipton* County, in the State of *Indiana*

CONVEY AND WARRANT to *John Goodknight*

of *Tipton* County, in the State of *Indiana* for the sum of *Six hundred* _____Dollars, the following Real Estate in *Tipton* County, in the State of Indiana, to-wit:

The West half of South forty of East fraction of the North West quarter of Section № nineteen (9) in Township № Twenty one (21) north of Range № three (3) East containing Twenty acres more or less

IN WITNESS WHEREOF, the said *Fulmoth Kearney and Charlotte Kearney his wife*

has hereunto set *their* hands and seals this *21* day of *December* A.D. 1871

Fulmoth Kearney
Charlotte Kearney mark

State of Indiana, *Tipton* County, ss:

BEFORE ME, *Titus M. Amos*, a *Notary Public* in and for said County, this *21* day of *December*, 1871 *Personally came Fulmoth Kearney and Charlotte Kearney his wife and* acknowledged the execution of the annexed Deed.

WITNESS my hand and *Notary* Seal.

This day of December 1871

Titus M. Amos
Notary Public

I CERTIFY, That the Deed of which the above and foregoing is a true copy, way duly stamped as provided by Act of Congress, and recorded on the *19* day of *January* 1872 at *2* o'clock, *P M*

N E Small , Recorder of *Tipton* County.

Record of sale of land in Tipton County by Fulmouth Kearney to John Goodknight, 1871.

to have visited the house. Indeed, Mr Dunham had a son named Dr Grover Cleveland Dunham, who practised medicine in Tipton and Clinton County, Indiana. On 3 May 2008, Barack Obama visited the house, which now styles itself "The Ancestral Home of President Barack Obama".

Jacob Mackey Dunham and Lousia Eliza Stroup were married in Tipton County, Indiana, in 1853, and over the ensuing years three of their sons would marry three of Fulmouth and Charlotte's daughters, the youngest of whom, Mary Ann, would become Barack Obama's second great-grandmother.

The Dunham's first child, David H. Dunham, was just short of his nineteenth birthday when, on 17 April 1873, he married Phoebe Kearney, the first child of Fulmouth and Charlotte, who was a little less than a year older than him. Three years later, Jeptha Dunham and Martha A. Kearney, both nineteen, were married.

> The wedding was an attractive feature of pioneer life. For a long time after the first settlement of the Territory, the people married young. There was no distinction of rank, and very little of fortune. On these accounts, the first impression of love generally resulted in marriage.[138]

Less than two years after Martha's wedding, both Kearney parents were dead: Charlotte died on 11 September 1877, when Mary Ann was eight and her younger brother Francis was four; Fulmouth died on 21 March 1878. It is not known where they were buried, but it is likely that they had left Indiana by the time of their deaths. Certainly they were in Tipton in 1870,[139] but no grave or records of their burial have been found in the Tipton area despite considerable research, and circumstantial evidence suggests that they moved to Kansas and are buried there.

Sometime between 1870 and 1880, Jacob Mackey Dunham, his wife Louisa and some of their children moved from Tipton County to rural Mount Pleasant in Labette County, Kansas.[140] David and Phoebe Dunham moved to nearby Oswego, just twenty miles away within Labette County, and with them, by the time of the Census of 1880, were Fulmouth and Charlotte's children – Mary Ann aged eleven in 1880, Fulmouth Jr aged fourteen, and Francis aged seven – and Fulmouth Jr was working as a labourer. It seems in the circumstances likely that Fulmouth and Charlotte moved from Indiana to Kansas with their three youngest children sometime before Fulmouth's death in September 1877.[141]

Jacob Mackey Dunham was a pioneer farmer, born in Virginia. In his twenties he had been part of one of the first pioneer families to settle the former Miami Indian Reserve in Indiana. In his fifties he and his family had undertaken the long, arduous journey of more than six hundred miles southwest from Indiana through Terre Haute, St Louis and Springfield to an isolated rural township in Labette County, Kansas. Now in his sixties, he and Louisa moved on again, sometime after March 1885,[142] following the extension of the western frontier, more than two hundred miles southwest to Oklahoma City, accompanied by three of their children. Here he established the first restaurant in Oklahoma City. He had prospered sufficiently to be able to offer to send all his sons to college, as a result of which his fourth son, Jacob William, known as Will, acquired a medical and pharmaceutical degree, probably from Kansas University. David and Phoebe and four of their children also made the move to Oklahoma.

In 1887, Jacob William married Mary Ann Kearney, now aged eighteen, and following their marriage they settled in Argonia City, Dixon Township, Sumner County, in Kansas.

Lying near the scenic banks of the Chikaskia River along

the BNSF railroad in western Sumner County, Argonia was a new city in the 1880s, having been first laid out in February 1881 in the midst of rich prairie farmland. William G. Cutler wrote in his *History of the State of Kansas* that "Argonia is a live little town, of about 100 inhabitants, located on the K. C. L. & S. K. Railroad, near the west line of the county . . . A drug store was opened by J. S. Baughman, who was the first physician to locate here."[143] Jacob William Dunham may well have been the second. The first child born in the town, on 13 February 1883, was Francis Argonia Salter; four years later, in 1887, Argonia, which had now grown to five hundred inhabitants, elected the child's mother, twenty-seven-year-old Susanna Medora Salter, America's first female mayor. It was in December of the following year that Mary Ann Kearney and Jacob Dunham had their first child, Harriet (Hattie); the second, Mabel, was born in February 1890.

With her two baby daughters, Mary Ann seems to have visited her in-laws in June 1890, and they were enumerated in the First Territorial Census of Oklahoma. Sometime after June 1890, Jacob Mackey and Louisa moved to Kickapoo, Lincoln County, Oklahoma, and they may have participated in one of the "Land Runs" of the time. Unassigned Lands were settled in the first Land Run of April 1889, and following this there was steady pressure for surrounding Indian reservations to also be opened up for white settlement.

To handle negotiations with the five tribes that owned roughly 1,503,360 acres of reservations, President Benjamin Harrison appointed a three-member Cherokee Commission, and they met with the tribal leaders in May and June 1890. Agreements were achieved with four of the five tribes, but negotiations with the Kickapoo became stalled and were not resolved until 1895.

Lincoln County dates its origins to the Land Run of 22

POPULATION.

480

Oklahoma City County No 2

Enumerated by me on the Thirteenth day of June 1890.

First Territorial Census of Oklahoma, June 1890, showing members of the
Dunham family at 476 and 477.

September 1891, which opened to public settlement three Indian reservations adjoining the former Unassigned Lands on the east. At noon that day, more than 20,000 settlers stood on horseback surrounding the three reservations where 6,097 160-acre homesteads were available, waiting for the starting signal for the rush to make their claims.

Was Jacob Mackey Dunham amongst the 20,000 settlers waiting that day in September to make their claims? Or did he have to wait for the Kickapoo impasse to be resolved?

The Kickapoo reservation lay in the southwest quarter of Lincoln County and was not opened for public settlement until May 1895. In this month he celebrated his seventy-first birthday; is it credible that at his age he was able to continue the rugged life of the pioneer? In Oklahoma City in 1890, he had been accompanied by his sons Joseph, aged twenty-four, and Samuel, aged nineteen; no doubt one or both of them may have taken the more active role in securing the family's fortunes and acquiring new land to settle. But by the Census of 1 June 1900, both Samuel and another son, Jeptha, were living beside Jacob Mackey and Louisa in Kickapoo. Jeptha, their second child, had married Martha ("Marthy") A. Kearney in 1876; she had died in March 1893, but Jeptha had married again and was living with his new wife Lottie and five children. Samuel had also recently married, to Carrie from Kansas, and they had an infant daughter, Pearl.

Louisa Dunham died on 26 October 1901 and is buried in Wellston cemetery in Lincoln County, Oklahoma. Jacob Mackey Dunham died on 12 June 1907 in Okmulgee County, Oklahoma. Both had lived the epic life of pioneers in the developing country. She had started her journey from Ohio, he from Virginia; together they had forged new paths into new territories, finding their final resting places in what was still frontier country.

— 12 —

The Post-Pioneer Family

Some of the pioneer Kearneys had remained on in the Scioto Valley in Ohio, where they largely prospered in what had become excellent farming land. In *A History of Ross County, Ohio,* Henry Holcomb Bennett was able to write in 1902 that:

> Deerfield township is one of the best agricultural districts in Ross county, and the thrifty farmers are profitably engaged in all classes of diversified farming. Considerable attention is given to the raising of fine stock, and some are buyers and shippers of the same. A very large proportion of the grain raised is fed to stock on the farms. There are many fine homes in the township, an evidence of thrift and prosperity.[144]

The pioneer life ebbed away, and in Argonia, Kansas, Mary Ann Kearney soon settled into urban life with her doctor husband. Dr Jacob William Dunham, who had acquired a medical/pharmaceutical degree at Kansas University, established himself as a druggist and drug manufacturer, and here he and

Mary Ann had five more children between 1892 and 1899: Frank Virgil, Ralph Waldo Emerson, Crystabel, Pearl and Earl Dewey Dunham. Some of the Dunhams remained in or around Labette County, Kansas, and at some stage Jacob William set up a drugstore in Altamont, Labette County, which later became Black's Drugstore.

By 1905, they had moved to Wellington, just twenty miles east of Argonia, and in 1907, the year of Jacob's father's death in Oklahoma, they moved thirty-five miles north to settle in Wichita, Sedgwick County.

Standing at the junction of the Arkansas Rivers, the site of Wichita had been a trading and meeting place for thousands of years, but there was no permanent settlement there until the Wichita Indians built a collection of grass houses in 1863. Pioneering white settlers developed the city of Wichita, which was incorporated as a village in 1870 and became the county seat of Sedgwick County. The railroad arrived in 1872, and Wichita then became the shipping point for Texas cattle being driven north along the Chisholm Trail for shipment to eastern markets. The burgeoning cattle, grain and milling markets resulted in rapid growth, and by 1886 Wichita had established itself as the region's principal city. In just ten years between 1880 and 1890, its population grew from 4,911 to 23,853. The two main ethnic groups were of German ancestry (38 per cent of present-day residents), and Irish (8 per cent).

Here Jacob and Mary Ann settled for the rest of their lives. From 1907 until sometime in the 1920s, they lived at 1150 North Market Street, Wichita, from which they ran a pharmacy. In 1928, they moved to open the Gem Pharmacy at 1201 West Douglas, in the heart of Wichita's Delano District, which proved to be busy and successful. Their son Ralph Waldo Emerson built the house at the back of the pharmacy at 103 South Dodge Street and raised his family there.

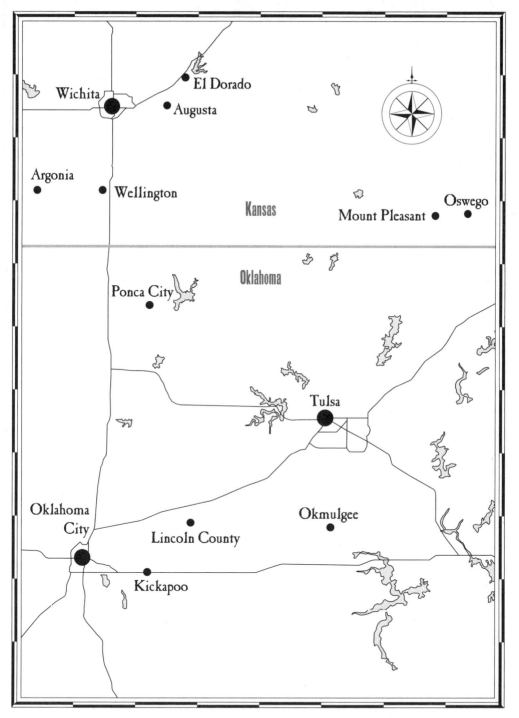

Places in Kansas and Oklahoma associated with the Kearney and Dunham families

Dr Jacob Dunham practised medicine in southern Kansas for forty years up to his death in 1930 at the age of sixty-seven. His grandson, Dr Ralph Emerson Dunham, eighty years later still recalls the circumstances of his death: standing out in the street near his house, he was challenged by a nine- or ten-year-old to a race around the block; unwisely, he accepted the challenge and suffered a heart-attack. He was a member of the Spiritualist church, as was his wife Mary Ann, who died in 1936 at the age of sixty-seven. Both are buried in Wichita Park cemetery.

Ralph Emerson Dunham was nineteen at the time of Mary Ann's death, and he remembers her well; he recalls that:

> All the men in the family had black hair, but she and all her daughters had red hair, and, you know, she had a bit of an Irish accent. Grandfather always called her Becky.[145]

"Like most women of the time," he says, "she was a good cook."[146] His grandfather Jacob made a practice of bringing the broader Dunham family together at picnics in the public parks, where they would pitch horseshoes and play games. After the death of his mother, he and his brother Stanley had gone to live with her parents in El Dorado, and it was mostly on the occasion of such family gatherings that Ralph met his grandmother Mary Ann.

Ralph's stepsister, Virginia Goeldner, was too young to have memories of her grandmother, but

> My mother, Marthamae Dunham, spoke to me many times about her and I can tell you that they were very close and she remained fond of her until she died. She also told me that she had to have her leg amputated due to complications from diabetes before she died . . . She also spoke of her religion

which was a spiritualism church. . . . I can tell you from what my father and mother said that Grandma Becky always preferred the Irish style of cooking. She liked things like cornbread, beef stew, boiled beef and cabbage. She also didn't consider it a proper dinner without potatoes.[147]

At the time of the death of Mary Ann Dunham in 1936, two of her three sons, Frank and Ralph Waldo Emerson, were living in Wichita, while Earl had moved to San Diego, California; of her four daughters, two were in Wichita, one in Beloit, Kansas, another in Melvern, Kansas. Two of her brothers, Francis and James Kearney, were living in Tulsa and Sperry in Oklahoma. Also living in Oklahoma were her husband's three brothers: Jeptha in Luther, Samuel in Tulsa and Joseph in Okmulgee, and his sister Mary was also in Tulsa.

The population of Wichita had grown nearly five-fold since Mary Anne and Jacob William had married forty-six years earlier. Wichita had first expanded in the wake of the Civil War; it expanded again during the two World Wars. In 1917, the first airplane, the Cessna Comet, was made in Wichita, and in the inter-war period the local aircraft manufacturing industry developed to such an extent that Wichita became known as the "The Air Capital of the World". The boom in employment saw the population rise from 72,000 in 1920 to 115,000 in 1940 and 168,000 in 1950. The development of Wichita Air Force Base created more jobs, and by 1960 the population stood at 255,000.

One of the sons of Mary Ann and Jacob Dunham, Ralph Waldo Emerson Dunham, born in Argonia on Christmas Day in 1894, married Ruth Lucille Armour, also of Wichita, when she was just fifteen. Her parents, Harry and Gabrielle (Clark) Armour, had settled in west Wichita, and Harry first appears in the Wichita city directory in 1908 as a travel agent in a building for the SV Clark Coal Company. He worked for the Colorado Fuel and Iron Company, which later became Rocky Mountain Steel Mills, and for over twenty years he worked as a roustabout for the Magnolia Petroleum Company in El Dorado.

Like many of the families associated with the Dunhams and Kearneys, he came from a farming background in Ohio, where his father was born in 1850. In about 1899, he married Gabriella Clark, who was born in Missouri in 1877, the daughter of Christopher Columbus Clark (1847–1937). The Clark side of the family was related to Jefferson Davis, the leader of the Confederacy. Susan Overall, the wife of Christopher Columbus Clark, was a daughter of George Washington Overall (1820–71), a farmer who in the census of 1850, the year Fulmouth Kearney arrived in America from Moneygall, was recorded as owning two slaves – a fifteen-year-old black female and a twenty-five-year-old black male – at his home in Nelson County, Kentucky. His wife, Louisiana Duvall (1826–55), was a daughter of Gabriel Duval (1787–1827), and his mother-in-law, Mary Duvall, owned a sixty-year-old black man and a fifty-eight-year-old black woman. If one traces that ancestral line back as far as the tenth great-grandparents, one finds Mareen Duvall, a major land owner in Anne Arundel County, Maryland, in the 1600s, the inventory of whose estate in 1694 names eighteen slaves.

While there might seem to be something sensational about some of Barack Obama's ancestors having been slaveowners, the truth of the matter is that slavery is very much part of American history. The majority of southern whites did not own slaves, but many of the wealthier families did. Gary Boyd Roberts, a senior research scholar at the New England Historic Genealogical Society, remarked: "If you have a white Southern mother, or a mother from the middle states who has ancestry in the South, it doesn't strike me that that should be very surprising."[148]

There is also little significance in the connections that may be established by going too far back into ancestry. Much has been made in the media about the fact that if you go back far enough in his maternal ancestry you can establish very distant relationships between Barack Obama and George Bush and Dick Cheney. It seems at first glance intriguing, but in truth the distance is so great that the relationship is of little or no significance. One distant cousin of Barack Obama was Wild Bill Hickok; another is Brad Pitt. The latter is a ninth cousin, the former was sixth cousins with Obama's fourth great-grandfather, Jacob Dunham. In a speech delivered to a packed hall in Springfield, Missouri, during the presidential election campaign, Senator Barack Obama laid down a challenge to his Republican opponent. "I'm ready to duel John McCain on taxes. Right here. Right now. I don't know if people are aware of the fact, but the family legend is that Wild Bill Hickok, he's a distant cousin of mine."

George Washington Overall's great-granddaughter, Ruth Armour, attended the old Wichita High School but dropped out when she was a junior to get married to Barack Obama's great-grandfather. They opened the City Cafe on William Street in downtown Wichita between the old firehouse and the old Wichita City Hall.

> "The area around City Hall was the hub of Wichita," said Wichita State University historian Jay Price. "This was the place to get your business done. Douglas and Main was the main shopping area."[149]

He worked as an auto mechanic there and at the El Dorado Garage, which sold Oakland automobiles. Later he went to Topeka and bought the Oakland Automobile Agency. After the demise of the Oakland car during the depression, he took over ownership of the Gem Pharmacy. For a time they also lived at 321 North Emporia in El Dorado.

Sadly, Ruth died by suicide at the age of twenty-six, her death allegedly stimulated by her husband's philandering. A contemporary Wichita newspaper report said she died of food poisoning (ptomaine poisoning in the terminology of the time), but the story of suicide seems to have been accepted within the family. She was buried in a cemetery in El Dorado.

She had given birth to two sons, the second of whom, Stanley Armour Dunham, was born in Wichita on 23 March 1918, named after the explorer Sir Henry Morton Stanley, whom Ruth had greatly admired and who was famous for his search for David Livingstone.[150] After her death, Ralph Waldo Emerson Dunham sent Stanley and his brother Ralph Emerson to live with his mother- and father-in-law, Harry and Gabrielle Armour, who were by now long-time members of Wichita's Westside Baptist Church. He married again, and Virginia May Dunham Goeldner (to give her her full name) was one of his daughters by his second wife, Marthamae Stonehouse.

Virginia recalled that he never appreciated being named for one of America's greatest writers. He liked the active, outdoors life of hunting and fishing, and he raised German shepherds for shows.

> "He was a very soft and gentle person, a very soft, sensitive type fellow," Goeldner said. "He told me once: If a dad has to tell their kids whether he loves them or not, he's not doing his job right.
>
> "He said, 'If you love your kids, they feel it.'
>
> "He never laid a hand on any of his kids," said Goeldner. "It wasn't like he would tell you what you should do. You did what you knew he wanted you to do just to make him pleased."[151]

Site of Market Street, Wichita house of the Dunhams
(Stephen MacDonogh)

Site of Gem Pharmacy on Douglas Street and Dunhams' house on Dodge Street, Wichita (Stephen MacDonogh)

El Dorado today (Stephen MacDonogh)

Stanley A. Dunham in England, Fall 1943 (Brandon)

Ralph and Stanley Dunham in London, February 1944 (Brandon)

Madelyn, Stanley Ann and Stanley (Obama for America)

Stanley, Stanley Ann, and Ralph Dunham in Richmond, California, May 1947 (Brandon)

Stanley and Madelyn Dunham in Richmond, California,
May 1947 (Brandon)

Stanley Ann, Stanley and Madelyn Dunham (Obama for America)

Barack Obama Sr
(Obama for America)

Ann and Barry in Hawaii in 1962

Barry on his tricycle

Barry in the sea

Lolo Soetero, Ann Dunham, Maya and Barry (Obama for America)

Ann Dunham, her daughter Maya, and Stanley A. Dunham, about 1968 (Brandon)

Madelyn and Stanley Dunham and Maya Soetoro (Brandon)

Barry with his father during his 1971 visit to Hawaii
(Obama for America)

Barack Obama Sr and Ann Dunham (Obama for America)

Barry Obama in Punahou School, 1971 (Punahou School)

Barry Obama in Ninth Grade at Punahou School 1976
(Punahou School)

Barry Obama and Stanley Dunham (Brandon)

Basketball team photo, Punahou School (Punahou School)

Senior Portrait, Punahou School, 1979 (Punahou School)

*Madelyn (Payne) Dunham; Maya Soetoro, Ann Dunham,
Stanley A. Dunham and Barack Obama* (Brandon)

Wilson Homestead (Strabane District Council)

Inside the Andrew Jackson Cottage (Carrickfergus Borough)

Ralph Dunham Sr worked, like most of his family, in the aircraft industry in Wichita, in the tooling department of Boeing Aircraft. He lived in Wichita until his death in 1970 and is buried at Resthaven Cemetery in west Wichita.

Stanley grew up with his maternal grandparents and Ralph Jr on Washington Street in El Dorado, a former oil boom town near Wichita. Living with them for the last fifteen years of his life was Madelyn's grandfather Christopher Columbus Clark, son-in-law of George Washington Overall, who had fought on the Union side in the Civil War as a private in the 69th Regiment of the Enrolled Missouri Militia.

Stanley, aged eighteen, was with him when he died at the age of ninety in 1937. Ralph, who describes him as "a really nice fellow" who was well liked by all the children of the neighbourhood, inherited his slippery elm cane, decorated with a snake's head, and uses it to this day.[152]

Stanley gained the reputation of being something of a wild child, which is perhaps not surprising, in the light of the fact that at eight years old it was he who apparently discovered his mother at the time of her suicide; she died in the Topeka hospital. Then again, some suggested that he was following in the footsteps of his father, who had a reputation for playing fast and loose. Either way, he spent much of his childhood in the care of his grandparents, just as he and Madelyn much later would care for their grandson, Barack Obama. At the age of fifteen he was suspended from El Dorado High School after punching the principal on the nose; though his class was 1935, he did not actually graduate until completing his credits after the war. He hopped railroad cars to California and Chicago, returned to Wichita and worked at odd jobs while enjoying himself out on the town.

On State Street, he met Madelyn Lee Payne, a young woman living in the neighbouring town of Augusta, whose parents considered him thoroughly unsuitable. Stanley and Madelyn were a study in contrasts. Stanley Dunham was well known to many in the area as a loud and gregarious young man – charming when he wanted to be, but wild with it. Madelyn, on the other hand, was sensitive and bookish. She was a middle-class Methodist; he was a blue collar Baptist. Her family disapproved of drinking, card-playing and dancing. Nevertheless, while still in school she hung out and smoked at a drug store on the corner of Main Street in Augusta and at the Augusta Theater. She became an enthusiast for the big bands that visited the local Blue Moon Dance Hall – Glenn Miller, Benny Goodman and Tommy Dorsey amongst them.

Madelyn had been born in 1922, the daughter of Rolla Charles Payne and Leona McCurry. Rolla, born 1892 in Olathe, Kansas, was a bookkeeper for an oil well supply company in Tulsa, Oklahoma, then for an oil company in Augusta. The Paynes had been farmers from Knox County, Missouri, and Rolla's father Charles had married into another farming family, his wife Della Wolfley having moved to Knox County from Ohio with her family. Her maternal grandparents, named Abbott, had – like Thomas Kearney and his family – moved from Maryland to Ohio (Licking County) in the early nineteenth century. Della's father, Robert Wolfley, was of German descent; his great-grandfather Johann Conrad Wolfley (originally Wolflin), born in 1729 in Besigheim, Württemberg (present day Baden-Württemberg), had immigrated in 1750 and settled in Pennsylvania. Robert Wolfley, born in Ohio in about 1835, served in Company A of the 145th Ohio Infantry (National Guard) as a Union soldier during the Civil War.

Madelyn's younger brother, Charles Thomas Payne, born in 1925, served during World War II in the US Army 89th Infantry Division. He worked later as the assistant director of the

University of Chicago's Library. In 2009, Payne spoke to *Der Spiegel* about his role in liberating Ohrdruf forced labor camp.

> Ohrdruf was in that string of towns going across, south of Gotha and Erfurt. Our division was the first one in there. When we arrived there were no German soldiers anywhere around that I knew about. There was no fighting with the Germans, no camp guards. The whole area was overrun by people from the camp dressed in the most pitiful rags, and most of them were in a bad state of starvation. The first thing I saw was a dead body lying square in the middle of the front gate . . . Inside the gate was an area where a bunch of the camp inmates had been machine gunned and were all lying on the ground. Each one had their tin cup in their hand or lying next to them.[153]

Madelyn's mother's parents, the McCurrys, also came from Missouri, though originally the family had emigrated from Scotland to Carolina, moving to Kentucky before settling in Missouri. Leona's paternal grandfather, Harbin Wilburn McCurry, born in 1823 in Indiana, lived much of his life in Missouri and married Elizabeth Edna Creekmore. In 1862, aged thirty-nine, Harbin McCurry was arrested in Arkanas on suspicion of being on the run to avoid serving in the forces of the Union. In a statement, however, he strongly rejected the charge, saying that he was in the area to visit a relative, and that "I am a Union Man and always have been. I am willing to take up arms in defense of the United States Government." He was released on parole after agreeing to take an oath of loyalty to the Union, enroll in the militia and put up a $1,000 bond.

He served seventy-eight days in the Enrolled Missouri Militia, but the war inflicted terrible suffering on his family when pro-slavery bushwackers led by the notorious William Quantrill attacked their home in Granby, Newton County. William Worth McCurry, the first-born child, who was looking after his younger siblings, including his baby sister Sophronia while his parents were in town getting supplies, recognised one of the raiders and appealed to him not to burn down their home. They killed him, set fire to the home and threw burning coals into the face of the baby girl lying on the bed.

As to why they were targetted for attack, it may have been because as Baptists they had sided with Northern congregations in opposing slavery. But it may have had to do with a story told in family lore about Harbin McCurry.

> "He brought a slave home, and Elizabeth threatened to beat him to death if he didn't turn him loose," Leon McCurry said. "So he turned the slave loose, and the slave took the McCurry name . . . I don't know if it was because she was against slavery, or he was black – could have been both."[154]

Harbin McCurry's son Thomas – Leona's father – was five at the time and remembered the traumatic events for the rest of his life. Not long after the attack, the family moved to St Joseph, Missouri, and from there to Longton, Kansas, by covered wagon. Ultimately, they moved into Indian territory that later became Oklahoma, where Harbin died in 1899, Elizabeth in 1918. Their son, Thomas Creekmore McCurry, had meanwhile moved to Peru, Kansas, where Leona McCurry was born in 1897. His wife, Leona's mother, was Margaret Belle Wright, born in 1869 in Dry Fork, Carroll County, Kansas, who was a daughter of Joseph Wright. Born in 1819 in Kentucky, Joseph became a farmer in Overton County, Tennessee, then in Carroll County, Arkansas, where he was the delegate to the constitutional convention of 1868 from that county. In later years he moved to Kansas, where he died in 1894 in Hale.

Madelyn believed that she had Cherokee blood through her mother's side. As Barack Obama writes in *Dreams from My Father,* she "would turn her head in profile to show off her beaked nose, which, along with a pair of jet-black eyes, was offered as proof of Cherokee blood". Circumstantial evidence lends support to the family lore. Steve Hammons writes in *American Chronicle*:

> During the 1700s . . . many Scottish pioneers, trappers, hunters and land-seekers made friends with the Cherokee whose homeland was then in the Appalachian Mountain region. Romantic encounters, marriages and babies resulted. . . .
>
> In 1838, the infamous "Trail of Tears" occurred after Cherokee were rounded up, put into temporary detention centers, then marched to Oklahoma. Approximately 4,000 men, women and children died in the process, primarily from disease, cold and starvation. . . .
>
> Although many of the mixed-blood Scottish-Cherokee went west, voluntarily or at the end of a bayonet, many stayed in the general region of their ancestral homeland and surrounding states. Some migrated into states like Kentucky and Ohio.
>
> As more generations came on the scene in the late 1800s and 1900s, and American society evolved, often just word of mouth and family stories reminded children that "we have Indian blood in the family" or "we have Cherokee back in our family tree." Obama's family is undoubtedly just like many, many other American families in this regard.[155]

In the spring of 1940, several weeks before Madelyn's graduation, she and Stanley secretly married. She remained living with her parents, not telling them about the marriage until she received her diploma in June. He and his brother Ralph kept in touch, although during 1941–42, Ralph was away teaching in Altamont in Labette County – where some of his relatives still lived.

Stanley promised Madelyn that they would live a life of adventure as free spirits. However, in December 1941, Pearl Harbor was attacked and the United States entered World War II; it was no time for free spirits. Stanley enlisted in the US Army Air Force (USAAF) at Fort Leavenworth, Kansas, and saw service in Europe – but not in Patton's army, as Barack Obama and others have suggested. He served in the 8th USAAF,[156] which was established in the UK as an intermediate command between US Army Forces in the British Isles (USAF-BI) and the AAF commands. Ralph was also in the armed forces, at first in the Replacement Depot on Classification Assignment, later as personnel officer in the 130th Ordinance MM Company. Madelyn meanwhile worked at Boeing's B-29 production plant in Wichita as a quality control inspector. The two brothers met in London in February 1944 and had their photographs taken together in uniform. Four months later, Ralph landed at Omaha Easy Red beach on D-Day plus four and took part in the battles of Normandy, northern France, the Rhineland and Germany. As the war drew to a close, he found himself waiting at the River Elbe for the Russians to capture Berlin. After the war, he remained in the reserves and retired as a lieutenant colonel.

On 29 November 1942, in Wichita Hospital, Madelyn gave birth to a girl, whom they named Stanley Ann Dunham – the Stanley because her father had wanted a son. Although it has been reported that she was born at Leavenworth camp,

Ralph is clear that this is incorrect, having visited mother and baby in the hospital in Wichita; Stanley Ann's birth certificate in Wichita County Hall, he says, confirms his recollection.

After the war, Stanley worked at a furniture store on Main Street in El Dorado, and Madelyn worked in restaurants, then used her secretarial skills at Casado Realty. He took some part-time courses in Wichita, and then the family moved to California, where Stanley attended the University of California at Berkeley on the GI Bill from September 1945 to December 1947. He did not declare a major, but took courses in geology, English, math, economics, French and journalism. Madelyn got a job working in the admissions office of the university.

Ralph was also in Berkeley at much the same time, studying for his doctorate in education from September 1946 through summer 1949. On his arrival, Stanley, Madelyn and Ann moved from their one-bed apartment to share a two-bedroomed apartment with Ralph. He recalls that Ann was aged four at the time. "In Berkeley," says Ralph, "we always called my niece Stanley Ann or Stannie."[157] He also recalls that his brother committed himself to his studies, and feels that Barack Obama was a little harsh in his description of Stanley in *Dreams from My Father,* in which he observed that "the classroom couldn't contain his ambitions, his restlessness". However, Stanley did not get a degree, and he did soon move on. While in Berkeley, Ralph got married to an Englishwoman from Essex he had met while in England in the army during the war. She sailed from England to Nova Scotia, and he drove more than 4,000 miles to meet her ship.

In 1948, Stanley secured a job as a salesman for Jay Paris Furniture in Ponca City, northern Oklahoma. He, Madelyn and Stanley Ann set up home at first on West Central and later on North 13th Street. He was described as "gregarious, friendly, impetuous, challenging and loud".

Bob Casey, who worked with Stanley Dunham at the furniture store described Stanley as

> ... a very smart guy with a long face and large shoulders who knew a lot about the furniture business and was one of Jay Paris' top salesmen at a time when the furniture company had six or seven salesmen. Stanley knew the technology of furniture, could analyze customers, and was one of the first salesmen to sell furniture as a full concept instead of by the item. "He could sell you a room full of furniture," says Casey. "And he could help you decorate it." Mr. Casey remembers a trip to Wichita with Stanley where they attended one of the first decorating seminars in the area. "Stanley was always working to improve himself," said Mr. Casey, adding jokingly that Stanley "was a smart guy who liked to tell you how smart he was."[158]

Stanley Ann, who was six years old when they arrived in Ponca City, attended first and second grade at old Jefferson Elementary School and third grade at Roosevelt Elementary School.

Stanley Dunham was a wanderer, for whom the grass was always greener, and in 1951 they left Ponca City. They then spent three years in Vernon and nearby Wichita Falls in Texas. They attended the Methodist church in Vernon during 1951, and some classmates remember playing with eight-year-old Stanley Ann.

> Kay Bellew says, "We were in fourth grade. She was in my bluebird group. She was a friend. Not a real close friend because she wasn't here very long. She was a very sweet girl that everyone liked."
>
> Francis Lowe was Dunham's classmate. She says, "She was very nice, and very straight forward.

We all liked her because she was very honest and very genuine."[159]

However, perhaps in Wichita Falls, Ann had some unhappy experiences in and around school. Barack Obama says that his mother made few friends at school and was "teased mercilessly for her name". Worse, she suffered a terrifying racist attack by other children when playing with a black friend in the grass outside her home. Her parents, too, encountered racism in Texas at their workplaces.

Ralph had visited once while they were living in Ponca City; he did not visit them in Texas but recalls mention of their time there in letters from Stanley. After a few years they moved back to Kansas, where they lived in El Dorado until 1955, and Stanley worked in the furniture department of the Powell Hardware Store on North Main at First Street. Then, when Stanley Ann was thirteen, Stanley and Madelyn Dunham moved with her to Seattle, and it was here she was to spend four formative years. Stanley had got work at Standard-Grunbaum Furniture, a large store in downtown Seattle at the corner of 2nd Avenue and Pine Street, where he was in charge of one of seven floors. "First in Furniture, Second at Pine," read its ad in the telephone directory.

Madelyn, who worked outside the home for most of her life, and clearly was a valued employee wherever she went, found a job in a banking real estate office, and the family settled into a two-bedroomed apartment near the lakeshore.

Soon after arriving in Seattle, Madelyn and Stanley set aside their Methodist and Baptist allegiances and began attending at the East Shore Unitarian Church in nearby Bellevue. In the McCarthyite 1950s, its association with liberal views led to it being sometimes referred to as "the little Red church on the hill". Ralph first heard about this change when Stanley was visiting him in Washington. Stanley said nothing to him directly, but several of Ralph's car pool group were Unitarians, and the subject came up one day.

Stanley Ann herself was an unconventional, questioning member of the Mercer Island High School. "She was not a standard-issue girl of her times. . . . She wasn't part of the matched-sweater-set crowd," said Chip Wall, a classmate and retired philosophy teacher.[160]

As an only child, Stanley Ann dealt directly with her uncommon first name. She hated it, but did not try to hide it. "My name is Stanley," she would say. "My father wanted a boy, and that's that."[161] Her mother called her Stanny or Stanny Ann, but at school she was known as Stanley. "She owned the name," recalled Susan Botkin, one of her friends on Mercer Island. "Only once or twice was she teased. She had a sharp tongue, a deep wit, and she could kill. We all called her Stanley."[162]

> In a high school culture of brawn and beauty, Stanley was one of the brains. Often struggling with her weight, and wearing braces her junior year, she had the normal teenage anxieties, according to her friends, though she seemed less concerned with superficial appearances than many of her peers. Her protective armor included a prolific vocabulary, free from the trite and clichéd; a quick take on people and events; and biting sarcasm.[163]

Her best friend in high school said:

> She touted herself as an atheist, and it was something she'd read about and could argue. She was always challenging and arguing and comparing. She was already thinking about things that the rest of us hadn't.[164]

Another classmate said:

> She wasn't a shouter, but sat and thought awhile
> before she put forth her ideas. She was one of the
> most intelligent girls in our class, but unusual in that
> she thought things through more than anyone else.[165]

She and her contemporaries undoubtedly absorbed the
spirit of the times, which included much questioning of established verities; the influence of the Beat generation may have
been felt, but it was not until the 1960s that the protest culture
and counter-culture amongst American youth developed.

Two teachers at Mercer High School – Val Foubert and Jim
Wichterman – encouraged their students to question authority
and challenge society's conventions. Foubert taught English,
Wichterman philosophy. Tim Jones quotes him:

> "I had them read *The Communist Manifesto*, and
> the parents went nuts," said Wichterman, adding
> that parents also didn't want any discussions about
> "anything to do with sex, religion and theology."[166]

Stanley Ann Dunham seems to have responded enthusiastically to the encouragement to think for herself. Intellectually
precocious and of an independent bent, she became interested
and engaged in the issues that would to a large extent define
the next decade: civil rights, racism, women's rights, war and
peace. She was an enthusiast for Adlai Stevenon, the liberal
Democrat who fought two unsuccessful campaigns for the
presidency in 1952 and 1956 and was defeated by Republican
Dwight D. Eisenhower. Tim Jones describes this independently
minded teenager:

> Boyish-looking, Stanley Ann was prone to rolling
> her eyes when she heard something she didn't agree
> with. She didn't like her nose, she worried about her

weight, she complained about her parents – especially her domineering father. Her sarcasm could be withering and, while she enjoyed arguing, she did not like to draw attention to herself. The bite of her wit was leavened by a good sense of humor.[167]

One friend, Susan Blake, said: "She had a world view, even as a young girl. It was embracing the different, rather than that ethnocentric thing of shunning the different. That was where her mind took her."[168]

Certainly the years in Seattle were important, formative years for Stanley Ann Dunham. In his article in the *Chicago Tribune,* Tim Jones went on to comment on the representation of Barack Obama's mother's story as "a tale of the Heartland" of America:

> Implicit in that portrayal is this message: If you have any lingering questions or doubts about the Hawaiian-born presidential candidate with a funny name, just remember that Mom hails from America's good earth. That's the log cabin story, or his version of Bill Clinton's "Man from Hope."
>
> That presentation, though, glosses over Stanley Ann Dunham's formative years, spent not on the Great Plains but more than 1,800 miles away on a small island in the Pacific Northwest.[169]

She graduated in June 1960, and she wanted to go to the University of Chicago, where she had been offered a place, but her father decided that at the age of just seventeen she was too young to go away. Meanwhile, Stanley Dunham had received an offer to run a furniture store in Honolulu and immediately decided to take it up. So, a few days after commencement, she left with her parents for Honolulu.

— 13 —

Hawaiian Marriage

Stanley Ann began classes at the University of Hawaii in 1960. There, in a Russian language class, she met the college's first African student, Barack Obama Sr, and fell in love with him. She was close to her eighteenth birthday; he was twenty-five. Around this time she wrote to friends that she now preferred to call herself Ann; he called her Anna. Years later she told her son a story about their first date, a story he tells in *Dreams from My Father.*

> He asked me to meet him in front of the university library at one. I got there and he hadn't arrived, but I figured I'd give him a few minutes. It was a nice day, so I laid out on one of the benches, and before I knew it I had fallen asleep. An hour later he showed up with a couple of friends. I woke up and three of them were standing over me and I heard him saying, serious as can be . . . "You see gentlemen, I told you she was a fine girl, and that she would wait for me."

It would not have been surprising if her parents had had reservations about the relationship. Interracial marriages were very uncommon in the America of the time and were even officially illegal in more than half the states, though these "miscegenation" laws were rarely enforced. Stanley, whose own view of himself included a certain pride in his liberal, even bohemian tendencies, seems to have been quite well disposed to the relationship. Madelyn Dunham, however, who was temperamentally sceptical in most things, had mixed feelings. She avoided interviews to a large extent, but she did speak to the *Chicago Tribune's* David Mendell, when he was researching his biography, *Obama: From Promise to Power.*

Mendell suggested to her that Barack Obama Sr had "a great deal of charm" and that his father, Hussein Onyango Obama, had been a medicine man.

> [S]he raised her eyebrows and nodded to herself.
> "He was ... ," she said with a long pause, "strange."
> She lingered on the *a* to emphasize "straaaaaange."
> She then continued: "He wasn't that handsome in a way, exceptionally dark-skinned, but he had a voice like black velvet ... with a British accent. And he used it effectively."

Stanley Ann and Barack clearly enjoyed each other's company as they engaged in debates about the issues of the day, listened to jazz and went to bars and cafés together.

Neil Abercrombie, a Democratic congressman from Hawaii who was part of their social set, describes Stanley Ann, who was the only woman in the group, as "the original feminist". She was extremely patient but nevertheless passionate in arguing for her beliefs. "I think she was attracted to his powerful personality, and he was attracted to her beauty and her calmness."[170]

But she was young, and Obama was confident and articulate, perhaps also somewhat overbearing.

She was a girl, and what I mean by that is she was only 17 and 18, just out of high school. And he brought her at different times. She mostly observed because she was a kid. Everybody there was pretty high-powered grad-student types. . . . Obama was much more in love with his intellect than a woman. Any female in his life, she was in his life, he was not particularly in hers.[171]

Barack Hussein Obama was in his second year at the University of Hawaii, having arrived as the first African student there almost a year before Ann and her parents moved to Honolulu from Seattle. He had come as one of eighty-one promising young Kenyans to be sent to US universities as part of a study programme organised by Tom Mboya, one of the leaders of the Kenyan independence movement. Kenya was emerging from the clutches of British colonialism, and the intention was to prepare educated young Kenyans to take up positions in the soon-to-be independent state. Mboya, who was, like him, a member of the Luo tribe, became Obama's mentor.

The Luo constitute the third largest ethnic group (13 per cent) in Kenya, after the Kikuyu (20 per cent) and the Luhya (17 per cent), and Obama had grown up in Nyang'oma Kogelo, a Luo village in Nyanza Province on the shores of Lake Victoria.

He was studying business administration and said that he wanted to help Kenya with its transition from tribal society to a modern economy. He spoke much about himself and his confident expectations of himself and his future role in the life of his country, but he never told his friends that he had a wife and two children back in Africa. He told Ann Dunham only that he was separated from his first wife.

Stanley and Madelyn Dunham were taken aback when, after the young couple announced their intention to marry, Barack Obama Sr's father Hussein Onyango Obama wrote to them a fiercely angry letter. Barack Obama quotes his mother telling him that "He didn't want the Obama blood sullied by a white woman."

Hussein Onyango Obama was born Onyango Obama in about 1895; he worked as a mission cook, and he joined the British Army during World War I. He visited Europe and India, and later lived for a while in Zanzibar, where he converted from Christianity to Islam, taking the name Hussein; his third wife, Sarah, remarked that he passed the name, not the religion, on to his children. His first wife was Helima, with whom he had no children. His second wife, Akumu Obama, was Barack Obama's paternal grandmother. She had three children: Sarah, Barack Hussein Sr and Auma Obama. She left the family while her children were still young, and Barack Obama Sr was as a result principally raised by Hussein Onyango Obama's third wife, Sarah Onyango Obama (also known as Sarah Ogwel or Sarah Hussein Obama). Known to Barack Obama as his "Granny Sarah", she lives in Nyang'oma Kogelo village, her husband's home place. Hussein Onyango Obama died in 1979.

Barack Obama also has an "Aunti Zeituni", Zeituni Onyango, who is the half-sister of his father and who was born in 1952 in Kenya. She worked as a computer programmer at Kenya Breweries in Nairobi, and, living in Boston since 2000, she has worked as a volunteer computer systems co-ordinator for the Experience Corps, a programme in which older adults mentor children in their communities. Some media attention was devoted to her in the final week of the 2008 US presidential election as a result of allegations that she was living in the United States without valid immigration status.

It transpired that she had applied for asylum but her request was rejected, and she was ordered deported in 2004. When her situation became public in November 2008, Barack

Obama said that he was unaware that his aunt had been living in the country illegally and that immigration law should be followed. His aunt confirmed that she had never asked Obama to intervene in her case and had not told him about her immigration difficulties. In May 2010, she was awaiting the outcome of a federal immigration hearing in Boston to determine her second application for political asylum.

Hussein Onyango Obama's father was named Obama and was born in Kendu Bay, Kenya. He had four wives and fathered many children; Onyango was the fifth son and his mother was Nyaoke.

Undaunted by opposition conveyed from Kenya, Ann and Barack flew to Maui where they got married on 2 February 1961, without any guests or family members present. Barack Hussein Obama Jr was born six months later, on 4 August at the Kapi'olani Medical Center for Women and Children in Honolulu.

Ann dropped out of school to take care of the baby. Barack graduated in June 1962, as a Phi Beta Kappa straight-A student. He had already been offered scholarships in graduate school at both the New School in New York and at Harvard. The scholarship on offer from the New School would have provided sufficient money for his wife and son to accompany him. However, although the monetary terms were less favourable, he opted for Harvard because of its international academic prestige. In May he had written to his mentor, Tom Mboya, about the Harvard offer. Mboya, who had recently been appointed minister of labour in Kenya, berated Obama for planning to leave his son behind. But before the end of June he was gone, leaving behind his wife and son.

Perhaps it was not, however, quite such a clear desertion. Late that summer, Ann arrived in Seattle with little Barry, as she called her baby son. Susan Botkin recalls:

> She was on her way from her mother's house to
> Boston to be with her husband . . . She had her baby
> and was talking about her husband, and what life
> held in store for her. She seemed so confident and
> self-assured and relaxed. She was leaving the next
> day to fly on to Boston.[172]

However, something happened in Boston, and Ann returned to Seattle. She stayed for a while and talked about enrolling in university there, but some time later she returned to Hawaii. There she resumed studies at the University of Hawaii, switching rather surprisingly to mathematics, and received her degree. As the marriage collapsed, Stanley and Madelyn proved very supportive of Ann and her son. Barack continued to write to her and inquire about their son, but their relationship further deteriorated, and in 1964 she filed for divorce.

Stanley Dunham, after many years in the furniture business, became an insurance salesman, but it seems that he was not particularly successful in this new line of work. Madelyn, however, provided a new financial stability to the family and to the material circumstances experienced by young Barry, as they called him. She once more established herself as a valued office worker, at the Bank of Hawaii in Honolulu, and her career there flourished as she worked her way up to become the bank's first woman vice-president.

Years later, in August 2008, Barack Obama spoke of her to a packed stadium in Denver on the night he accepted the Democratic presidential nomination. "She's the one who taught me about hard work," he said. "She's the one who put off buying a new car or a new dress for herself so that I could have a better life. She poured everything she had into me."

His father, Barack Obama Sr, had met a woman at Harvard named Ruth Nidesand, a teacher with money. He had begun to drink heavily and had gained the nickname "Mr Double Double" from his taste for Johnnie Walker Black whisky. He told friends that he was attracted to Ruth Nidesand partly because, "she was able to pay for some of the social activities that he could not afford", said Leo Odera Omolo, a journalist and friend.[173]

Meanwhile, Barack Obama received his master's degree in economics in 1965, without completing his PhD, and returned with Ruth Nidesand to Kenya, where he hoped to realise his dreams of taking a place in the Kenyan government. The couple married there, but Obama also resumed his relationship with his first wife, Kezia Obama, whose two children, Auma and Roy, moved in with him. He had two more children with Kezia and two with Nidesand. He maintained contact with Ann in Hawaii and would proudly show to his Kenyan family photos and certificates and school reports of his son, "Barry". He secured a job as an economist in the Ministry of Economic Planning and Development, headed by Tom Mboya.

Dreams from My Father is a book of three parts, in which the third part concerns Barack Obama's Kenyan family. Malik, also known as Abongo or Roy, and Auma Obama were the two children of Barack Obama Sr's first marriage, to Kezia, before he went to America and married Ann Dunham. Malik was born in 1958 in Nairobi, Kenya. He graduated with a degree in accounting from the University of Nairobi and later moved to Washington, DC. Malik and his half-brother Barack were best men at each other's weddings. Auma, who was born two years later, studied German at the University of Heidelberg from 1981 to 1987, and she gained a PhD from the University of Bayreuth. She moved to London, and in 1996 married an Englishman, Ian Manners.

On his return to Kenya, Barack Obama Sr and Kezia had two more sons, Abo and Bernard. Born in 1968, Abo Obama is an international telephone store manager in Kenya. Bernard Obama, born in 1970, was for a time an auto parts supplier in Nairobi, and converted to Islam as an adult. He now lives in Bracknell, England, with his mother.

When Barack Obama Sr had moved back to Kenya, he had brought with him Ruth Nidesand, whom he had met at Harvard. Adopting the name Ruth Ndesandjo, she worked as a private kindergarten director in Kenya, and later she and Barack Obama Sr were married and had two sons, Mark and David, who took their mother's surname. Mark Ndesandjo runs an Internet company called WorldNexus that advises Chinese companies about international marketing. He studied physics at Stanford University and has lived in Shenzhen, China, since 2002 and is married to a Chinese woman. David Ndesandjo was killed in a motorcycle accident.

Barack Obama Sr also had a relationship with a woman named Jael, with whom he had a son, George, just six months before he died in an automobile accident in 1982. George Hussein Onyango Obama was raised in Nairobi by his mother and a French stepfather. He later lived in South Korea for two years with his mother before returning to Nairobi. When it was reported during the presidential election campaign that George was living in poverty, this was seized on by conservative critics of Barack Obama. One columnist sought donations for George Obama from his readers; another made a trip to Kenya to give him a cheque for $1,000 but was expelled by immigration authorities.

Two years after her divorce in 1964 from Barack Obama Sr, Ann remarried, when her son was five. Her new husband was also a foreign student at the university, Lolo Soetoro, from Indonesia. In 1966, following the political turmoil surrounding the rise of Suharto, Lolo Soetoro was summoned home to Jakarta by a government nervous of students abroad who might provide a locus for oppositional politics. Ann followed with Barack, who attended local schools until the age of ten. There Ann's second child, Maya, was born, in August 1970.

Ann's marriage to Lolo had, however, begun to fade. A source of tension lay in the fact that she wanted to work, while her husband wanted more children. She decided to send her son, Barack, to Honolulu to live with his grandparents. There he attended, on scholarship, the prestigious Punahou School from the fifth grade until his graduation from high school in 1979. His grandparents became strong influences in his life. As a child he learned many of the fundamentals from them. As he later wrote in his autobiography, Madelyn, his grandmother, "read me the opening lines of the Declaration of Independence and told me about the men and women who marched for equality because they believed those words put to paper two centuries ago should mean something".

In late 1971 Ann returned, with Maya, to Honolulu, where she became a graduate student of anthropology. Soon after her return, Barack Obama Sr paid a month-long visit to see his ten-year-old son; this month now constitutes Barack Obama's sole memories of his father, but the visit was, perhaps inevitably, somewhat uneasy.

In 1977, Ann went back to Indonesia to work as an anthropological field worker. Barack, now aged sixteen, chose to remain in Honolulu with his grandparents: Stanley, known as Gramps, and Madelyn, known as Tutu or Toot, from the Hawaiian word for grandparent. They provided stable and loving support for much of his childhood and undoubtedly helped him keep his bearings through the teenage years.

Later, Ann worked with international relief agencies, focused on women's development. She earned an international reputation in the development community, playing a particularly important role in developing microfinancing networks. These provided credit to female artisans in rural communities around the world. She began her work in this area in Jakarta in the early 1980s, working for the Ford Foundation, but she also worked in Pakistan, in Lahore; in New York and New Delhi. Her work remains extremely relevant to the challenges facing the developing world and the key potential economic role of women.

David Maraniss writes:

> Her dissertation, published in 1992, was a masterwork of anthropological insight, delineating in 1,000 pages the intricate world of peasant metalworking industries in Indonesia, especially traditional blacksmithing, tracing the evolution of the crafts from Dutch colonialism through the regime of General Suharto, the Indonesian military strongman. Her deepest work was done in Kajar, a blacksmithing village near Yogyakarta. In clear, precise language, she described the geography, sociology, architecture, agriculture, diet, class structure, politics, business and craftsmanship of the village, rendering an arcane subject in vivid, human terms.
>
> It was a long time coming, the product of work that had begun in 1979, but Dewey [Alice Dewey, chair of the University of Hawaii anthropology department, where Ann did her doctoral dissertation] said it was worth the wait: Each chapter as she turned it in was a polished jewel.[174]

Nancy Barry, a former president of Women's World Banking, an international network of microfinance providers, where Ann Soetoro worked in New York City in the early 1990s, has said of her:

> She was a very, very big thinker. I think she was
> not at all personally ambitious, I think she cared
> about the core issues, and I think she was not afraid
> to speak truth to power.[175]

Another person who worked with her at Women's World
Banking, said:

> I feel she taught me how to live. She was not par-
> ticularly concerned about what society would say
> about working women, single women, women mar-
> rying outside their culture, women who were fearless
> and who dreamed big.[176]

Barack Obama's sister, Maya Soetoro-Ng, said of her
mother:

> She gave us a very broad understanding of the
> world. She hated bigotry. She was very determined
> to be remembered for a life of service and thought
> that service was really the true measure of a life.[177]

Ann returned to Hawaii in 1994 and died of ovarian cancer in 1995.

A teenage mother who had met and married a Kenyan
fellow-student, who then divorced him and married another
foreign student and brought her young son to his country,
Indonesia, (Stanley) Ann Dunham had been absent from
Barack Obama's life for some time during his childhood, and
she had relied upon her parents to help her raise both her children. But he describes her as "the kindest, most generous spirit
I have ever known", and "the single constant in my life".[178]

The rootlessness that arose from her somewhat wander-
ing, exploratory life may well have encouraged Barack
Obama, by contrast, to seek to put down roots. In an interview he observed: "We've created stability for our kids in a

way that my mom didn't do for us. My choosing to put down roots in Chicago and marry a woman who is very rooted in one place probably indicates a desire for stability that maybe I was missing."[179]

Although Obama chose in his memoir to focus on his father, there is little evidence that he inherited or learned his political and other approaches to life principally from his father. There is ample evidence, however, of elements in Ann Dunham's character that are suggestive of some of her son's characteristics. She was a gifted intellectual, and she was a dreamer who was intellectually curious and open to new experience. She had in particular a great openness to other cultures and nationalities and a special capability in observing them. He wrote of her: "The values she taught me continue to be my touchstone when it comes to how I go about the world of politics."[180]

— 14 —

Obama and Ireland: The Personal and the Political

Barack Obama's autobiography was entitled *Dreams from My Father*, not *Dreams from My Mother*; its subtitle *A Story of Race and Inheritance* referred principally to his paternal, African inheritance. Perhaps he could have explored inheritance on his maternal side, but he didn't, and so he did not explore his Irish ancestry. In the preface to the 2004 edition, he wrote of his mother: "I think sometimes that had I known she would not survive her illness, I might have written a different book – less a meditation on the absent parent, more a celebration of the one who was the single constant in my life."

In *Dreams from My Father*, he documents the struggle to come to his own understanding of his personal family circumstances, and it is clear that this was linked with his developing understanding of the role of ethnicity and race in American society and politics.

It is commonplace in American politics that candidates for public office seek to engage with the many ethnic sectors and lobbies that play significant social, cultural and political roles; often ethnic associations have operated as power-brokers in American political history. Within the Democratic Party, an

Irish element has often been important, from Tammany Hall in Chicago to the Catholic Church in Boston and the iconic role of the Kennedys.

Barack Obama became part of Chicago life and politics not because of any familial connections with the place, still less because of the famously prominent Irish element in the city's make-up and history. He arrived in Chicago because it was the one place that would offer him a job as a community organiser. Its importance in his life is indicated in the fact that almost one third of his inspiring 1995 autobiography, *Dreams from My Father,* concerns his experience in the city.

In June 1985, at the age of twenty-four, he arrived in Chicago, an idealist seeking to immerse himself for the first time during his relatively privileged life in a working-class African-American community. He took up a poorly paid position as principal organiser for the Developing Communities Project, a campaign established and funded by South Side Catholic churches in the wake of the decline of southeast Chicago steel plants.

During his three years as an organiser, he built up community activism in Roseland and the nearby Altgeld Gardens public housing complex, securing for residents a place at the table of discussions and decision-making about job-training initiatives; the question of asbestos and lead paint in local schools was successfully addressed, and the development of the area's landfills was subjected to community interests. It was a positive, learning experience for Obama, but it had its frustrations. As David Mendell writes in *Obama: From Promise to Power:*

> It opened his eyes to both the complexities and the shortcomings of a unique racial culture, as well as to the cruel reality of American priorities. But after three years of working close to the "streets" he had so longed for, Obama felt shackled by the

limited power of a small nonprofit group to create expansive change.[181]

He left Chicago to pursue a law degree at Harvard, from which he graduated magna cum laude. He broke new ground by becoming the first African-American president of the *Harvard Law Review,* the most influential legal publication in America. This brought him to considerable public notice, with profiles in the *New York Times* and other major national newspapers, and brought him a book publishing contract which led to the publication, in 1995, of *Dreams from My Father.*

He had promised to return to Chicago after completing his law studies, and return he did. Writing in the epilogue to *Dreams From My Father,* he observed:

> Upon my return to Chicago, I would find the signs of decay accelerated throughout the South Side – the neighborhoods shabbier, the children edgier and less restrained, more middle-class families heading out to the suburbs, the jails bursting with glowering youth, my brothers without prospects. All too rarely do I hear people asking just what it is that we've done to make so many children's hearts so hard, or what collectively we might do to right their moral compass – what values *we* must live by. Instead I see us doing what we've always done – pretending that these children are somehow not our own.
>
> I try to do my small part in reversing this tide. In my legal practice, I work mostly with churches and community groups, men and women who quietly build grocery stores and health clinics in the inner city, and housing for the poor.

In the course of both his community activity and legal work, he inevitably encountered the presence of the Irish in local politics, and in them he found a people with long experience in building coalitions among other racial, ethnic and religious groups.

For over one hundred and fifty years, the Irish had played a leading political and cultural role in Chicago. Drawn initially to the area in the late 1830s as labourers to work on the construction of the Illinois and Michigan Canal, connecting the Great Lakes to the Mississippi River, the Irish participated in the creation of the city in the great numbers that came in the wake of the Famine. Not all Irish in nineteenth-century Chicago were labourers, nor were they all Catholic. Irish physician Dr William Bradford, born in Kerry, became one of Chicago's first real estate speculators. Cork native James Lane opened the first meat market in 1836 in the city which was to become America's foremost centre of meat production.

The editor of the *Chicago Tribune,* who was descended from Ulster Presbyterians, frequently attacked Irish Catholics: "Who does not know that the most depraved, debased, worthless and irredeemable drunkards and sots which curse the community are Irish Catholics?"[182]

By the 1870s, the Irish constituted 25 per cent of the population of Chicago. By the 1880s, 30 per cent of Chicago's police force and other civil service jobs were held by Irish Americans. Yet the Irish were just one of many ethnic groups in the city, to which Germans, Poles, Jews and other eastern Europeans flocked in large numbers. But it was characteristic of the mid- and late-nineteenth-century Irish in Chicago that they brought with them and maintained a strong concern about the cause of freedom for Ireland, and the revolutionary republican organisation Clan na Gael enjoyed strong support in the city.

The Catholic Irish in Chicago became associated with narrow-mindedness, racism and violence. The most infamous of the Irish gangsters was Deanie O'Banion, who proudly carried a rosary in his pocket and a carnation in his jacket; another was Bugs Moran. But the Irish also made more progressive contributions. John Fitzpatrick, president of Chicago's Federation of Labor, and Margaret Haley, America's first teacher union leader as president of the Chicago Teachers Federation, were two prominent Irish labour leaders. The famous radical, trade union organiser and socialist, "Mother" Jones, who was born Mary Harris on the northside of Cork city, also settled in Chicago after the death of her husband and young children during a yellow fever epidemic in Tennessee. Under the leadership of Chief Francis O'Neill, from rural County Cork, Chicago became the centre for the revival of Irish traditional music.

The Irish, from early days, played prominent roles in the politics of the Windy City, which has boasted twelve Irish mayors, the most powerful of whom was Richard J. Daley, who ran Chicago for over twenty years from 1955; his son, Richard M. Daley, was elected Chicago mayor in 1989.

Not long after his return to Chicago, where he joined a law firm headed by Judson Miner, Mayor Washington's corporation counsel, Barack Obama became involved in Project Vote, a very successful grassroots voter-registration campaign which was aimed primarily at African Americans. It added an estimated 125,000 voters to the voter rolls.

Through Judson Miner and Project Vote, Obama came to know many of the black political activists on the South Side, and in 1995 an opportunity arose for him to run for public office. State Senator Alice Palmer, a widely respected progressive African American, proposed to run for Congress and supported Obama to succeed her in the state senate. Things turned fractious when Palmer realised she would not succeed in being elected to Congress and her people asked Obama to step aside. He declined, and went on, after much shenanigans, to be elected.

As David Mendell remarked in *Obama: From Promise to Power*:

> The whole episode showed that Obama was an extraordinarily ambitious young man willing to do whatever it took to advance not only his agenda of community empowerment but his own political career.[183]

Later, however, he took on more than he could chew when contesting an election with Congressman Bobby L. Rush, a legendary figure in the African-American working class of Chicago's South Side. Barack Obama was ultimately trounced in this South Side race, and learned that when it came to Windy City politics, he still had a good deal to learn. But he did learn: he saw that Bobby Rush had got support from the Irish. He understood the importance of the political machine operated by Richard Daley; they underestimated him, but soon he manoeuvred very well around them. When they realised his qualities, they embraced him.

In his political life, Barack Obama has participated in Irish events, such as St Patrick's Day parades, but he has made no attempt to approach the substantial Irish-American con-stituency with any assertion of ethnic connection, nor has he courted any Irish lobby. However, he emerged from Chicago politics with much more experience of an Irish milieu than Bill Clinton had when he became president. And he appointed as his chief-of-staff Rahm Emanuel, former cog in the Daley machine. He also appointed as his vice president Joe Biden, a solid Irish Catholic in the key state of Delaware. Nevertheless, the spectacular failure in January 2010 to win for the Democrats the Massachusetts US Senate seat previously held by Ted Kennedy caused some to suggest that Barack Obama had failed to learn enough from his experience of working alongside the Irish in Chicago.

During his campaign for the Democratic presidential nomination, he was criticised for his failure to engage with the Irish lobby and criticised in the pages of Irish-American newspapers which, of course, sided firmly with Hillary Clinton.

This may seem surprising, in the light not just of the Kennedy Democratic tradition but also the high priority given to Ireland and the Irish peace process by President Bill Clinton. After all, Bill Clinton had described his visit to Ireland at the end of November 1995 as "two of the best days of my presidency".[184] However, it is consistent with Obama's overall political approach, which sees the USA as a patchwork of many colours.

As an issue, Ireland does not rate a mention in *The Audacity of Hope,* Obama's personal political manifesto. For the previous Democratic president, Bill Clinton, Ireland represented a highlight, an issue to which he devoted an enormous amount of attention and which he chose to mention frequently. Clinton engaged with the Irish issue during his campaign for the presidency and, once elected, he used the office to intervene in relation to the Irish peace process with major effect. It would be entirely fair to say that he went out on a limb for Ireland and for the resolution of the centuries-old conflict.

Barack Obama avoided giving much attention to Ireland in his campaign for the presidential nomination or, indeed, for the Democratic nomination. Amongst Irish-American Democrats, the attention devoted by Bill Clinton to the Irish issue gave overwhelming reason to support Hillary Clinton for the party's nomination. In addition, Hillary Clinton herself consistently maintained sympathetic contact with Irish-American lobbies.

The principal lobby group was the Irish Lobby for Immigration Reform (ILIR), co-founded by Niall O'Dowd, publisher of *The Irish Voice* and *Irish America,* and Ciaran Staunton, a long-time immigration activist and member of Noraid, who had played a leading role in the US implementation of Sinn Féin's peace strategy, accompanying Gerry Adams on visits to the White House.

In June 2007, Barack Obama proposed amendments to the Comprehensive Immigration Reform Bill, which had been crafted by a surprising but powerful coalition including President George W. Bush, Edward Kennedy (Democrat) and Senator John McCain (Republican). His attempt to amend the bill was blamed for undermining the delicate agreement between Democrats and Republicans, and thus scuppering a real opportunity to achieve a resolution to the legal limbo affecting thousands of Irish immigrants in the US. He was, however, just one of many who wanted to get the legislation off the table, and he had seen the way the emotional wind was blowing regarding amnesty.

While Hillary Clinton accepted invitations to attend some ILIR events, Barack Obama did not. Ciaran Staunton remarked, in an *Irish Voice* interview: "We're disappointed with the lack of reaction from the Obama campaign to date."

There was also criticism from Irish-American activists that although Obama made some overseas visits, he did not include Ireland in his itinerary. Some Irish activists were inclined even to move towards support for Republican candidate John McCain, who had expressed his support for immigration reform and who had attended some Irish lobby events.

The ILIR was considerably disconcerted when Irish

Taoiseach Bertie Ahern seemed by his statements to undermine their campaign.

In August 2008, Obama issued a statement in which he said that, the crisis having passed in Northern Ireland, he would "consult with the Taoiseach, the British prime minister, and party leaders in Northern Ireland to determine whether a special envoy continues to be necessary".

This caused consternation in some Irish-American circles. In New York, the head of the Emerald Isle Immigration Center, Brian O' Dwyer, an attorney who was a prominent Hillary Clinton supporter, said he was "profoundly disappointed to the point of being shocked . . . I notice in the statement no mention has been made of any provision to cure the historic inequity discrimination felt by the Irish and the immigration laws." He also interpreted the statement as "calling for a detachment of American involvement in Northern Irish affairs". And he insisted that a US envoy was as important today as when President Clinton first appointed one. He added: "I must say that those of us who have worked regularly in the field of helping to bring peace to Northern Ireland know that there is still a lot of work to be done."[185]

The Ancient Order of Hibernians (AOH) and Sinn Féin also expressed objections. Sinn Féin's principal representative in America, Rita O'Hare, said:

> In terms of the claim that the crisis in the North is over I would ask which crisis is over? What is coming down the line here is that there has not been a meeting of the Executive for six weeks. I would very firmly say that the crisis is not over and there's very great concern about the Democratic Unionist Party (DUP) refusing to do business that isn't DUP business.[186]

John McCain saw an opening, and intervened to say that the role of the special envoy was critical; he suggested that Obama's statement showed his "total lack of experience and profoundly poor judgement on matters of foreign policy". Obama's campaign responded by announcing the setting up of an advisory panel on Irish issues, including two unquestionably heavy hitters, Edward Kennedy and George Mitchell. On 8 September, it was announced that Barack Obama, if elected president, would appoint a "senior envoy" to Ireland.

Later in September, Ciaran Staunton again criticised Obama. "We've had great access to Senator McCain. Every event we've invited him to over the past two years, both in Washington and in the Bronx, he has shown up to," he said. "I spent half an hour talking with him about the issue and other Irish-American issues and he didn't need notes or staff. He gets the issue. This is in contrast to his opponent. We have as yet been unable to get a hold of Barack Obama to turn up to any campaigns," Mr Staunton said. "We don't endorse candidates but we certainly thank them and as of now there's certainly only one who's shown an interest."[187]

Nevertheless, the Kennedys chose at a crucial point to throw their support in the race for the Democratic nomination behind Barack Obama, who owes them an enormous debt for the way in which they kept the superdelegates from going over to Hillary Clinton. In effect, Edward Kennedy handed the torch of Irish-American politics over to Obama. Clearly he did not do so on the basis of any commitment the candidate had shown towards Irish causes or the Irish-American political sector. Rather, he was convinced by Barack Obama's vision, personal qualities and ability to deliver on his vision for Americans of all ethnic backgrounds, and particularly on those key issues, such as healthcare, to which Edward Kennedy had devoted a long political lifetime.

Obama and Ireland: The Personal and the Political

An issue that concerned establishment political circles in Ireland considerably more than immigration reform was the question of tax changes that might render it less attractive for US companies to locate in Ireland. Barack Obama proposed to prevent US multinationals from sheltering their profits in low-tax economies such as Ireland. Despite Ireland's small size, it plays host to some 580 US multinationals, and the concern was that Obama's proposal to broaden the US tax base to prevent the flow of capital and profits away from the US, and make it more difficult for US companies to shelter their overseas income, would cause them to relocate outside Ireland, to pull back operations to the US or to otherwise scale back their activities in Ireland. This would, it was feared, have serious consequences for the Irish economy, as these US companies produce goods and services valued at some $60 billion annually and pay corporation tax of around $2.5 billion to the Irish exchequer.

On the eve of the election, an Irish tax consultant, Conor Begley, sounded a serious warning in an article in *The Irish Times*:

> Income from outbound investments earned by separately incorporated foreign subsidiaries of US corporations are generally not subject to US tax until that income is repatriated. It is this deferral mechanism that Ireland has benefited and grown from, playing off the tax differential of mainstream US corporation tax of 35 per cent versus Irish corporation tax of 12.5 per cent.

He outlined the threat posed to Ireland as he saw it:

> Obama's proposals are to tighten rules involving tax havens and offshore activities in his sweeping Stop Tax Haven Abuse Act and the Obama Patriot Act.

He wants to penalise companies that abuse the US tax code and stop the use of tax havens. Ireland would not, technically, be considered a tax haven, however. Obama's Patriot Act, which he co-sponsored and introduced in to the Senate in August 2007 when he was already running for the White House, seems to have been forgotten about. However, it deserves a significant amount of attention as it has the potential to completely torpedo Ireland's corporation tax policy.

The Act would provide a tax credit equal to 1 per cent of taxable income to employers who fulfill the condition of maintaining their corporate headquarters in the US.

To finance this tax break, the taxing mechanism of US corporate profits earned abroad may be revisited.

In addition, the Act states that employers must not decrease their ratio of full-time workers in the US to full-time workers outside the US.

An intervention by the US government to influence companies' decisions about respective domestic and foreign employment levels and the location of their headquarters through fiscal disincentives would have serious consequences for the Irish economy and would lead to a haemorrhaging of jobs. Begley goes on to say:

> The sweeping changes that Obama is proposing, if implemented, could severely damage Ireland's attractiveness to US foreign direct investment. We can ill afford to lose US investment at a time when our public finances are under so much threat.[188]

Following the election, the Industrial Development Authority, IDA Ireland, engaged in discussions with senior members of Obama's campaign team in relation to their position. It also indicated that it would lobby members of the US Congress and Senate, particularly public representatives with strong ties to Ireland.

Brian Lenihan, the minister for finance, said there would be "continuous liaison with the business community through diplomatic and overseas channels" to monitor any potential changes to the US tax system.

Opinions varied about the degree of threat posed by Obama's proposals. Speaking in Ireland, Massachusetts congressman William Delahunt, chairman of the House of Representatives' Foreign Affairs Subcommittee, and one of Obama's most high-profile Irish American supporters in the Democratic Party, said:

> "We want to make sure there is an agreed playing field for American companies abroad. If there are American companies headquartered here, we recognise they have to have subsidiaries abroad if they are international companies," says Delahunt. "We understand the need for growth of American companies overseas. I don't think we'll do anything to diminish that. I'd advise you to relax."

He was upbeat about prospects for immigration reform that would resolve the situation of the undocumented Irish in the US:

> "Senator Kennedy, Senator McCain and Senator Obama have all endorsed comprehensive reform legislation. For those of us who are Irish-American or have Irish-American constituencies, it's an important goal. I think we'll see it happen in 2009."[189]

The presidential election campaign was observed and reported on in Ireland to an unprecedented extent. It even seemed to engage people's attentions more than the politics of Ireland itself. And the attention was not focused upon Irish issues such as the peace process, immigration or tax reform. Attention was focused on the dramatic contest for the most powerful position in the world. As a drama, it gained much from the fact that for the first time ever a person of colour seemed poised to achieve that highest office. But in Ireland as in America, many people – and especially younger people – were effectively colour-blind; what stimulated their attention was largely Obama's charismatic articulation of a message of hope.

The intense interest in the prospect of Barack Obama becoming president was international. Neither in Ireland, America or anywhere else was that interest seriously focused on the fact that his ancestry was partly Irish. And yet behind the drama exhaustively acted out in the present media lay another drama, of the past. It was a drama that included an eighteenth-century Dublin businessman, an early nineteenth-century Irish bishop, a shoemaker from Moneygall, Methodists in Baltimore, pioneers in Ohio, Indiana, Kansas and Oklahoma . . . It was a story of a maternal ancestry that mingled Irish, German, Scottish, Native American and English elements. As such it was an archetypal American story, in which the classic narrative of log cabin pioneers held centre stage.

The fact that Barack Obama, great-great-great-grandson of Fulmouth Kearney of Moneygall, stood on the brink of being elected president was emblematic of the unique American capacity to combine the ordinary and the extraordinary. As the presidential campaign entered its final two weeks, Barack Obama seemed on the verge of an astonishing success. His campaign showed no relaxation of effort as the long journey approached ever closer the destination of the White House.

Yet suddenly Barack Obama deserted the campaign. On the brink of public greatness, he took the decision to leave the campaign to spend time in Hawaii with his grandmother Madelyn Dunham, "Toot", who had become seriously ill. On 23 and 24 October, he simply exited the campaign to turn his attention to the private matter of saying goodbye to one of the great influences in his life, who, together with her husband Stanley, had been a pillar of his childhood and teenage years.

Michael Powell of the *New York Times* commented:

> To leave the trail at this juncture, when the bell lap is upon both Mr. Obama and his Republican rival, Senator John McCain, carries an element of risk. Mr. Obama is running ahead in every national poll, but his lead in some recent polls is not large.[190]

On the morning of 3 November, on the very eve of the election, Madelyn Lee Payne Dunham died. In a speech later that day in North Carolina, Obama spoke of her as "a quiet hero". He and his sister Maya released a statement:

> It is with great sadness that we announce that our grandmother, Madelyn Dunham, has died peacefully after a battle with cancer. She was the cornerstone of our family, and a woman of extraordinary accomplishment, strength, and humility. She was the person who encouraged and allowed us to take chances. She was proud of her grandchildren and great-grandchildren and left this world with the knowledge that her impact on all of us was meaningful and enduring. Our debt to her is beyond measure.

As president, Barack Obama immediately faced a daunting array of challenges at home and abroad. Healthcare reform headed the legislative list of priorities, while intervention to begin dealing with the extraordinarily deep economic and financial crisis vied only with the wars in Iraq and Afghanistan for urgent attention.

The Irish political conflict was quiescent and off the radar of American political life. However, the question of the administration's approach to the issue of a special envoy to Northern Ireland was resolved in September 2009 when Secretary of State Hillary Clinton announced the appointment of Declan Kelly as economic envoy to Northern Ireland. Meanwhile, she herself took responsibility for handling the political issues around the peace process. "Secretary Clinton did a great thing when she assumed the role of the envoy for herself," said Denis McDonough, deputy national security adviser and chief-of-staff of the US National Security Council. "It underscores her commitment to it, and frankly it underscores the president's commitment to it."[191]

The issue of immigration, while of immense concern to Irish-American lobbyists and campaigners, was also a touchstone question for Latino voters, whom Barack Obama had promised during the election that he would deliver comprehensive immigration reform.

In November 2009, the Obama administration's agenda for immigration reform in 2010 was outlined in a speech by Homeland Security Secretary Janet Napolitano. She expressed the need for immigration reform on economic, national security and humanitarian grounds, and she described the administration's approach as a three-legged stool: effective enforcement, improved legal/approval processes for workers and employers and a "firm but fair way to deal with those who are already here".

Some commentators welcomed the speech as indicating that major priority would be given to the issue. As Deborah White wrote in *Deborah's US Liberal Politics Blog*:

Without doubt, immigration reform will be to 2010 what healthcare reform has been to 2009: the headline-grabbing dominant issue, hotly debated, replete with plenty of ugly Republican rhetoric, and will ultimately culminate in some Congressionally-negotiated form of landmark legislation.[192]

Then, on 27 January 2010, President Obama included mention of the issue in his State of the Union address. The mention was brief, but such a major international issue as the situation in the Middle East was not mentioned at all. Leading Irish-American campaigner Niall O'Dowd responded:

Barack Obama came out fighting last night in his State of the Union and made it clear that issues such as immigration reform are still very much on his agenda.

It was great to see the Commander in Chief recapture some of the fire and fury that brought him to the White House in the first place . . .

On immigration reform he was clear that he will pursue what has become one of the most contentious issues of his presidency. For tens of thousands of undocumented Irish his message was good news.[193]

However, views of Obama's approach and commitment varied. *Irish Echo* editor Ray O'Hanlon wrote that "President Obama's focus on reform during the lengthy address to both houses of Congress struck many observers as being little more than perfunctory."[194]

Illinois Democrat Rep Luis Gutierrez, whose Comprehensive Immigration Reform for America's Security and Prosperity Act of 2009 was at the time before the House of Representatives, told the *Washington Post* that there was "disillusionment" among immigration advocates. "There's almost universal consensus that what the president said – it was too little. He was very weak on immigration, lackadaisical."

By February 20, Niall O'Dowd's opinion had radically changed:

> Comprehensive immigration reform for 2010 and beyond is dead . . . As the founder of the Irish Lobby for Immigration Reform, a movement that took thousands of Irish to Capitol Hill to lobby for reform, it gives me no pleasure whatsoever to say this . . . But the math does not lie. There is no chance in hell that a filibuster-proof majority exists in the U.S. Senate for most anything right now, let alone immigration reform.[195]

In relation to this issue and many others, the president's room for manoeuvre has been reduced by Republican Scott Brown's victory over Democrat Martha Coakley in the Massachusetts Senate race. Nevertheless, in the immediate wake of the passage of the healthcare reform legislation in March 2010, Obama chose to raise the question of immigration reform and his commitment to it.

Inevitably, Barack Obama has been experiencing the difficult transition from articulating hopes and aspirations to dealing in the everyday world of politics as the art of the possible. Equally inevitably, his opinion poll ratings have slipped. He has shown leadership and succeeded in achieving reform on an exceptionally divisive issue that has defeated other presidents and bedevilled US politics for many decades. There was always a real danger that his presidency would fail to surmount this substantial first hurdle, but following this success, all the other issues on his agenda are still to be played for.

Throughout most of Europe a strongly positive appreciation of Barack Obama holds sway, modified principally by disappointment on foreign policy issues. Probably nowhere is more positively attuned to him than Ireland. There is perhaps no great political substance to this positive feeling, but there is in Ireland a special sense of affinity with the United States – a fellow feeling that derives from the historic connection through emigration. Most Irish people were heartened and grateful for President Clinton's engagement with Ireland. Most felt, regretfully, that his successor and Obama's predecessor George W. Bush represented the US in an outstandingly negative fashion, and so the hope represented by Barack Obama has been amplified by the comparison. In addition, his qualities as US leader shine particularly brightly against the backdrop of the widespread public perception that in Ireland a catastrophic failure of political leadership lies behind the collapse of the economy and the absence of good governance.

— 15 —

Carnival of Reaction in America:
Birthers, Tea Parties and Racists

Barack Obama's Irish ancestors had arrived in America over a period of about seventy years from a country riven by discord, inequality, despair and poverty. In their new home they experienced the welcome challenge of new opportunities, and participated in the making of the United States as the frontier moved westward. In Ireland they experienced in Offaly something of the political tensions and sectarian division between Protestant and Catholic that were to constitute the historic tragedy of Ireland. In Maryland they encountered the slavery and racism that were to prove the great historic stain on American democracy, before moving to settle in Ohio. The question of what it meant to be American was taking shape and began to be forged in large part by images from the frontier; as yet it failed to include either the Native Americans or black Americans. The question of what it meant to be Irish was beginning to be redefined in rather different exclusivist terms.

Neither in Ireland nor America have these divisions and differences been dispelled. The people of Ireland have breathed a collective sigh of relief at the resolution achieved in its peace process, but the politics of Northern Ireland remain defined by essentially Catholic and Protestant parties, and the Southern state remains a Catholic state in painful transition.

In the United States of America, the election of a person of colour, with mixed ancestry, has thrown a challenge in the face of the racial prejudice that underlies much conservative opinion. It has also inspired people of colour in a powerful way, while also inspiring those American citizens of all backgrounds who wish for a nation in which, to paraphrase Frederick Douglass, people are measured and esteemed according to their moral and intellectual worth, and not according to the colour of their skin or their ethnic origins. However, the election of President Obama cannot on its own usher in the end of racism, because no one individual can sweep away a social reality experienced daily by millions of people.

Indeed, to an extent Obama's election has served as a focus for racist sentiment. Dr Maya Rockeymoore, president and CEO of Global Policy Solutions, a Washington DC-based think-tank, said the election offered a

> . . . fascinating look at how issues of race, ethnicity and religion are playing out in America.
>
> Clearly we have a generational divide in terms of people's perspective on race relations in this country. Younger people don't necessarily see the country in Black and White terms as the older generations have in the past, so we see an historic turning to the Barack Obama campaign by younger voters who don't necessarily have the baggage. At the same time we have seen that race is still a factor.[196]

A report by *Scientific American* on research presented to the Council for the Advancement of Science Writing concluded:

Amazingly, white Americans did see a European like Hugh Grant as being somehow more American than the Asian-American Connie Chung. And similar research in 2008 found that whites thought of ex-British Prime Minister Tony Blair as somehow more American than Obama. So the mental framework to believe that Obama is foreign probably was, to use a health care term, a pre-existing condition.[197]

Former president Jimmy Carter, a son of the segregated South, observed that "There is an inherent feeling among many in this country that an African-American should not be president."[198] And in a country where whites have enjoyed power and privilege, it is hardly surprising that there are those who will react violently to advances by blacks. The end of the Civil War and slavery saw black political progress, but it also saw the rise of the night riders, the Ku Klux Klan, Jim Crow laws and Black Codes. When black boxer Jack Johnson defeated white former heavyweight champion James J. Jeffries in 1910, race riots broke out. Campaigns in the 1950s to desegregate schools, businesses and neighbourhoods were met with attacks, as was school bussing in the 1970s.

At "tea party" rallies since the election of Barack Obama, ostensibly organised in opposition to healthcare reform, racist placards have been carried. The campaign of "Birthers", alleging that Barack Obama was really born in Kenya rather than Hawaii and is therefore not qualified to be commander-in-chief, has assumed a virulent character. A white congressman from the Deep South shouted, "You lie!" at the first black president; many believed he would not have done so had the president been white.

Birthers have brought many lawsuits claiming that Obama is ineligible to be president because he is not a bona fide US citizen. His valid birth certificate and his mother's citizenship establish his own citizenship, and such lawsuits have been thrown out. As the judge in one such case, US District Judge David O. Carter of California, said:

> Plaintiffs have encouraged the Court to ignore ... mandates of the Constitution; to disregard the limits on its power put in place by the Constitution; and to effectively overthrow a sitting president who was popularly elected by "We the People" – over *sixty-nine million* of the people. Plaintiffs have attacked the judiciary, including every prior court that has dismissed their claim, as unpatriotic and even treasonous for refusing to grant their requests and for adhering to the terms of the Constitution which set forth its jurisdiction. Respecting the constitutional role and jurisdiction of this Court is not unpatriotic. Quite the contrary, this Court considers commitment to that constitutional role to be the ultimate reflection of patriotism.[199]

A challenge faces the United States of America in dealing with its deeply seated tendencies to deny equal citizenship to all, and the election of the first president of colour marks an important point in the evolving relationship of America with questions of race. Ireland's tragedy is that it took the road of sectarian division, but some believe it is beginning to face the consequences, North and South, and perhaps to move beyond them.

In the last two decades, the southern state in Ireland has undergone a new transformation of its population. For so long a country of net emigration, it suddenly received proportionally large numbers of immigrants. "Catholic Ireland" now contains not only Protestants but also Muslims and those of other religions and none, and Irish citizens now include those with Polish, Lithuanian, Nigerian and other origins.

When Fredrick Douglass visited Ireland in 1845, his mind and soul were refreshed by the fact that he encountered no racial prejudice. He came then as an individual on a short-term basis and was perceived, presumably, as posing no threat. Those who have arrived in recent decades – as asylum-seekers and as economic migrants – have sought what Irish people sought in America, Great Britain and Australia over the course of centuries: better opportunities for themselves and their families. They arrived in large numbers at a time when unemployment had reached an all-time low, when the economy was expanding at by far the fastest rate in Europe and when all economic commentators agreed that there was a need for substantial immigration to meet the labour needs of the economy. Despite these propitious circumstances, the greeting they received did not resemble the welcome afforded Frederick Douglass.

The cliché that the Irish people are friendly and the appellation "Ireland of the Welcomes" both have a real basis in long experience. Nevertheless, the majority of the Irish people have received educations in exclusivism, and it is difficult to say whether the Catholics of the South or the Protestants of the North are the more qualified graduates in that particular school. As Marianne Elliott observes, the Catholic prejudice may be subtler. But both brands have prepared people to be in general more focused on how others may differ from their norm than on what may be held in common. The unity of people, whether born in Ireland or not, has failed to be realised, just as the unity of Protestant, Catholic and Dissenter envisaged by the United Irishmen was frustrated.

However, there is in Ireland now a tendency amongst younger people and amongst many of a progressive disposition to wish to move beyond the differences of the past. Some of those who were subjected to inhuman treatment in institutions run by the religious orders have fought back heroically. The civil rights movement, the women's movement, campaigns for divorce and contraception rights have been amongst elements that have shaken the consensus, undermining the basis of the divisive construction of Irish identity. As Dermot Keogh observes in "Catholicism and the Formation of the Modern Irish Society", the crises in Southern society over the issue of divorce during the 1980s and 1990s formed part of "a shift from confessional to consensus democracy", involving a change in "the very definition of 'Irishness' ".[200]

Irish people in recent generations have made a notable contribution to developing world charities and have shown a remarkable commitment to non-governmental activism. The institutions are widely perceived to have failed, and many identify a need to turn to themselves, in the community, for leadership. Many of these – in common with people in other countries – identify Barack Obama as a beacon of hope. Perhaps in part it is because he comes from a background in community self-activity; perhaps because he goes against the grain simply by being a person of colour; perhaps because he is young; perhaps because he is articulate, handsome and personable. It is probably in part a combination of such factors, but perhaps what accounts most significantly for his appeal is his constant articulation of the unity of people. If young and not-so-young people are disenchanted with politics, ideologies and institutions based upon division and exclusivity, it is likely that they have identified in Obama someone who has resonance for them and does not so much give them hope as accord with their own feelings of hope and aspiration.

Dean Victor Griffin of the Church of Ireland suggests in *Untold Stories*:

> When Irishness is seen as transcending religion and politics, more a sense of place, of belonging, of being at home in a common homeland, then all can rejoice in the victory of inclusiveness over exclusiveness, of a common unity not limited but enhanced by diversity.[201]

Ireland has a long way to go to achieve such transcendence, especially because the existence of the problem is scarcely recognised; but where does the USA stand in relation to "a common unity not limited but enhanced by diversity"? The words echo those of President Barack Obama when he said in his Inaugural Address:

> ... we cannot help but believe that the old hatreds shall someday pass; that the lines of tribe shall soon dissolve; that as the world grows smaller, our common humanity shall reveal itself ...

He also spoke about the role of America in the world, and the question of equal respect for all ethnic and religious strands is not just an internal American matter. Long before 9/11, many of the various elements within the Islamic world had perceived the US government to be not only pro-Israeli but anti-Arab and anti-Islam. While instances of Arabs cheering at the news of the 9/11 attacks were isolated and unrepresentative, some within the Arab world undoubtedly felt that the US was suffering in the attack something analagous to the experiences of the people of Beirut, Baghdad and Gaza. Even within America, there were those like Susan Sonntag who saw 9/11 as a "coming home" of an imperial US foreign policy. George W. Bush described the US intervention in Iraq as a "crusade", and many observers internationally considered that Islam did not hold the copyright in fundamentalism.

One of the clearest dividing lines drawn by President

Obama between his international policy and that of his predecessor was the line of including the Islamic world within the arena of a dialogue of equals. This contrasted sharply with the clumsy attribution of "axis of evil" to a variety of states of varying characters and with the attempt of the Bush administration to cast Islam in the role of a pro-terrorist ideology. It was this rhetorical initiative by Barack Obama that was the principal reason why he was awarded the Nobel Peace Prize. Despite the fact that the award was something of a political embarrassment to him at the time, it was based on a recognition by the Nobel committee that words of inclusiveness and equality can sometimes be as significant as actions. In the future, it may well be seen as fitting that a president influenced by orators such as Frederick Douglass, Arthur O'Connor and Martin Luther King should be presented with laurels for his articulation of hope and aspiration.

— 16 —

Carnival of Reaction: Ireland in the Twentieth Century

Ireland today is shaped by the great turning point of the defeat of universal republicanism at the turn of the eighteenth and nineteenth centuries, and by the Famine. In the half century after Thomas Kearney's emigration to Maryland, the United States had advanced to consolidate its democracy, ratifying the Bill of Rights and establishing new states. Ireland, on the other hand, had lost its opportunity to advance into a democracy based upon the separation of religion and politics. In America, defeated Irish republican exiles combined with other elements of both Protestant and Catholic Irish origin to contribute greatly to the character of American democracy. In Ireland, however, the great defeat was followed by a period in which sectarian division took hold.

As the era of the pioneers came to an end in America, Ireland underwent a transformation. The Protestant ascendancy, which had been in decline for the whole of the nineteenth century, was about to give way. Home Rule seemed to be inevitable, but the new confidence of the nationalist opponents of British rule rested on an insecure foundation of defeat and demoralisation. The defeat of the republican idea had been followed by Famine and by the opening of the floodgates of emigration. All over Ireland, a nation reeling from the impact of the successive years of disaster, individual stories were written during a collective tragedy, as families and individuals set out to make new lives in England, Australia and America.

In the Kearneys' homeland of Offaly, the large drop in the population between 1841 and 1851 was followed by further decline over each succeeding decade and generation. Between 1851 and 1860, nearly 21,000 people emigrated from Offaly. The population of the county fell from almost 147,000 in 1841 to 90,043 in 1861; to 72,852 in 1881, and just 53,000 in 1926. The 1841 Census showed that there were 8,175,124 people living in Ireland. By 1881, forty years later, the population had fallen by over three million to 5,174,836. By 1926, the number had fallen further to just 4,228,553.

The gaping wound of the Famine gave rise to fierce simplicities, forging a mythical image of Irish identity that has been largely sustained through to the present generations. Landlords, who were often tenants of larger operators, existed at almost every level of the social scale and of all religious persuasions. Catholics constituted an influential section of landed society, and indeed the great Liberator, Daniel O'Connell, was a landlord. But most of the larger, more prominent landlords were Protestants, and the pre-eminence of the established Protestant religion in England had been imposed on Irish public life through the Church of Ireland. Therefore, the simplified story had it, all Catholics were assumed to be landless – having been dispossessed by the Protestant English – and native Irish. By much the same token, all Protestants were assumed to be landlords and essentially English.

Writing in *Irish Life in the Seventeenth Century*, Edward McLysaght observed:

[A]s the cause of Church and nation became ever more closely identified and the idea of nationality grew up in Europe, the stereotyped division which has lasted till our own time developed. In Ireland the words Catholic and Irishman became almost synonymous, and the word "English" was often used to denote a Protestant, even though his family might have been in Ireland for several generations.

Catholicity in Ireland was thus greatly strengthened by its association with what we now call patriotic and national feelings: it became the proud heritage of a people steeped in tradition, and it was immensely intensified by persecution, since it happened that the people persecuted had and have an innate dislike of brooking any tyranny imposed by strangers.[202]

Irish Protestants such as the Kearneys came to be regarded by the incipient Catholic establishment as foreigners in their own country, denoted in Irish as *gall*. At a meeting in Moneygall in January 1881, the parish priest recited a verse:

> May we all live to see Moneygall
> Clothed in splendour and free from (en)thrall,
> Thy name subdivided as now I forestall [foretell],
> Money in plenty while dropping the gall.

Of course, all the Kearneys had been gone from Moneygall and from Ireland for thirty years by then, but had they remained they might well have experienced a sharp discomfort in their lives. A new Catholic triumphalism gained much of its vigour from the long period of Protestant ascendancy, during which Catholics had been discriminated against in a wholesale fashion. In the aftermath of the Famine, Ireland and Irishness began to be redefined as a Catholic monoculture. Some relations of the Kearneys, the Healys, remained in Offaly, but soon many of them were no longer Protestant.

A new exodus from Ireland began, and it was an exodus of the Kearneys' co-religionists. In the few years between 1911 and 1926, the Protestant population was drastically reduced. In the twenty-six counties of "southern Ireland", or the Free State as it then was, a census was taken in 1926.

> It revealed that thousands of Protestants had decided they had no future in Catholic Ireland and had left: in 1911 there had been 327,000 Protestants in what eventually became the Free State, but by 1926 there were only 221,000. This, and not the events in Belfast in 1920–2, or, indeed in 1969–72, represents the biggest movement of population in twentieth-century Irish history.[203]

It was a decline that was to continue.

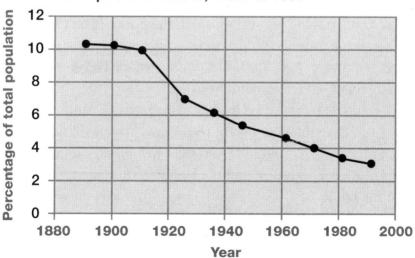

The declining Protestant population in the Republic of Ireland,* 1891 to 1991

*For the period before 1921, these figures are for the 26 counties that later constituted the Republic of Ireland.

A revival of radical republicanism in Ireland surrounding the 1916 Rising and War of Independence had swiftly been dissipated by counter-revolution, civil war and the partition of the country into two sectarian states. The result was the antithesis of universal republicanism: rather than Catholic, Protestant and Dissenter being united under the common name of Irish people, they were to be formally, politically, constitutionally and socially divided. In 1798, the backbone of the United Irish rebellion had been provided by Presbyterian merchants and tenant farmers, yet by the twentieth century the Protestants of the North were fighting to maintain their link with the British Crown and empire.

Leader of the 1916 Rising and ideological leader of the Irish left, James Connolly, had predicted that partition would result in a carnival of reaction on both sides of the border. While reaction took different forms in each of the two states, he was proved correct.

Everything was explicit and clearly rigged in the north-eastern six-county state: voting was gerrymandered to deny Catholics equal representation; a "Protestant parliament for a Protestant people" was established; the police forces included a Protestant militia, the B-Specials, backed by the draconian Special Powers Act; Catholics were denied equal access to employment, education and housing.

Excluded from equal rights as citizens, Catholics were driven to despair. Many were terrorised, attacked and driven from their homes. Isolated from their neighbours south of the border and deprived of political power, they were delivered into the hands of a hostile government that was intent on ruling for the benefit only of Protestants. Later, civil rights demonstrations were violently suppressed by the sectarian state and by the British army. Moves to ameliorate the lack of democratic rights for Catholics were met by a reactionary mass movement of Protestants that was mobilised to prevent power-sharing.

In the Southern twenty-six counties, exclusion of Protestants was less explicit and matters were for the most part less bluntly administered. As Marianne Elliott observes:

> Catholic sectarianism is no less real for being less easy to identify, and the belief that they have been history's victims puts Catholics in denial. It often takes the form of post-colonial speak: Protestant-planter-settler-coloniser victimizer versus Catholic-native-Irish-Gaelic victim.[204]

The new southern state did not legislate to exclude Protestants: it did not need to. Partition had consigned the majority of the island's Protestants to the northern state; about a third of those who remained in the southern state chose to leave. And for many of those who continued to make their lives in the new state, there was an inescapable feeling that they had been expelled to a form of internal exile.

> Since Irishness became linked in people's minds with Catholicism, so Protestants were considered foreign "blow-ins," settlers, planters, associated with the Big House and landlordism in the South, and the Stormont regime in the North. However hard Irish governments in post-independence Ireland sought to be inclusive, the emphasis on Catholic identity all but expelled Protestants from the "nation."[205]

In *Obstacles to Peace Building in the Republic of Ireland*, published by the Irish Peace and Reconciliation Platform in 2000, the authors write about "a fostering of selective cultural and historic amnesia . . . allowing whole swathes of people to be 'airbrushed' out of history".[206]

Indeed, so deeply did the process of historical misrepresentation and myth-making embed itself that Irish non-Catholics have long had to endure assumptions that if they are not Catholic they are not really Irish or, in some instances, *as* Irish as their Catholic neighbours.

This process succeeded despite the fact that both the ideological and activist leaders of Irish republicanism and Irish nationalism were largely Protestant. The Gaelic language movement, which constituted such a vitally important element of the nationalist movement, was largely founded by Protestants. The first Bible in Gaelic was translated by Church of Ireland Bishop William Bedell in the seventeenth century. The Presbyterian church was the only church in Ireland to require, at the end of the nineteenth century, that candidates for the ministry should be able to speak Gaelic.

In its literature, Ireland had seen a pre-eminent contribution by Protestants, and one significant but largely forgotten figure in the Irish literary revival, who came from County Offaly, was Thomas William Hazen Rolleston (1857–1920), a writer, translator and founder of the *Dublin University Review*. Born in Glasshouse, Shinrone, he published *Poems and Ballads of Young Ireland* (1888), and his most important works were *Celtic Myths and Legends* and *The High Deeds of Finn Mac Cumhail*. He was also a journalist and a civil servant involved with agriculture, and he was a colleague of Douglas Hyde in the Gaelic League. However, despite his deep love of Irish culture, he emigrated in 1908, like many Protestant Irish, to England.

In the situation created by the new partitioned states, the northern state was to be defined as Protestant, the southern as Catholic. Although W. B. Yeats sought to argue in the South that the Protestants were "no mean people", they were rendered irrelevant to the triumphant creation of a Catholic southern state. However, they experienced nothing like the suppression and repression visited upon the Catholics in the northern state.

The Catholic and Protestant churches alike had assiduously promoted over centuries a sense of difference between Catholics and Protestants, creating an atmosphere in which people of the two religious persuasions found it all but impossible to intermarry. Nothing was more damaging to the position and sense of security of Protestants in Ireland than *Ne Temere,* a papal decree of 1907 that was rigorously enforced by the Catholic church in the newly independent twenty-six-county Irish state. When a Catholic married a non-Catholic, it was required that both partners commit to raising any children of their marriage solely as Roman Catholics. And this was what happened to most of the relatives of the Kearneys who did not emigrate, the Healys of Moneygall and Shinrone. *Ne Temere* has been described as "the Irish answer to ethnic cleansing", a hyperbole that seems unbalanced in the light of the sectarian slaughters carried out in other religious conflicts, but the seriousness of this assault upon the rights and freedoms of all non-Catholics in Ireland was confirmed by the state.

The Irish constitution of 1937 reserved a special place for the Catholic church, and the courts supported the operation of the *Ne Temere* decree in judgements such as that of Judge Gavan Duffy in *Tilson v. Tilson.*[207]

The most highly publicised occasion related to *Ne Temere* arose in the fishing village of Fethard-on-Sea near Hook Head in County Wexford. Sheila Kelly and Seán Cloney had grown up as neighbours in Fethard-on-Sea, but when they decided to get married in 1949, they chose to do so in London, because she was Protestant and he Catholic, and Ireland was hostile to "mixed" marriages. On their return to Fethard, they had two daughters, but one day in 1957, as the time approached for their first daughter to go to school, Sheila Cloney was visited by a local priest of the Catholic church, who demanded that her children be raised and educated as Catholics, in accordance with *Ne Temere*. "Eileen's going to the local Catholic school and there's nothing you can do about it," he told her. She responded by leaving Fethard-on-Sea with her two daughters. As her husband later put it, "Sheila didn't fancy being ordered." She travelled first to Belfast, then to the Orkney Islands in Scotland. Back in Fethard-on-Sea, the Catholic priest called for a boycott of Protestant-owned local businesses, which swiftly gained the backing of the bishop and various Catholic publications. On the other side of the argument, liberals such as Hubert Butler, Owen Sheehy Skeffington and Eoin O'Mahony weighed in.

As is made clear in a recent account of the affair – *The Fethard-on-Sea Boycott* by Tim Fanning – the social divisions that fuelled local Catholic support for the boycott went back to that same period when in Moneygall the parish priest was reciting the verse about "dropping the gall". That was the time when the rising Catholic middle class and its church took to characterising Protestants as not being Irish, exploiting the centuries-old injustice of colonial land-grabbing to drive a wedge between Catholic and Protestant neighbours.

Seán Cloney followed his wife to Scotland, and after some months Sheila and their two daughters returned; the two elder daughters did not go to school at all, but stayed at home, working on the farm for the whole of their childhood. Later, their younger sister was baptised in the Church of Ireland and attended the local Catholic school.

In the 1980s, Fethard-on-Sea suffered further at the hands of a priest when the paedophile Father Seán Fortune was appointed as curate to the parish. One man who stood up to him was Seán Cloney, who tried to expose his activities.

Neither of Seán Cloney's conflicts with the Catholic church was isolated. *Ne Temere* was a bitter experience for many of the Protestants who remained in the southern twenty-six counties of Ireland. As Lynne Adair and Colin Murphy write in the preface to *Untold Stories: Protestants and the Republic of Ireland 1922–2002*:

> Who knows the breadth and depth of the damage done to the Protestant minority in the community, not to speak about the individual parents, children and extended family members who were sundered by its tenets? How many marriages were blighted even before they were solemnised? The ministries of how many priests and ministers were challenged and compromised as they struggled to preserve a modicum of Christian love as they implemented this dehumanising and degrading process?[208]

A more recent study, *Outside the Glow*[209] confirms that the application of *Ne Temere* in Ireland inflicted a deep and widespread sense of hurt upon Protestants, an injury of which almost all Catholics remain largely unconscious.

The establishment of sectarian paradigms in the two separate states took place in thousands of small and large ways through many instances in many localities. In County Offaly in 1924, just as the two new partitioned states in Ireland were stabilising themselves, the Catholic bishops of the area united to oppose the establishing of a county library in Daingcan (formerly Philipstown) with the aid of the Carnegie Trust. A Father Burbage referred with strong disapproval to the writings of the poet W.B. Yeats and the playwright and Abbey Theatre director Lennox Robinson (both Protestants), who were connected with the Advisory Committee of the Carnegie Trust in Ireland. In view of their involvement, he could not have anything to do with it.

In Mayo in 1930, Dean Edward D'Alton of Ballinrobe denounced the Local Appointments Commission's selection of a Protestant as county librarian. Eamon de Valera, leader of Fianna Fáil, was amongst those who argued that a Protestant librarian was not properly qualified to deal with Catholics, any more than a Protestant doctor would be qualified to deal with Catholic patients.

Even a Catholic, just because he had been educated at the Protestant university, Trinity College Dublin (TCD), was forced to surrender his appointment as professor of gynaecology at University College Galway (UCG) and emigrate.

One of the first pieces of legislation to be enacted by the southern state was the Censorship of Publications Act. Under the specific influence of the Catholic church, almost all contemporary Irish writers had books banned, not to mention many of the most prominent international authors.

Placed in untrammelled power by the creation of a partitioned southern state, the Catholic church soon grew accustomed to its unquestioned authority. The social, intellectual, political and educational spaces of the new state were taken over by Catholicism, leaving no secular public space and effectively spancelling critical debate. A forceful anti-intellectualism established a firm grip and engendered a kind of infantilised public discourse. Although in 1949 the twenty-six-county Free State declared itself a republic, it resembled in its make-up nothing at all like a state representing Protestant, Catholic and Dissenter united under the name of Irish people. This did not prevent political leaders trotting out the republican mantra, but rhetoric could not make up for substance.

A kind of politics of false appearances took hold. The attempt to win the republic had failed, but twenty-six counties out of thirty-two would be called the Republic of Ireland anyway. The state claimed that its territory was the island of Ireland, despite the fact that another state functioned in six of the counties. So later the name of the state became "Ireland", as if it administered the whole island. Gaelic (now called the Irish language) was to be the "first language" of the state; yet in practice it was used as a means of communication by very few of the people; the principal language of instruction in schools was English; almost all parliamentary debates were conducted in English; the vast majority of the business of the state and of the courts was conducted in English.

There were no false appearances, however, when it came to the dominant position of the Catholic church. Politicians and sportsmen alike bowed the knee to kiss the rings of the princes of the church. The pulpits of Catholic churches were used to denounce socialism and promote support for General Franco in Spain. Catholic bishops interfered in political matters at will, perhaps most notably – because the matter was, unusually, aired in public – during the Mother and Child controversy of 1951. Minister for Health Dr Noel Browne proposed to introduce a welfare programme for mothers and young children, but privately the Catholic hierarchy told Taoiseach John A. Costello that such an intervention by the state would be "in direct opposition to the rights of the family". The response of the taoiseach was to defer, as he informed the Dáil: "I, as a Catholic, obey my church authorities and will continue to do so." Noel Browne was left with no option but to resign, and mothers and children were denied the intended benefits of the legislation.

Amongst the institutions run by the various elements of the Catholic church have been children's homes, institutions for the incarceration of unmarried mothers, and reformatories and industrial schools such as Letterfrack in Donegal and Daingean in County Offaly.

In 1946, Father Edward Flanagan, founder of Boys Town in Nebraska, paid a visit to his home country. He was at the time one of the most famous living Irishmen and had been played by Spencer Tracy in an Oscar-winning performance. He had unrivalled experience of helping young people, and he was shocked at what he found. "Your institutions are not all noble, particularly your borstals, which are a disgrace." However, his words were first criticised, then ignored, and thirty years of misery ensued for the young people who passed through the doors of institutions such as Daingean Reformatory in County Offaly.

In 2009, following a wide-ranging enquiry, the Ryan Commission into Child Abuse conclusions on Daingean Reformatory were published. Amongst its findings were:

- Daingean was not a suitable location or building for a reformatory. The refusal by management to accept any responsibility for even day-to-day maintenance led to its complete disintegration over the years.
- Daingean did not provide a safe environment. Management failed in its duty to ensure that all boys were protected. They lived in a climate of fear in which they were isolated, frightened and bullied by both staff and inmates.
- Flogging was an inhumane and cruel form of punishment . . . but the management did nothing to stop it . . .
- Corporal punishment was a means of maintaining control and discipline, and it was the first response by many of the staff in Daingean for even minor transgressions . . .
- The Department of Education knew that its rules were being breached in a fundamental way and management in Daingean operated the system of punishment

in the knowledge that the Department would not interfere.

- Sexual abuse of boys by staff took place in Daingean, as complainant witnesses testified.
- The full extent of this abuse is impossible to quantify because of the absence of a proper system of receiving, handling and recording complaints and investigations.
- The system that was put in place tended to suppress complaints rather than to reveal abuse or even to bring about investigations.
- The Congregation in their Submission and Statements have not admitted that sexual abuse took place or even considered the possibility, but instead have directed their efforts to contending that it is impossible to find that such abuse actually occurred.[210]

Daingean was by no means an exception. All over the twenty-six counties, the Catholic church presided over, ran and operated institutions that systematically brutalised and abused the children and adults placed in their care. In addition, Irish Catholicism exported to the Unites States a phenomenon of sexual abuse by Irish priests and cover-up by the institutions of the Church. Partitionist Catholic nationalism had succeeded in creating an almost seamless identity of interest between the institutions of the southern Irish state and of their church. The authority of the leaders of the church could not successfully be challenged.

The division of national identity into two religiously defined camps lay at the foundation of the carnival of reaction. It was not that Catholicism held within itself a particular evil; after all, one of the worst instances of child abuse, at Kincora in Northern Ireland, was an entirely Protestant affair. In 1980, three members of staff at Kincora children's home were charged with the systematic abuse of children in their care over a number of years; all three were later convicted. One of them was also the leader of a loyalist paramilitary group, called Tara.

In the North, state schools and even Queen's University Belfast simply ignored Irish history; anything smacking of Gaelic culture was regarded as suspect. Education in the southern state was almost entirely controlled by a Catholic ethos, its texts such as the *Irish History Reader* providing the ideological building-blocks of a network of exclusionary mythologising.

"The sectarian Catholic reading of Irish identity was the core theme of such texts, drip-feeding anti-Protestant propaganda into modern nationalism . . ."[211]

In *Obstacles to Peace Building in the Republic of Ireland*, the authors report on their finding that:

> School curricula, especially the teaching of history, were sufficiently defective to allow a student to complete an entire education cycle without really learning the history, culture and beliefs of any other tradition or religion [than the Roman Catholic tradition].[212]

Such reference as was made to Protestants in the course of the teaching of history mostly conformed to the character of an odious absentee landlord bogeyman, though there were occasional references to the Protestant republican Wolfe Tone in terms that accorded him the status of "honorary Catholic".

Even in 2010, 91 per cent of primary schools in the twenty-six-county state are controlled not by the state – as one would expect in the case of a republic – but by the Catholic Church. In an opinion poll in *The Irish Times* on 25 January 2010, 61 per cent of respondents were of the opinion that the church should give up control of the primary school system. But the state has no plans to make this a reality, and Cardinal Seán Brady responded that:

> We should not apologise for who we are. In an increasingly diverse culture the future lies in ensuring that our schools become more authentically Catholic, both in terms of the authentic Catholic doctrine they teach and the Christian environment which they create.[213]

Not only have schools in the South been controlled by the church for decades, but their control has been unchecked by any appropriate oversight by state institutions. The state has simply deferred to the church. When instances – such as those of sexual abuse by clergy – have arisen that demanded the intervention of the police, the Gardaí have failed to carry out their duty.

If the Kearneys had remained in Ireland, what would have been their fate? Irish Protestants have learned to live with their exclusion from the national narrative, and many, thanks in particular to *Ne Temere,* are no longer Protestants. The Church of Ireland church at Templeharry, where the Kearneys were baptised, is closed. The school in Moneygall where they worshipped is now a private house. The Shinrone church in which Thomas Kearney was baptised in 1765 was replaced in 1820 by a larger church which is now floodlit at night. In 1835, 450 parishioners attended service each Sunday morning, and another fifty-five in the evening. In 2010, weekly services are attended by congregations of just thirty. Dunkerrin Church of Ireland, where the Minchins and Rollestons worshipped, has weekly congregations of between ten and fifteen.

— 17 —

The Irish American Presidents

Ancestry, especially in America's renowned melting pot, is often a matter of degrees. President Obama's paternal ancestry is quite clearly and simply Kenyan. His maternal ancestry, however, shows multiple national and ethnic strands; in this respect, he is typical both of many American presidents and many American people in all walks of life.

The fact that his Irish ancestry is Protestant will seem unusual to many in Ireland, and in Irish America, where Irishness and Catholicism are so generally regarded as synonymous. However, the majority of those in America who indicate an Irish background are in fact Protestant. Gallup in the 1980s put the proportion of Protestants at 54 per cent. The National Opinion Research Centre in 2006 revealed that of those who described their first ethnic identity as Irish, 48 per cent were Protestant, 29 per cent were Catholic, and 23 per cent were unaffiliated or other or no religion. The notion that Irish and Catholic are one and the same thing in America is a myth.

This can be difficult for people in both America and Ireland to accept, and while the Irish Catholic vote has been studied assiduously, the Irish Protestant vote has hardly been studied at all. The fact is that Irish Protestants tended to get on with being Americans and did not define themselves politically as a distinct group with its own interests. They defined themselves by their class interests, occupations, and religious and ideological convictions rather than their ethnic origins. Interestingly, Barack Obama unconsciously expresses this Protestant Irish tradition by his emphasis on what unites Americans and his avoidance of the politics of ethnic interest groups.

The many presidents who have been Irish American to one degree or another count among their number a large proportion who were Presbyterians, Baptists or Methodists from northern counties of Ireland: Jackson, Arthur and McKinley from Antrim, Polk from Coleraine, Buchanan from Donegal, Grant and Wilson from Tyrone. More than a third of all presidents have had ancestral links to the north of Ireland – far more than from any other immigrant group.

George Washington, 1st President 1789–97

Burke's Peerage observes of George Washington's ancestry:

> The Washingtons are of unusual antiquity in European terms, let alone American ones. A direct male ancestry has been traced back to William de Wessington or Wessyngton (i.e., Washington, a town in Tyne and Wear, formerly County Durham, in northern England), who was living in the late 12th century. The remoter ancestry is not absolutely certain but a detailed argument has been put forward for William de Wessington's descent in the male line from Eochu Mugmedon, High King of Ireland in the mid-4th century, through his son Niall of the Nine Hostages . . . From Eochu and Niall descend the O'Neills, the oldest family traceable in the male line

in Europe. If the link between William de Wessington and Eochu is accepted, it makes Washington the first of many American presidents with direct male line Irish ancestry.[214]

In *Irish-American Heritage Month, 1995: A Proclamation by the President of the United States of America* it is stated that "Nine of the people who signed our Declaration of Independence were of Irish origin, and nineteen presidents of the United States proudly claim Irish heritage – including our first president, George Washington."

Despite this Irish link, much evidence suggests that George Washington's ancestry was overwhelmingly English, and so he is frequently not included in lists of Irish-American presidents.

Andrew Jackson, 7th President 1829–37

In 1765, the year Thomas Kearney was born in Shinrone, Andrew Jackson and Elizabeth "Betty" Hutchinson, both Presbyterians from Carrickfergus in County Antrim, left Ireland and emigrated to America.

Andrew Jackson Jr was born two years later, in a backwoods settlement in the Carolinas. He went on to become an outstanding and prosperous young lawyer in Tennessee, where he built a mansion near Nashville and bought slaves. He was the first man elected from Tennessee to the House of Representatives, and he served briefly in the Senate. A major general in the War of 1812, Jackson became a national hero when he defeated the British at New Orleans.

Acquiring the nickname "Old Hickory", he began in 1824 to gain the support of several state political factions, and by 1828 that support had grown to win numerous state elections and control of the Federal administration in Washington.

Jackson was elected seventh president of the United States in 1829 and was the first president not rooted in the eastern aristocracy. He was primarily associated with the American frontier west of the Appalachians, and more than any of his predecessors, he was elected by popular vote. National politics became polarised around Jackson and the opposition to him, and two parties now grew out of the old Republican Party – the Democratic Republicans, or Democrats, who were with Jackson; and the National Republicans, or Whigs, who were against him.

James Knox Polk, 11th President 1845–49

In 1845, the year of Andrew Jackson's death, James Knox Polk, a Jacksonian Democrat, was elected eleventh president. Like Jackson, he came from a settler background in the North Carolina mountains, and he was a Presbyterian whose parents had immigrated from Ireland in 1740, from Coleraine. Like Jackson, too, he was a lawyer who entered politics and served in the Tennessee legislature.

He served as speaker of the House of Representatives between 1835 and 1839, leaving to become governor of Tennessee. He won the Democratic nomination for president in 1844 on the basis of the expansionist issue, asserting that Texas should be "re-annexed" and all of Oregon "re-occupied"; he also favoured acquiring California.

In office, President Polk added an enormous area to the United States, but its acquisition precipitated a bitter quarrel between the North and the South over the expansion of slavery. He continued in office until 1849, the year in which Joseph Kearney arrived in Ohio from Moneygall.

James Buchanan, 15th President 1857–61

Buchanan was, like his two immediate Irish-American predecessors, a Presbyterian, and he was born in 1791 in a log cabin in Franklin County, Pennsylvania; his

father, James Buchanan Sr, had been born in Donegal in Ireland thirty years earlier and emigrated to America in 1783.

Elected five times to the House of Representatives, he
served briefly as minister to Russia, then for a decade in the
Senate. He was President Polk's secretary of state and President Pierce's minister to Great Britain. And so he was a
remarkably experienced candidate when he won the Democratic nomination in 1856. However, it is generally agreed
amongst historians that he was the worst US president. He was
unable to hold his own Democratic Party together, which
made a Republican victory in the 1860 election inevitable. His
ditherings and failings are generally regarded as having rendered the Civil War inevitable, too.

Ulysses S. Grant, 18th President 1869–77

Born into a Presbyterian family in Point Pleasant,
Ohio, in 1822, Grant was general-in-chief of the Union Army
from 1864 to 1869 during the American Civil War. His maternal grandfather, John Simpson, was born in 1738 at Ballygawley, County Tyrone, in the north of Ireland and emigrated
to America in 1760. The farmhouse at Ballygawley may be visited today.[215] The cottage has two rooms with mud floors and
has been restored and furnished with functional period pieces,
including a settle bed and dresser. There is also a display of
typical agricultural implements: ploughs, turf creels and a
horse-drawn cart. The adjoining visitor centre tells the full
story of Ulysses S. Grant.

After graduating from West Point, he fought in the Mexican War under General Zachary Taylor. He later left the army,
but at the outbreak of the Civil War, he was appointed to command an unruly volunteer regiment, and by September 1861
he had risen to the rank of brigadier general of volunteers. In
1862, Grant was appointed to the Army of Tennessee. In

Vicksburg, Mississippi and Chattanooga, he impressed Abraham Lincoln with his tenacity and self-reliance, and early in 1864 he was placed in charge of all Northern Armies and promoted to lieutenant general. He put Sherman in charge of the west, and worked closely with George G. Meade's Army of the Potomac. Together they led the driving advances against General Robert E. Lee, whom Grant was finally able to corner at Appomattox Court House.

After the war, he was advanced to general-in-chief and served momentarily as secretary of war under Andrew Johnson, but he quarrelled with the president and aligned himself with the Radical Republicans for whom he was their logical candidate for president in 1868. He became the first president since Andrew Jackson to serve for two terms. A nominal Presbyterian throughout his life, he attended Metropolitan Methodist church while he was president.

Chester Alan Arthur, 21st President 1881–85

The son of a Baptist preacher who had emigrated from County Antrim, Ireland, Arthur was born in Fairfield, Vermont, in 1829. He practised law in New York City and was appointed collector of the Port of New York by Ulysses S. Grant in 1871. He served briefly as vice president in the Republican administration of James Garfield, and when Garfield was assassinated, he succeeded him as president. The principal issue of his presidency was civil service reform, and the successful passage of the Pendleton Act earned him the title of "The Father of Civil Service". Publisher Alexander K. McClure wrote, "No man ever entered the Presidency so profoundly and widely distrusted, and no one ever retired . . . more generally respected."[216]

Grover Cleveland, 22nd and 24th President 1885–89, 1893–97

Stephen Grover Cleveland was born in 1837 in New Jersey. His father was a Presbyterian minister, originally from Connecticut, and on his mother's side, he was descended from Irish Protestants and German Quakers from Philadelphia. Working as a lawyer in Buffalo, he was elected mayor of Buffalo in 1881 and later governor of New York. He won the presidency with the support both of Democrats and reform Republicans, known as the "Mugwumps", who had strong reservations about the record of his opponent James G. Blaine of Maine.

In 1887, he courted unpopularity on the issue of reducing high protective tariffs, and he was defeated in 1888; although he won a larger popular majority than the Republican candidate Benjamin Harrison, he received fewer electoral votes.

He was re-elected in 1892 at a time of economic depression, and in his second tenure was noted for his forceful treatment of striking railroad workers. He lost the support of his own party, who nominated William Jennings Bryan in 1896.

William McKinley, 25th President 1897–1901

William McKinley was born in 1843 in Ohio, to William and Nancy Alison McKinley from Dervock, County Antrim, Ireland. He is described in some instances as Presbyterian, in other instances as Methodist.

He enlisted as a private in the Union Army in 1861 and rose to the rank of brevet major. Later he studied law, was admitted to the bar in 1867 and served as a Republican in the House of Representatives. He was the foremost proponent of protectionist legislation, favouring a high tariff to keep out imports. From 1892–96, McKinley served as governor of Ohio, and in 1896 he was nominated as the Republican candidate for the presidency.

His administration spanned the important period in which America moved on to the world stage as a major player, principally as a result of the Spanish American War, which resulted in the United States taking possession of Puerto Rico, the Philippines and Guam. Spain capitulated and gave independence to Cuba – the stated goal of the war. McKinley also approved the annexation of Hawaii.

He stood successfully for a second term in 1900, but in 1901 he was shot by an assassin and died.

Theodore Roosevelt, 26th President 1901–09

Some include Roosevelt as an Irish-American president; some do not. With a Dutch paternal grandfather, he was Irish on his mother's side. He himself "was proud of his Dutch roots . . . He was also quick to point out his Scottish, English, French, German, Irish, and Welsh ancestors, and not just at election time."[217] Theodore Roosevelt described his maternal "Scots-Irish" ancestry as "this stern and virile" heritage.

He was a hero of the Spanish-American War, when he served as lieutenant colonel of the Rough Rider Regiment. He also became celebrated for his achievements as a naturalist, explorer, hunter and author. He was elected Republican governor of New York in 1898 and was regarded as a considerable success in the job; two years later he was elected vice president of the United States. Following the assassination of President McKinley, he became, at forty-two, the youngest ever president (John F. Kennedy was the youngest to be *elected* president, at the age of forty-three). He energetically led Congress and the American people toward progressive reforms and a strong foreign policy. His favourite proverb that one should "Speak softly and carry a big stick" remains oft-quoted, and he negotiated an end to the Russo-Japanese War, for which he won the Nobel Peace Prize.

He left the presidency in 1909, but in 1912 he ran for president again under the aegis of his new progressive Bull Moose Party.

Woodrow Wilson, 28th President 1913–21

Woodrow Wilson's paternal grandfather James Wilson emigrated at the age of twenty from the rural townland of Dergalt, in the foothills of the Sperrin Mountains in north Tyrone, Ireland, in 1807. The Wilson Ancestral Home may be visited during the months of July and August and gives an insight into the history of the rich Ulster-American connections. There is a traditional hearth fire, and the carefully conserved rooms are furnished with authentic artefacts.[218]

James Wilson had just completed his apprenticeship as a printer at Gray's Shop at Bridge Street, Strabane, the same print shop which had earlier employed John Dunlap, printer of the first copies of the 4 July 1776 Declaration of Independence and founder of the first American daily newspaper *The Pennsylvania Packet*.

Woodrow Wilson's maternal grandfather, the Rev. Thomas Woodrow, was a Presbyterian native of Paisley in Scotland who moved to America in 1835. Speaking at a St Patrick's Day rally in New York in 1909, when he was president of Princeton University, Woodrow Wilson said: "I myself am happy that there runs in my veins a very considerable strain of Irish blood."

Franklin D. Roosevelt, 32nd President 1933–45

The fifth cousin of President Theodore Roosevelt, Franklin D. Roosevelt also had a Dutch grandfather and an Irish element in his ancestry. Like his cousin, he is regarded by some, but by no means all, as an Irish-American president. He won election to the New York Senate in 1910 and was then appointed assistant secretary of the navy by President Wilson; in 1920 he became the Democratic nominee for vice president. At the 1924 Democratic Convention, he nominated Alfred E. Smith, the first Catholic candidate for the presidency, who failed to get the nomination. Al Smith was born in Manhattan, had Irish, German, Italian and English grandparents, but he became the leading spokesman of the Irish-American community in the 1920s. He won the Democratic nomination in 1928 but was defeated in a landslide by Herbert Hoover. In 1928, Roosevelt succeeded him as governor of New York, and in 1932 was elected president, for the first of four terms.

There were thirteen million unemployed, and almost every bank was closed. He swiftly proposed a sweeping programme to bring recovery, and Congress enacted it. In 1936, he was re-elected with a large majority.

He sought to keep the United States out of the war in Europe, but when the Japanese attacked Pearl Harbor in December 1941, he organised the resources of the United States for war. He sought to plan for a United Nations, in which international difficulties could be resolved, but in April 1945, he died of a cerebral haemorrhage.

John Fitzgerald Kennedy, 35th President 1961–63

The second of nine children born to Joseph and Rose Kennedy, and the great-grandson of eight Irish immigrants, John Fitzgerald Kennedy was the youngest man elected president and the first Catholic; he was also the youngest to die. His great-grandfather, Patrick Kennedy, was born in about 1823 in Dunganstown, County Wexford, Ireland. As the first Catholic president, he was always likely to be celebrated in mostly Catholic Ireland, but he was also young, articulate and seemed a unique beacon of hope in a tired and fearful world; his iconic image resonated with Catholic and Protestant alike.

A Democratic congressman from the Boston area, he moved in 1953 to the Senate. In 1960, he was a first-ballot nominee for president, and he won the election by a narrow margin.

His presidency, though tragically cut short, was full of crucial issues and conflicts: civil and human rights, economic expansion, the role of the arts, world peace, the arms race, the exploration of space, the Bay of Pigs and the Cuban missile crisis, the blockade of Berlin, the Vietnam war.

When he was killed, it was for many in America, Ireland, Europe and the rest of the world as if hope itself had been extinguished.

Lyndon Baines Johnson, 36th President 1963–69

Lyndon Baines Johnson was a son of Samuel Ealy Johnson Jr. and Rebekah Baines, and the Johnson family were originally of Ulster Protestant and English ancestry. On his mother's side, he was descended from a pioneer Baptist clergyman, George Washington Baines.

In 1937, he campaigned successfully for the House of Representatives on a New Deal platform, and after six terms in the House was elected to the Senate in 1948. In 1953, he became the youngest minority leader in Senate history. The following year he became majority leader, and he secured passage of several key Eisenhower measures.

In 1960, Johnson, as John F. Kennedy's running mate, was elected vice president. On 22 November 1963, when Kennedy was assassinated, Johnson was sworn in as president. In 1964, he won the presidency with 61 per cent of the vote, the widest popular margin in American history.

Congress rapidly enacted his Great Society programme, and millions of elderly people benefitted through the 1965 Medicare amendment. However, his presidency was marked by unrest and rioting in black ghettoes at home and the Vietnam War abroad. When he left office, peace talks had started but had not concluded when he died suddenly of a heart attack in early 1973.

Richard Milhous Nixon, 37th President 1969–74

Born in 1913 in California to Francis Anthony Nixon, a Methodist, and Hannah Milhous Nixon, a Quaker. The Nixons were "Scots-Irish", the Milhouses of Irish and English descent. His Milhous ancestors came from Timahoe, County Kildare, Ireland, where Thomas Millhouse was born in 1699 and married Sarah Miller; they emigrated to the Pennsylvania colony in Philadelphia just before the war of the American Revolution. Both were Quakers, and a map of Kildare for the year 1752 shows a Quaker Meeting House in Timahoe near the ruins of the castle of the Fitzgeralds.

After a brilliant academic career, he took up law and in World War II served in the navy. After the war he was elected to Congress, in 1950 to the Senate. Two years later, at only thirty-nine, he was selected by General Eisenhower as his running mate and served as an active vice president. He ran for the presidency in 1960, losing out narrowly to John F. Kennedy. In 1968, he defeated Democratic Vice President Hubert H. Humphrey and third-party candidate George C. Wallace to become president. In 1972, he defeated George McGovern by a wide margin.

Within months, he was embattled over the "Watergate" scandal, which stemmed from a break-in at the offices of the Democratic National Committee during the election campaign. However, during this period he achieved much in the pursuit of greater world stability, reducing tensions with China and the USSR, announced an agreement with North Vietnam to end American involvement in Indochina, and in 1974 his secretary of state, Henry Kissinger, negotiated accords between Israel and its opponents, Egypt and Syria. But in the same year, facing impeachment, he announced his resignation.

James Earl Carter, 39th President 1977–81

A Baptist of Irish ancestry; the first of the "Scotch-Irish" Carters arrived in Virginia in the eighteenth century some time before the Revolutionary War, and later the family moved to the southwestern Georgia hamlet of Plains, where James Earl was born in 1924.

After seven years as a naval officer, Jimmy Carter served two terms in the Georgia Senate, and in 1970 he was elected governor of Georgia. He ran a successful campaign to be the Democratic candidate for the presidency in 1976 and was elected in 1977 after defeating the incumbent President Ford.

He is widely perceived to have achieved more after his presidency than during it, and he is the only US president to have received the Nobel Peace Prize after leaving office. For more than the last year of his administration, his presidency was dominated by the Iran hostage crisis, which contributed to his loss of popularity and his defeat in the presidential campaign of 1980 by Ronald Reagan.

Ronald Wilson Reagan, 40th President 1981–89

Ronald Wilson Reagan was born in 1911 to Nelle and John Reagan in Tampico, Illinois, and his great-grandfather, Michael Reagan, is thought to have come from Ballyporeen, County Tipperary, which lies just about fifty miles south of the birthplace of the Kearneys, Moneygall. His father was a Catholic and his mother a Protestant, and he was raised a Protestant while his brother was raised a Catholic.

He made more than fifty films during twenty years in Hollywood, where he became president of the Screen Actors

Guild. Elected governor of California in 1966, he was re-elected in 1970. He won the Republican presidential nomination in 1980, and voters disenchanted with Jimmy Carter, inflation and the Iran hostage crisis elected him and his vice presidential running mate George Bush by a large majority. They won again in 1984 with an unprecedented number of electoral votes.

Tax reform was a hallmark of his domestic policy, and in foreign policy he sought to achieve "peace through strength".

George Herbert Walker Bush, 41st President 1989–93

A great-great-great-great-grandfather of George Bush was William Holliday, born in Rathfriland, County Down, about 1755, while a great-great-great-great-great-great-grandfather, William Shannon, was born in Cork about 1730. However, the Bush ancestry is overwhelmingly English.

Born in Milton, Massachusetts, in 1924, he flew fifty-eight combat missions during World War II and was awarded the Distinguished Flying Cross. He worked in the oil industry of west Texas, and he served two terms as a representative to Congress from Texas. He was appointed to a series of high-level posts: ambassador to the United Nations, chairman of the Republican National Committee, chief of the US Liaison Office in the People's Republic of China, and director of the Central Intelligence Agency. In 1980 he campaigned for the Republican nomination for president, losing out to Ronald Reagan, who chose him as his vice presidential running mate.

In 1988, he won the Republican nomination for president and defeated Michael Dukakis in the general election. His presidency was marked by the collapse of the Soviet Union and the war against Saddam Hussein's Iraq known as "Desert Storm". In 1992, he failed to be re-elected, losing out to Bill Clinton.

William Jefferson Clinton, 42nd President 1993–2001

Clinton's ancestry is principally English and Southern, but with Irish elements. Two of his great-great-grandparents, named Ayers and Hayes, were born in Ireland. His mother Virginia Dell Cassidy's ancestry has been traced back to Zachariah Cassidy, born about 1750, probably in South Carolina, whose father may have come from the north of Ireland.

President Clinton was born William Jefferson Blythe III in 1946, in Hope, Arkansas, three months after his father died in a traffic accident. When he was four years old, his mother married Roger Clinton, and William took the family name.

He received a law degree from Yale University and entered politics in Arkansas. In 1974, he was defeated in his campaign for Congress, but in 1976 he was elected Arkansas attorney general, and in 1978 he became governor. He failed to be elected for a second term, but four years later was governor again, serving until he defeated George Bush and Ross Perot in the 1992 presidential election.

George W. Bush, 43rd President 2001–09

Inheriting much the same ancestry as his father, George W. Bush was born in 1946, in New Haven, Connecticut, to Barbara and George H.W. Bush. Barbara Pierce Bush is the daughter of publisher Marvin Pierce, whose ancestor, an early New England colonist of English origin named Thomas Pierce, was also an ancestor of Franklin Pierce, the 14th president of the United States. In 1948, the family moved to Texas, where George Bush Jr grew up in Midland and Houston.

In 1994, George W. Bush was elected the 46th governor of Texas; he was re-elected in 1998. In 2000, he was elected president and faced the greatest challenge of his first term on 11 September 2001. He engaged the United States in wars in

Afghanistan and Iraq, reformed the intelligence community and established the Department of Homeland Security.

There is relatively little consciousness in Ireland of the Irish ancestry of most of these presidents. So it was perhaps not surprising that when in 2009 an Irish television station broadcast a six-part documentary series on Irish-American attempts to win the presidency, it ignored all but one of the Irish-American presidents, and focused exclusively on Catholic Irish Americans.[219]

John F. Kennedy, the one Catholic president, occupies an iconic position in Irish consciousness. His story is a narrative of which Irish people can feel proud, can celebrate a triumphant emergence out of the catastrophe of the Famine and the decades of emigration that followed it. It is the story of the triumph of hope and achievement after tragedy and desolation. And the triumph stands not just in isolation as one man's achievement but as a kind of vindication and emblem of those millions who emigrated from Ireland and engaged in the struggle to make lives for themselves and their families in a new world.

So, what does it matter if the Protestant Irish presidents are ignored? It matters because the true story of the Irish in America – and the Irish in Ireland – encompasses Irish people of various religious and ethnic backgrounds. Ireland, which in recent centuries experienced so little immigration and so much emigration, is a country made up of many elements, and its exiles have also reflected this variety. The Old English in Ireland were Catholics; amongst the Old Irish were both Protestants and Catholics. Elizabethan English settlers came to be "more Irish than the Irish themselves". Many of the most prominent Irish families were of Norman origin – Fitzgeralds, Burkes and so on. There were the Gaelic-speaking people of

Dalriada, who came to be called "Scotch-Irish"; the Huguenots who came to Ireland in search of religious freedom; the Cromwellian soldiers granted lands; the lowland Scots who came as settlers to secure Ireland as a British colony; the Quakers who led the fight to end slavery. All were or became Irish.

In recent years, between about 1995 and 2008, a great many immigrants arrived and settled in Ireland; children of African and eastern European parentage were born as Irish citizens. Whatever Irishness or Irish identity may have been in the past was always more diverse than the monocultural myth of "Catholic Ireland". Now the people of this small island have gained new diversity; and Irishness – so often associated with its development outside Ireland – continues to grow and develop in its home place.

Appendix 1

COMPTON CEMETERY INSCRIPTIONS

1. "SACRED/ To the Memory of/
THOMAS KEARNEY Sen./ who was born in Moneygall
Kings/County Ireland/ Apr 15 1765/ Died Sep 23 1846
Aged 81 Yrs/ 5 months & 8 days"

2. "SACRED/ To the Memory of/ SARAH/ Consort of
Thomas Kearney/ Born in Frederick Co Virginia/July 23
1774, died Jan 3/ 1845 Aged 71 years 7 months"

3. "SARAH/ Wife of/ F. Kearney:/ Died/ Apr 15 1893/
Aged/ 82 Years"
(and on the other side of the stone)
"Francis Kearney/ Died/ Feb 3 1848/
aged/ 44 YRS 1 MO/ 8 Ds"
(Francis is also on a large flat stone that is broken and lying
on its back)

4. "SACRED/ To the Memory of/ FRANCIS KEARNEY/
Who was born in Moneygall, Kings County/ Ireland Dec 26
1803 & Died/ Feb 3 1848/ Age 44 Years/ 1 Month & 8
Days"

5. "SACRED/ To the Memory of/ THOMAS KEARNEY/

Who was born in Moneygall, Kings County/Ireland Oct 22 1800 Died/ July 26 1845/ Aged 44 Years 9 Mo & 4 Ds"

6. "SACRED/ To the Memory of/ SARAH wife of/ Richard Hunt/ Was born in Moneygall/Kings County Ireland June/ 1793 and Died May 6/ 1852 Aged 58 Years 11 Months"

7. "RICHARD HUNT/ Died/ July 10 1873/ Aged 63 Years"

8. "In Memory of/ THOMAS KEARNEY/ Who was born in Moneygall Kings County/ Ireland July 1808 & Died April 27"

9. "To the Memory of/ JOSEPH KEARNEY Sen./ ????/ Moneygall Kings County Ireland/Died Oct 30 1861/ Aged 67 Years"

10. "To the Memory of/ WILLIAM KEARNEY/ Born in Moneygall/ Kings County/ June 24th 1833/And departed this life/ October 1st 1855/ Aged/ 22 years 3 Mo & 6 Days"

11. "Deborah/ Wife of/ J. Kearney/ Died/ Nov 3 1870/ Aged 92 Years"
(And on the other side:)
"John Kearney/ Died / Dec 20 1870/ Aged/ 89 Years"
(On the front of a post style stone)

12. "SARAH/ wife of/ F. Kearney/ Died/ Apr 15 1893/ Aged/ 82 years"
(On the back)
"Francis Kearney/ died/ Feb 3 1848/ aged/ 44 yrs 1 mo/ 8 ds"
(The same Francis was also listed on one of the large flat stones)

13. "SACRED/ To the memory of/ Francis Kearney/ Who was born in Moneygall, Kings County/Ireland Dec 26 1803 & Died/ Feb 3 1848 Aged 44 Years/ 1 Month & 8 Days"

14. "Joseph/ Son of/ J. & D. Kearney/ died/ Aug 11 1868/ Aged 54 yrs"

15. "Phebe/ wife of/ Joseph Kearney/ died/ May 25, 1876/ Aged/ 72 years"

16. "SACRED/ To the memory of/ John Kearney/ who died Feb 13 1839/ aged 20 years 6 months"

17. "SACRED/ In the memory of/ Mary wife of/ Samuel Hays/ Born Aug 3 1797 Died/ June 21 1835/ Aged/ ????"

18. "In memory of/ ???? Son of/ Francis & Sarah/ Kearney was born/ April 5, 1847/ and died July 13/ aged 3 mos & 8 days"

19. "In memory of/ Frances dau of/ Francis & Sarah/ Kearney/ ???? 1848/ Died 22 ??? Aged 17/ days"

20. "Jesse, son of/ J & E Kearney/ died/ Aug 12 1854/ aged/ 11 mos 5 dys"

21. "Alice/ wife of/ Wm Kearney/ Died/ Mar 2 1869/ Aged 41 yrs 9 mo/ & 2 da"

22. "Wm Kearney/ died/ Sept 13 1868/ aged/ 56 yrs 4 mos/ & 12 Ds"

23. "Little Willie/ Son of/ Wm & M/ Clary/ died/ July 13, 1851/ aged 6 mos"

24. "William/ CLEARY/ Died/ Sep 8 1862/ Aged/ 60 years"

25. "Mary Kearney/ wife of/ John F. Hill/ May 29 1866/ Aged/ 28 yrs 6 ms 5 dys"

NEW HOLLAND CEMETERY INSCRIPTIONS
1.
ELEANOR R.A.
WIFE OF J. KEARNEY
DIED
SEPT. 24, 1890
AGED
68 YEARS
JAMES KEARNEY
DIED
FEB 5, 1887 [*Sic:* actually 1888; ref diary of Abraham
Lincoln Kearney]
AGED
76 Y 2M 21D
2.
[Right side inscription]
WILLIAM
KEARNEY
Aug 17, 1842
Nov 27, 1897
[Inscription on top]
Alice

Feb 14, 1866
Sept 26, 1881
Lillie Dean
Sept 14, 1896
Jan 26, 1897
3.
FATHER
Wm Kearney
Co. H
The metal star and flag holder:
Our Defender 61–65

Endnotes

1. Inaugural Address, 20 January 2009.
2. Tom Inglis, *The Irish Times*, 24 August 2009.
3. "Irish-American a Key Member of Obama's Inner Circle", *The Irish Times*, 1 March 2010.
4. See Richard K. MacMaster, *Scotch-Irish Merchants in Colonial America* (Belfast: Ulster Historical Foundation, 2010).
5. LeRoy James Votto, "Social Dynamism in a Boom Town: The Scots-Irish in Baltimore 1760 to 1790," MA thesis, University of Virginia, 1969.
6. Audrey Lockhart, *Some Aspects of Emigration from Ireland to the North American Colonies Between 1660 and 1775* (New York, 1976), quoted in Richard K. MacMaster: *Scotch-Irish Merchants in Colonial America* (Ulster Historical Foundation, Belfast, 2010).
7. *Londonderry Journal,* 4 June 1773, quoted in Richard K. MacMaster: *Scotch-Irish Merchants in Colonial America* (Ulster Historical Foundation, 2010).
8. *Maryland Journal and Baltimore Advertiser,* 16 October 1773, quoted in Richard K. MacMaster: *Scotch-Irish Merchants in Colonial America* (Ulster Historical Foundation, 2010).
9. Richard K. MacMaster, *Scotch-Irish Merchants in Colonial America* (Ulster Historical Foundation, 2010).
10. Timothy Meagher, *The Columbia Guide to Irish American History.* (New York: Columbia University Press, 2005).
11. W.E. MacClenny, *The Life of Rev. James O'Kelly* (Suffolk: Cushing-Malloy, Inc., 1950; first pub. 1910).
12. Abel Stevens, *History of the Methodist Episcopal Church in the United States of America* (Nampa, Idaho: Wesley Center for Applied Theology of Northwest Nazarene University, 2000).
13. The quotations are from letters of "John Shillington, Esq., of Ireland, in the possession of the author" (Abel Stevens).

14. Quoted in Abel Stevens, *History of the Methodist Episcopal Church in the United States of America* (Nampa, Idaho: Wesley Center for Applied Theology of Northwest Nazarene University, 2000).

15. Abel Stevens, *History of the Methodist Episcopal Church in the United States of America* (Nampa, Idaho: Wesley Center for Applied Theology of Northwest Nazarene University, 2000).

16. Dee Andrews, *The Methodists and Revolutionary America, 1760–1800* (Princeton: Princeton Univesity Press, 2000).

17. Abel Stevens, *History of the Methodist Episcopal Church in the United States of America* (Nampa, Idaho: Wesley Center for Applied Theology of Northwest Nazarene University, 2000).

18. Dee Andrews, *The Methodists and Revolutionary America, 1760–1800* (Princeton: Princeton Univesity Press, 2000).

19. Russel Richey, *Early American Methodism* (Bloomington: Indiana University Press, 1991).

20. Gregory A. Stiverson, *Poverty in a Land of Plenty: Tenancy in Eighteenth-Century Maryland* (Baltimore: Johns Hopkins University Press, 1977), p. xiii.

21. Grady McWhiney, *Cracker Culture* (Tuscaloosa: University of Alabama Press, 1988), p. 6.

22. Edward MacLysaght, *Irish Life in the Seventeenth Century* (Dublin: Talbot Press, 1939), p. 280.

23. http://www.nyaoh.com/History_Articles/09%2007%20Washington's%20Irish.pdf.

24. *Ibid.*

25. Samuel Hood, George Campbell, Joseph Jones, A Brief Account of the Society of the Friendly Sons of St. Patrick (Philadelphia: Hibernian Society, 1844).

26. Kerby A. Miller, *Emigrants and Exiles: Ireland and the Irish Exodus to North America* (Oxford: Oxford University Press, 1985), p. 132.

27. *Ibid.*, p. 133.

28. Edward T. McCarron, "In pursuit of the 'Maine' chance: the North family of Offaly and New England, 1700–1776 in William Nolan and Timothy P. O'Neill (eds.), *Offaly: History and Society.* (Dublin: Geography Publications, 1998.).

29. Anthony Cronin, *Heritage Now: Irish Literature in the English Language.* (Dingle: Brandon, 1982).

30. Dunbar to Board of Trade, 9 October 1729, *Baxter Manuscripts*, x, p. 440.

31. Edward T. McCarron, "In pursuit of the 'Maine' chance: the North family of Offaly and New England, 1700–1776 in William Nolan and Timothy P. O'Neill (eds.), *Offaly: History and Society.* (Dublin: Geography Publications, 1998.).

32. James Ware, Walter Harris (ed. and trans.) *The Whole Works of Sir James Ware Concerning Ireland,* Volume I, (Dublin, 1739).

33. Rev. James B. Leslie *Ossory Clergy and Parishes* (Enniskillen, 1933).
34. *Guild of Barber Surgeons & Periwig makers, Minute Book 1706–57*, TCD Library, Manuscripts Dept. Ms. 1447/8/1.
35. See Early Printed Books, in the Trinity College Library.
36. Fergus Whelan, *Dissent into Treason* (Dingle: Brandon, 2010), chapter 8.
37. Michael Kearney, *Lectures Concerning History Read during the Year 1775* (Dublin: William Hallhead, 1776).
38. Quoted in the Oxford Dictionary of National Biography (Oxford: OUP, 2004).
39. http://www.heritagecouncil.ie/about-us/headquarters/.
40. Miller, *Emigrants and Exiles*.
41. Ruan O'Donnell, "King's County in 1798" in William Nolan and Timothy P. O'Neill (eds.), *Offaly: History and Society* (Dublin: Geography Publications, 1998).
42. *Ibid.*
43. Colin Murphy and Lynne Adair (eds.), *Untold Stories: Protestants and the Republic of Ireland 1922–2002* (Dublin: The Liffey Press, 2002).
44. Whelan, *Dissent into Treason*, chapter 18.
45. Marianne Elliott, *When God Took Sides* (Oxford: Oxford University Press, 2009), pp. 42–43.
46. Timothy Meagher, *The Columbia Guide to Irish American History* (New York: Columbia University Press, 2005).
47. *Journal of American Ethnic History*, vol. 28, no. 4 (Summer 2009).
48. Miller, *Emigrants and Exiles*.
49. M. A. Jones, "Ulster Emigration, 1783–1815" in E. R. R. Green (ed.), *Essays in Scotch-Irish History* (London: Humanities Press Intl., 1969), p. 67.
50. Andrew Lee Feight, "Land Speculation, Lawlessness, and the Establishment of Seats of Government in Ohio's Scioto Country, 1783–1807" from *Borderland and Backcountry: Frontier Communities in Comparative Perspective,* University of Dundee, Scotland, July 2009.
51. *Ibid.*
52. Alan Taylor, "Land and Liberty on the Frontier", in David Thomas Konig ed. *Devising Liberty: Preserving and Creating Freedom in the New American Republic* (Stanford: Stanford University Press, 1995).
53. Feight, "Land Speculation, Lawlessness, and the Establishment of Seats of Government in Ohio's Scioto Country, 1783–1807".
54. *Ibid.*
55. R. T. Stevenson, *One Hundred Years of Methodism in Ohio* (Cincinnati: 1898), p. 8.

56. Isaac J Finley and Rufus Putnam, *Pioneer Record and Reminiscences of the Early Settlers and Settlement of Ross County, Ohio* (Cincinnati: R. Clarke & Co., 1871).
57. George Perkins, *Pioneer Sketches: Life in the Northwest Territory and Ross County, Ohio, 1600s–1896* (Chillicothe: Ross County Genealogical Society, 1999).
58. Henry Holcomb Bennett, *A History of Ross County, Ohio, from the Earliest-Days, with Special Chapters on the Bench and Bar, Medical Profession, Educational Development, Industry and Agriculture and Biographical Sketches.* (Madison: 1902).
59. *Ibid.*
60. *Ibid.*
61. Isaac J Finley and Rufus Putnam, *Pioneer Record and Reminiscences of the Early Settlers and Settlement of Ross County, Ohio* (Cincinnati: R. Clarke & Co., 1871).
62. *Ibid.*
63. Bennett, *A History of Ross County, Ohio.*
64. *Ibid.*
65. T. A. Jackson, *Ireland Her Own* (London: Lawrence & Wishart, 1976), p. 164.
66. Bennett, *A History of Ross County, Ohio.*
67. *Ibid.*
68. Samuel Wesley Williams, *Pictures of Early Methodism in Ohio* (Cincinnati: 1909), p. 35.
69. Stevenson, *One Hundred Years of Methodism in Ohio*, p. 3.
70. *Ibid.*, p. 5.
71. *Ibid.*, p. 10.
72. Merle C. Rummel, *Four Mile Community* (1998), http://www.union-county.lib.in.us/GenwebVA4mile/Table%20of%20Contents%204M.htm.
73. Stevenson, *One Hundred Years of Methodism in Ohio*, p. 10.
74. Rummel, *Four Mile Community.*
75. Walter A. Hazen *Everyday Life: The Frontier* (Tucson: Good Year Books, 1998).
76. Stevenson, *One Hundred Years of Methodism in Ohio*, p. 10.
77. Williams, *Pictures of Early Methodism*, p. 40.
78. *Ibid.*, p. 35.
79. *Ibid.*
80. *Ibid.*
81. *Ibid.*
82. *Ibid.*
83. *Ibid.*
84. *Ibid.*
85. Stevenson, *One Hundred Years of Methodism in Ohio*, p. 11.

86. Sir Charles Coote, *Statistical Survey of the King's County* (Dublin: Graisberry & Campbell, 1801).

87. *Ibid.*

88. *Ibid.*

89. *Ibid.*

90. Jonathan Binns, *Miseries and Beauties of Ireland* (London: 1836), pp. 60–61.

91. Valentine Trodd, *Midlanders* (Banaher: 1994), pp. 13–14.

92. Binns, *Miseries and Beauties of Ireland*, p. 62.

93. Donald Harmon Akenson, *Small Differences: Irish Catholics and Irish Protestants,1815–1923* (Dublin: Gill and Macmillan, 1991), p. 26.

94. Cormac O'Grada, "Did Ulster Catholics Always Have Larger Families?", *Irish Economic and Social History*, vol. 12 (Londonderry: University of Ulster, 1991), p. 86.

95. A.C. Hepburn, "Work, Class and Religion in Belfast, 1871–1911", *Irish Economic and Social History* vol. 10 (Londonderry: 1983), p. 52.

96. Akenson, *Small Difference*, p. 37.

97. J. J. Lee, *Modernisation of Irish Society, 1848–1918* (Dublin: Gill and Macmillan, 1973), p. 6.

98. *First Report of the Commissioners Supplement to Appendix B* (369) XXXII, Part II (1835).

99. *Farnham Papers*, Ms. 18604/2 N. L. Manuscript Room.

100. W. R. LeFanu, *Seventy Years: Being Anecdotes and Reminiscences.* (London: Edward Arnold, 1893).

101. Binns, *Miseries and Beauties of Ireland.*

102. Asenath Nicholson, *Ireland's Welcome to the Stranger* (New York: 1847), pp. 146–49.

103. *Ibid.*

104. *Ibid.*

105. *Ibid.*

106. *Ibid.*

107. Pliny A. Durant, *History of Union County, Ohio* (Chicago: W. H. Beer & Co., 1883).

108. *Ibid.*

109. Ann Hagedorn, *Beyond the River: The Untold Story of the Heroes of the Underground Railroad* (New York: Simon & Schuster, 2002).

110. *Ibid.*

111. Frederick Douglass, Philip S. Foner (ed.), *Life and Writings of Frederick Douglass,* vol. 1 (New York: International Publishers, 1950), p. 120.

112. Patricia J. Ferreira, "Frederick Douglas in Ireland: The Dublin Edition of His Narrative", *New Hibernian Review / Iris Éireannach Nua,* 5:1 (Spring / Earrach, 2001), pp. 53–97.

113. Douglass, *Life and Writings of Frederick Douglass.*
114. Ferreira, "Frederick Douglas in Ireland: The Dublin Edition of His Narrative".
115. *Ibid.*
116. Douglass, *Life and Writings of Frederick Douglass.*
117. Ferreira, "Frederick Douglas in Ireland: The Dublin Edition of His Narrative".
118. William S. McFeely, *Frederick Douglass* (New York: Simon and Schuster, 1991), p. 119.
119. Ferreira, "Frederick Douglas in Ireland: The Dublin Edition of His Narrative".
120. Therese Abbott, "Quakerism in the Edenderry Area 1673–1831", *Offaly Heritage, Journal of the Offaly Historical and Archaeological Society*, vol. 2 (2004).
121. Rev. M. Comerford, *Collections Relating to the Dioceses of Kildare & Loughlin*, 3 vols. (Dublin: 1883), vol. i, p. 270.
122. Abbott, "Quakerism in the Edenderry Area 1673–1831".
123. Rev. J.P. Holmes of Gallan (Ferbane), cited in Timothy P. O'Neill, "The Famine in Offaly" in *Offaly: History and Society*, p. 686.
124. Marianne Elliott, *When God Took Sides* (Oxford: Oxford University Press, 2009), p. 2.
125. *Tipperary Vindicator*, 22 August 1846.
126. Quoted in Steuart W. Trench, *Realities of Irish Life* (London: 1869).
127. *Transactions of the Central Relief Committee of the Society of Friends during the Famine in Ireland, in 1846 and 1847* (Dublin: Hodges and Smith, 1852).
128. Thomas P. Power, *Land, Politics, and Society in Eighteenth-Century Tipperary* (Oxford: Oxford University Press, 1993).
129. Timothy P. O'Neill, "The Famine in Offaly" in Nolan, William and O'Neill, Timothy P. eds. *Offaly: History and Society* (Dublin: Geography Publications, 1998).
130. The Will of Francis Kearney (Recorded at the Pickaway County Courthouse, Circleville, Ohio. Case No. 4093).
131. *New Ross Standard* 30 April 1851.
132. Irene Whelan, "Religious Rivalry and the Making of Irish-American Identity", in J.J. Lee and Marion Casey, eds., *Making the Irish American* (New York: NYU Press, 2006), p. 279.
133. Alan Taylor, "Land and Liberty on the Frontier", in David Thomas Konig ed. *Devising Liberty: Preserving and Creating Freedom in the New American Republic* (Stanford: Stanford University Press, 1995).
134. Hon. W.S. Haymond, *History of Indiana* (Indianapolis: 1879).
135. *Ibid.*
136. *Ibid.*
137. *Ibid.*

138. *Ibid.*
139. See Census.
140. Census of 1880.
141. Note: Labette County records for the 1870s are unavailable.
142. See Census.
143. William G. Cutler, *A History of the State of Kansas* (Chicago: A. T. Andreas, 1883).
144. Bennett, *A History of Ross County, Ohio.*
145. Interview with the author, February 2010.
146. Interview with the author, March 2010.
147. Interview with the author, October 2009.
148. Quoted from David Nitkin and Harry Merritt, "A new twist to an intriguing family history" in the *Baltimore Sun*, 2 March 2007.
149. http://www.kake.com/home/misc/38157259.html.
150. Ralph E. Dunham, letter to the author, 13 March 2010.
151. *Chicago Sun-Times* interview with Scott Fornek, 9 September 2007.
152. Interview with the author, 29 March 2010.
153. http://www.spiegel.de/international/germany/0,1518,626703, 00.html.
154. Leon Wilburn McCurry, quoted by Scott Fornek, "Harbin Wilburn McCurry: 'I am a Union Man'", *Chicago Sun-Times*, 9 September 9, 2007.
155. Steve Hammons, "Obama's Scottish, Cherokee ancestry has meaning" in *American Chronicle,* October 08, 2008 http://www.americanchronicle.com/articles/view/76976.
156. Ralph E. Dunham, notes to the author, 13 March 2010.
157. Ralph E. Dunham, letter to the author, 13 March 2010.
158. http://peacecorpsonline.typepad.com/poncacitywelovey-ou/2009/02/barack-obamas-mother-lived-in-ponca-city-for-two-years.html.
159. http://texomashomepage.com/content/fulltext/?cid=32911.
160. Quoted from Tim Jones, "Barack Obama: Mother not just a Girl from Kansas; Stanley Ann Dunham Shaped a Future Senator", in the *Chicago Tribune*, 27 March 2007.
161. Quoted in David Maraniss, "Though Obama Had to Leave to Find Himself, It Is Hawaii That Made His Rise Possible", *Washington Post*, 22 August 2008.
162. *Ibid.*
163. *Ibid.*
164. Maxine Box, quoted in Tim Jones: "Barack Obama: Mother not just a Girl from Kansas.
165. John W. Hunt, quoted in David Maraniss, "Though Obama Had to Leave to Find Himself, It Is Hawaii That Made His Rise Possible".
166. Quoted in Tim Jones, "Barack Obama: Mother not just a Girl from Kansas".

167. *Ibid.*
168. Quoted in: Janny Scott, "A Free-Spirited Wanderer Who Set Obama's Path", *The New York Times,* 14 March 2008.
169. Tim Jones, "Barack Obama: Mother not just a Girl from Kansas".
170. Neil Abercrombie, quoted in David Maraniss, "Though Obama Had to Leave to Find Himself, It Is Hawaii That Made His Rise Possible".
171. Quoted *ibid.*
172. David Maraniss, "Though Obama Had to Leave to Find Himself, It Is Hawaii That Made His Rise Possible".
173. *Ibid.*
174. *Ibid.*
175. Quoted in Janny Scott, "A Free-Spirited Wanderer Who Set Obama's Path".
176. *Ibid.*
177. *Ibid.*
178. Barack Obama, *Dreams from My Father* (New York: Crown, 2004).
179. Amanda Ripley, "The Story of Barack Obama's Mother", *Time,* 4 April 2008.
180. Quoted in Tim Jones, "Barack Obama: Mother not just a girl from Kansas; Stanley.
181. David Mendell, *Obama: From Promise to Power,* p. 82.
182. Quoted in John Patrick Koval (ed.), *The New Chicago: a Social and Cultural Analysis* (Philadelphia: Temple University Press, 2006).
183. David Mendell, *Obama: From Promise to Power,* p. 110.
184. Bill Clinton, *My Life,* p. 686.
185. http://www.irishabroad.com/news/irish-voice/news/Articles/obama-statement280808.aspx.
186. *Ibid.*
187. Interview in *The Irish Times,* 25 September 2008.
188. Interview with Conor Begley, tax director with the international accounting and consulting company Grant Thornton, in *The Irish Times,* 3 November 2008.
189. Interview in the *Sunday Tribune,* 9 November 2008.
190. http://thecaucus.blogs.nytimes.com/2008/10/20/obama-leavingtrail-to-visit-ailing-grandmother/.
191. "Irish-American a key member of Obama's inner circle" *The Irish Times,* 1 March 2010.
192. http://usliberals.about.com/b/2009/11/17/2010-immigrationreform-agenda-set-by-obama-administration.htm.
193. http://www.irishcentral.com/story/news/periscope/obama-saysyes-we-can-to-immigration-reform-82872537.html.
194. Ray O'Hanlon, *The Irish Echo,* 3 February 2010.

195. http://www.irishcentral.com/story/news/periscope/?month=February&year=2010.

196. www.finalcall.com/artman/publish/National_News_2/Obama_candidacy_exposes_race_hatred_in_America_5399.shtml.

197. http://www.scientificamerican.com/podcast/episode.cfm?id=whats-behind-birthers-obama-belief-09-08-10.

198. http://althouse.blogspot.com/2009/09/jimmy-carter-says-there-is-inherent.html.

199. Barnett v. Obama. Case No. SACV 09–0082 DOC (ANx), United States District Court for the Central District of California, 29 October 2009.

200. Dermot Keogh, *Irishness in a Changing Society* (Gerard's Cross: 1988); quoted in Elliott, *When God Took Sides*, p. 47.

201. Colin Murphy and Lynne Adair (eds.), *Untold Stories: Protestants and the Republic of Ireland 1922–2002* (Dublin: The Liffey Press, 2002).

202. MacLysaght, *Irish Life in the Seventeenth Century*, pp. 281–82.

203. Akenson, *Small Difference*, p. 4.

204. Elliott, *When God Took Sides*, p. 14.

205. *Obstacles to Peace Building in the Republic of Ireland* (Irish Peace and Reconciliation Platform, 2000).

206. *Ibid.*

207. Ernest Tilson, a father of three children, was Protestant, but on his marriage to a Catholic had agreed that his children be raised Catholic. When the marriage hit problems, he removed the children. The judge ruled in favour of the Catholic mother on the grounds that the special position of the Catholic church in the constitution meant that the judicial system should reflect Catholic canon law.

208. Colin Murphy and Lynne Adair (eds.), *Untold Stories: Protestants and the Republic of Ireland 1922–2002* (Dublin: The Liffey Press, 2002).

209. Heather K. Crawford, *Outside the Glow: Protestants and Irishness in Independent Ireland* (Dublin: University College Dublin Press, 2010).

210. *Report of the Commission to Inquire into Child Abuse* (Dublin, Government Publications, 2009).

211. Elliott, *When God Took Sides*, p. 28.

212. *Obstacles to Peace Building in the Republic of Ireland* (Irish Peace and Reconciliation Platform, 2000).

213. *Independent Catholic News*, 29 January 2010 http://www.indcatholicnews.com/news.php?viewStory=15553.

214. http://www.burkespeerage.com/articles/america/APF-WASHINGTON-1-FESS-nonsub.aspx.

215. See http://www.geographia.com/northern-ireland/ukiher01.htm.

216. http://www.whitehouse.gov/about/presidents/ChesterArthur.

217. Hans P. Vought, *The Bully Pulpit and the Melting Pot: American Presidents and the Immigrant, 1897/1933* (Macon: Mercer University Press, 2004).
218. See http://www.irishtourist.com/details/the_wilson_ancestral_home. shtml.
219. *Bóthar go dtí an White House* (The Road to the White House), TG4.

Bibliography

Abbott, Therese. "Quakerism in the Edenderry Area 1673–1831", *Offaly Heritage, Journal of the Offaly Historical and Archaeological Society,* vol. 2. Tullamore, 2004.

Akenson, Donald Harman. *Small Difference: Irish Catholics and Irish Protestants, 1815–1922.* Dublin: Gill and Macmillan, 1991.

Andrews, Dee E. *The Methodists ad Revolutionary America, 1760–1800: The Shaping of an Evangelical Culture.* Princeton: Princeton University Press, 2002.

Bennett, Henry Holcomb. *A History of Ross County, Ohio, from the Earliest-Days, with Special Chapters on the Bench and Bar, Medical Profession, Educational Development, Industry and Agriculture and Biographical Sketches.* Madison: 1902.

Binns, Jonathan. *Miseries and Beauties of Ireland.* London: 1836.

Brundage, David. "Recent Directions in the History of Irish American Nationalism", *Journal of American Ethnic History,* vol. 28, no. 4, Summer 2009.

Clinton, Bill. *My Life.* London: Arrow Books, 2005.

Coleman, Carole. *The Battle For The White House.* Dublin: Liffey Press, 2009.

Comerford, Rev. M. *Collections Relating to the Dioceses of Kildare and Loughlin,* 3 vols. Dublin: 1883.

Connolly, S. J. *Religion, Law and Power: The Making of Protestant Ireland 1660–1760.* Oxford: Oxford University Press, 1992.

Coote, Sir Charles *Statistical Survey of the King's County* Dublin: Graisberry & Campbell, 1801.

Crawford, Heather K. *Outside the Glow: Protestants and Irishness in Independent Ireland.* Dublin: University College Dublin Press, 2010.

Cronin, Anthony. *Heritage Now: Irish Literature in the English Language*. Dingle: Brandon, 1982.

Cutler, William G. *A History of the State of Kansas*. Chicago: A. T. Andreas, 1883.

Douglass, Frederick; Foner, Philip S. ed. *Life and Writings of Frederick Douglass*, vol. 1. New York: International Publishers, 1950.

Douglass, Frederick. *Narrative of the Life of Frederick Douglass*. Dublin: 1845.

Durant, Pliny A. *History of Union County, Ohio*. Chicago: W H. Beers & Co., 1883.

Eckert, Allan W. *The Frontiersmen*. Ashland, Kentucky: The Jesse Stuart Foundation, 2001.

Eckert, Allan W. *That Dark and Bloody River*. New York: Bantam, 1995.

Eckert, Allan W. *The Wilderness War*. Ashland, Kentucky: The Jesse Stuart Foundation, 2003.

Elliott, Marianne. *When God Took Sides*. Oxford: Oxford University Press, 2009.

Fanning, Tim. *The Fethard-on-Sea Boycott*. Cork: Collins Press, 2010.

Farnham Papers, Ms. 18604/2 N. L. I. Manuscript Room.

Feight, Andrew Lee. "Land Speculation, Lawlessness, and the Establishment of Seats of Government in Ohio's Scioto Country, 1783–1807", from *Borderland to Backcountry: Frontier Communities in Comparative Perspective*, University of Dundee, Scotland, July 2009.

Ferreira, Patricia J. "Frederick Douglas in Ireland: The Dublin Edition of His Narrative", *New Hibernian Review / Iris Éireannach Nua*, 5:1, Spring / Earrach, 2001.

Finley, Isaac J. and Putnam, Rufus. *Pioneer Record and Reminiscences of the Early Settlers and Settlement of Ross County, Ohio*. Cincinnati: R. Clarke & Co., 1871.

First Report of the Commissioners Supplement to Appendix B (369) XXXII, Part II, 1835.

Foster, Emily ed. *American Grit: A Woman's Letters from the Ohio Frontier*. Lexington: The University Press of Kentucky, 2002.

Foster, Emily ed. *The Ohio Frontier: An Anthology of Early Writings*. Lexington: The University Press of Kentucky, 1996.

Gallagher, Thomas. *Paddy's Lament: Ireland 1846–47: Prelude to Hatred*. New York: Harcourt, 1982.

Bibliography

Gribben, Arthur and Harris, Ruth-Ann M. eds. *The Great Famine and the Irish Diaspora in America*. Amherst: The University of Massachusetts Press, 1999.

Griffin, Patrick. *The People with No Name*. Princeton: Princeton University Press, 2001.

Guild of Barber Surgeons & Periwig makers, Minute Book 1706–57, TCD Library, Manuscripts Dept. Ms. 1447/8/1.

Hagedorn, Ann. *Beyond the River: The Untold Story of the Heroes of the Underground Railroad*. New York: Simon & Schuster, 2002.

Haymond, Hon. W.S. *History of Indiana*. Indianapolis, 1879.

Hazen, Walter A. *Everyday Life: The Frontier*. Tucson: Good Year Books, 1998.

Hepburn, A. C. "Work, Class and Religion in Belfast, 1871–1911", *Irish Economic and Social History* 10, 1983.

Hood, Samuel, Campbell, George and Jones, Joseph, *A Brief Account of the Society of the Friendly Sons of St. Patrick*. Philadelphia: Hibernian Society, 1844.

Hurt, R. Douglas. *The Ohio Frontier: Crucible of the Old Northwest, 1720–1830*. Bloomington & Indianapolis: Indiana University Press, 1998.

Jackson, T. A. *Ireland Her Own*. London: Lawrence & Wishart, 1976.

Jones, M. A. "Ulster Emigration, 1783–1815" in E. R. R. Green, ed. *Essays in Scotch-Irish History*. London: Humanities Press Intl, 1969.

Kearney, John. *Alphabet of the Irish Language and Catechism*. See Ó Cearnaigh, Seán. *Aibidil Gaoidheilge agus Caiticíosma*.

Kearney, Michael. *Lectures Concerning History Read during the Year 1775*. Dublin: William Hallhead, 1776.

Keogh, Dermot. "Catholicism and the Formation of the Modern.

Irish Society" *Irishness in a Changing Society*. Gerard's Cross: Colin Smythe Ltd., 1988.

Konig, David Thomas ed. *Devising Liberty: Preserving and Creating Freedom in the New American Republic*. Stanford: Stanford University Press, 1995.

Koval, John Patrick (ed.). *The New Chicago: a Social and Cultural Analysis* Philadelphia: Temple University Press, 2006.

Lee, J. J. *The Modernisation of Irish Society, 1848–1918*. Dublin: Gill and Macmillan, 1973.

Lee, J. J. and Casey, Marion R., eds. *Making the Irish American*. New York: New York University Press, 2007.

LeFanu, W. R. *Seventy Years: Being Anecdotes and Reminiscences.* London: Edward Arnold, 1893.

Leslie, Rev. James B. *Ossory Clergy and Parishes.* Enniskillen: R. H. Ritchie, 1933.

McBride, Ian ed. *History and Memory in Modern Ireland.* Cambridge: Cambridge University Press, 2001.

McCarron, Edward T. "In pursuit of the 'Maine' chance: the North family of Offaly and New England, 1700–1776 in William Nolan and Timothy P. O'Neill (eds.), *Offaly: History and Society* Dublin: Geography Publications, 1998.

MacClenny, W.E. The Life of Rev. James O'Kelly and the Early History of the Christian Church in the South. 1910 and Suffolk, Va.: Cushing-Malloy, Inc., 1950.

McFeely, William S. *Frederick Douglass.* New York: W. W. Norton & Co., 1991.

McGuinne, Dermot. *Irish Type Design.* Dublin: Irish Academic Press, 1992.

MacLysaght, Edward. *Irish Life in the Seventeenth Century.* Dublin: Talbot Press, 1939.

MacMaster, Richard K. *Scotch-Irish Merchants in Colonial America.* Belfast: Ulster Historical Foundation, 2010.

McWhiney, Grady. *Cracker Culture.* Tuscaloosa: University of Alabama Press, 1988.

Meagher, Timothy. *The Columbia Guide to Irish American History.* New York: Columbia University Press, 2005.

David Mendell. *Obama: From Promise to Power.* New York: HarperCollins, 2008.

MacMahon, Noel. *In the Shadow of the Fairy Hill: Shinrone and Ballingarry – A History.* Kilcommon Press, 1998.

Matthew, H. C. G. (ed), Harrison, Brian (ed) *Oxford Dictionary of National Biography.* Oxford: OUP, 2004.

Miller, Kerby A. *Emigrants and Exiles: Ireland and the Irish Exodus to North America.* Oxford: Oxford University Press, 1985.

Murphy, Colin and Adair, Lynne eds. *Untold Stories: Protestants and the Republic of Ireland 1922–2002.* Dublin: Liffey Press, 2002.

Newman, Harry Wright. *Maryland Revolutionary Records.* Baltimore: Genealogical Publishing, 2002.

Nicholson, Asenath. *Ireland's Welcome to the Stranger.* New York: Baker and Scribner, 1847.

Nolan, William and O'Neill, Timothy P. eds. *Offaly: History and Society.* Dublin: Geography Publications, 1998.

Obama, Barack. *The Audacity of Hope.* New York: Crown, 2006.

Obama, Barack. *Dreams from My Father.* New York: Crown, 2004.

Obstacles to Peace Building in the Republic of Ireland, Irish Peace and Reconciliation Platform, 2000.

Ó Cearnaigh, Seán. *Aibidil Gaoidheilge agus Caiticíosma.* Baile Átha Cliath [Dublin]: 1571.

O'Donnell, Ruan. "King's County in 1798" in Nolan, William and O'Neill, Timothy P. eds. *Offaly: History and Society.* Dublin: Geography Publications, 1998.

O'Grada, Cormac. "Did Ulster Catholics Always Have Larger Families?", *Irish Economic and Social History,* vol. *12.* Londonderry: University of Ulster, 1991.

O'Neill, Timothy P. "The Famine in Offaly" in Nolan, William and O'Neill, Timothy P. eds. *Offaly: History and Society.* Dublin: Geography Publications, 1998.

Ó Riain, Séamus. *Dunkerrin: A Parish in Ely O Carroll.* Dunkerrin: Dunkerrin History Committee, 1988.

Ó Tuathaigh, Gearóid. *Ireland Before the Famine 1798–1848.* Dublin: Gill and Macmillan, 2007.

Peden, Henry C. Jr. *A Guide to Genealogical Research in Maryland.* Baltimore: Maryland Historical Society, 2001.

Perkins, George. *Pioneer Sketches: Life in the Northwest Territory and Ross County, Ohio, 1600s–1896.* Chillicothe: Ross County Genealogical Society, 1999.

Power, Thomas P. *Land, Politics, and Society in Eighteenth-Century Tipperary.* Oxford: Oxford University Press, 1993.

Report of the Commission to Inquire into Child Abuse. Dublin, Government Publications, 2009.

Reynolds, Joshua, Sir, *Discourses* Chicago: A.C. McClurg, 1891.

Richey, Russell. *Early American Methodism.* Bloomington: Indiana University Press, 1991.

Ripley, Amanda. "The Story of Barack Obama's Mother", *Time,* 4 September 2008.

Rummel, Merle C. *Four Mile Community.* 1998. *www.union-county.lib.in.us/GenwebVA4mile/Table%20of%20Contents%204 M.htm.*

Stanage, Niall. *Redemption Song: An Irish Reporter Inside the Obama Campaign.* Dublin: Liberties Press, 2008.

Bibliography

Stevens, Abel. *History of the Methodist Episcopal Church in the United States of America* Nampa, Idaho: Wesley Center for Applied Theology of Northwest Nazarene University, 2000.

Stevenson, R. T. *One Hundred Years of Methodism in Ohio.* Cincinnati: 1898.

Stiverson, Gregory A. *Poverty in a Land of Plenty: Tenancy in Eighteenth-Century Maryland.* Baltimore: Johns Hopkins University Press, 1977.

The Baltimore Directory for 1799, containing the names, occupation, and places of abode of the citizens. (Arranged in alphabetical order by John Mullin.) Baltimore: Warner & Hanna.

The New Baltimore Directory and annual Registers for 1800 and 1801. Baltimore: Warner & Hanna.

The Baltimore Directory for 1802. (By Cornelius William Stafford.) Baltimore: John W. Butler.

The Baltimore Directory for 1803. (By Cornelius William Stafford.) Baltimore: John W. Butler.

The Baltimore Directory for 1804. (By James Robinson). Baltimore: Warner & Hanna.

Thomas, Garen. *Yes We Can.* New York: Fiewel & Friends, 2008.

Tipperary Vindicator, 22 August 1846.

Transactions of the Central Relief Committee of the Society of Friends during the Famine in Ireland, in 1846 and 1847 Dublin: Hodges and Smith, 1852.

Trench, Steuart W. *Realities of Irish Life.* London: 1869.

Trodd, Valentine. *Midlanders.* Banaher: Scéal Publications, 1994.

Vought, Hans P. *The Bully Pulpit and the Melting Pot: American Presidents and the Immigrant, 1897/1933.* Macon: Mercer University Press, 2004.

Ware, James. *The Whole Works of Sir James Ware Concerning Ireland,* Volume I, ed. and trans. Walter Harris, Dublin, 1739.

Webb, Jim. *Born Fighting: How the Scots-Irish Shaped America.* New York: Broadway Books, 2005.

Whelan, Fergus. *Dissent into Treason.* Dingle: Brandon, 2010.

Whelan, Irene. "Religious Rivalry and the Making of Irish-American Identity", in Lee, J. J. and Casey, Marion R., eds. *Making the Irish American.* New York: New York University Press, 2007.

Williams, Samuel Wesley. *Pictures of Early Methodism in Ohio.* Cincinnati: 1909.

Acknowledgements

Ancestry.com, the online resource for family history, broke the story on 12 March 2007 that Barack Obama has Irish branches in his family tree. Megan Smolenyak, Chief Family Historian for Ancestry.com, remarked that "This research will once and for all put to rest any perceptions that Barack Obama is a first generation American. Like most of us he has an interesting mix of ancestry, including some impressively early all-American roots." Further research was published by Eneclann.ie, where the genealogists were Fiona Fitzsimons and Helen Moss. William Addams Reitwiesner Genealogical Services, better known as *www.wargs.com*, compiled a very detailed "Ancestry of Barack Obama". I am indebted to all of them for their researches.

The story that appeared in the media and online centred on Fulmouth (Falmouth or Fulmoth) Kearney, who left Ireland for America in 1850. But I also learned about Thomas Kearney, Fulmouth's uncle, who had left Ireland for Maryland some sixty years earlier. My source for information about Thomas was Roger Kearney of Troy in Ohio, and his website *www.onthesquare.com/kearney*. Roger is a descendant of Joseph Kearney and Sarah Healy, who were married in Shinrone, County Offaly in 1761. Rev. Stephen Neill in

Acknowledgements

Cloughjordan, County Tipperary showed me the parish registers of Shinrone and Templeharry that recorded the marriages, baptisms and burials of several of the Kearneys and Healys.

On his website Roger Kearney provided invaluable resources: the inscriptions on the Kearney gravestones at Compton Cemetery in Ohio; background information on Thomas Kearney; James G. Kearney's Civil War Diaries; an autobiographical letter from John Brough Kearney, grandson of Thomas Kearney; genealogical profiles of the descendants of Joseph Kearney, William Kearney (son of Joseph and Sarah); Thomas Kearney (son of Thomas and Sarah Baxley Kearney); plat maps of Perry Township and Deerfield Township; the wills recorded in Pickaway and Ross Counties of Thomas, Francis, John and Joseph Kearney; an obituary of the James Kearney who died in 1888. He also presented on the website detailed information about the Baxley family of Baltimore.

Roger was kind enough to meet me in Troy and to give me directions about places I might visit. With his help I was able to find records of Kearney land and tax transactions, and later he took the trouble to read my manuscript. He has been a true keeper of the family flame.

I want to express my special thanks to Roger, and also to Ralph Dunham and Virginia Goeldner, who were very helpful in giving me insight into their family backgrounds. Unfortunately I didn't get to meet Ralph or Virginia, but we had conversations on the phone which helped me greatly, and Ralph provided some wonderful photos and carefully typed notes, and was good enough to read the proofs.

I used many sources for my study of Offaly history, but I must record my great indebtedness in particular to two fine local histories: Noel MacMahon's *In the Shadow of the Fairy Hill: Shinrone and Ballingarry – A History* and Séamus Ó Riain's *Dunkerrin: A Parish in Ely O Carroll*.

Acknowledgements

I had learned about Michael Kearney, the wig-maker and his son John, the bishop, at Eneclann, the genealogical service based in Trinity College Dublin, and I garnered further information about this branch of the family through the *Oxford Dictionary of National Biography* and *Ossory Clergy and Parishes* by Rev. James B. Leslie. My thanks, too, to Dr Susan Hood, Assistant Librarian and Archivist at the Church of Ireland RCB Library.

Rev. Stephen Neill, Henry Healy, Rev. Michael Johnston, and Andrew Lee Feight all helped establish context.

In Maryland, Ohio, Indiana and Kansas public officials in courthouses, county halls, libraries and museums were unfailingly professional, helpful and courteous.

Terry Fitzgerald, Cleo Murphy, Ciaran Reilly and Fergus Whelan offered helpful editorial advice. Terry Foley provided the maps.

Thanks to George Saltz, Ryan Rosenberger, J. D. Lindsey, Jostin Beachler and Chad Martin at Dogtown Road. Thanks to Shawn Clements at the Dunham House and to Niall O'Dowd in New York. Thanks to the staff at the National Library and the Genealogical Office in Dublin; to Colm Murray and Martina Malone at the Heritage Council, Kilkenny; to Bishop Michael Burrows in Kilkenny; to Elizabeth Keyes at St Canice's in Kilkenny; to Provost Dr John Hegarty, Olivia Waters and Catherine Gilltrap at Trinity College Dublin; to Joseph Mischyshyn.

SOME OTHER READING

from

BRANDON

Brandon is a leading Irish publisher of new fiction and non-fiction for an international readership. For a catalogue of new and forthcoming books, please write to Brandon/Mount Eagle, Cooleen, Dingle, Co. Kerry, Ireland. For a full listing of all our books in print, please go to

www.brandonbooks.com

Fergus Whelan. *Dissent Into Treason*
Unitarians, King-killers and the Society of United Irishmen
The fascinating untold story of the Cromwellian roots of Irish republicanism.

Fergus Whelan reveals the hidden history of the Protestant Dissenters whose Dublin congregations were established in the Cromwellian era and who went on to contribute their republican ideas to the United Irishmen.

Paperback 9780863224294

Tom Reilly. *Cromwell: An Honourable Enemy*

"Make no mistake, this is a very important reappraisal." *Sunday Tribune*
"He is scrupulous in his examination of evidence, he has the necessary scepticism, he is assiduous in research and he quotes primary sources extensively." *Sunday Times*

Paperback 9780863223907

Sean O'Callaghan. *To Hell or Barbados*

"An illuminating insight into a neglected episode in Irish history, but its significance is much broader than that. Its main achievement is to situate the story of colonialism in Ireland in the much larger context of world-wide European imperialism." *Irish World*

Paperback 9780863222870

Gerard Ronan. *'The Irish Zorro': the extraordinary adventures of William Lamport (1615-1659)*

"Comprehensive and enthralling... Lamport's story is truly extraordinary... Sometimes historical biography can be a dry read. Ronan's is anything but. He provides interesting insights into the lives of large Irish enclaves in France and Spain in the first half of the 17th century along with harrowing ones of those accused of heresy and subjected to the *auto da fe* of the Inquisition. Ronan's passion and sympathy for his subject shine through so it reads like a novel. A 'must read'."
Irish Independent

Hardback 9780863223297

www.brandonbooks.com

Kevin Connolly. *Yeats and Sligo*

A beautifully illustrated book to illuminate the world of Ireland's most admired and celebrated poet.

"A brilliantly evocative twinning of the physical landscape of a county and the mental landscape of the great poet... No lover of Yeats should be without [it]." Dermot Bolger

Hardback 9780863224195

Michael Murphy. *At Five in the Afternoon*

"A brave and absorbing piece of work." *Irish Independent*

"A fine literary memoir ... a well crafted memoir that speaks out unflinchingly about his fight against prostate cancer. Michael Murphy eloquently illustrates all aspects of his battle with his illness through the lives and experiences of the people around him. This book will strike a chord with those whose lives have been affected by cancer." *Ireland's Own*

Paperback 9780863224263

Alan Simpson. *Duplicity and Deception*

Policing the Twilight Zone of the Troubles
A leading detective reveals the truth behind the headlines of some of Northern Ireland's most violent crimes.

"I had many unique experiences, which, in order to protect certain people, I felt I could not write about until a sufficient period of time had elapsed. I believe that time has now arrived..."

Hardback 9780863224164; paperback 9780863224287

William Campbell. *Here's How*

Creative solutions for Ireland's economic and social problems.
Ireland is in crisis, and snowed under with opinions on what went wrong and who is to blame. *Here's How* focuses on the solutions.
Using lateral thinking and challenging concepts, William Campbell offers sometimes simple, sometimes very inventive solutions to Ireland's economic and social problems.

Paperback 9780863224270

www.brandonbooks.com